WINNING TRIAL ADVOCACY

How to Avoid Mistakes Made by Master Trial Lawyers

Julius B. Levine

PRENTICE HALL
Englewood Cliffs, New Jersey 07632

Prentice-Hall International (UK) Limited, *London*
Prentice-Hall of Australia Pty. Limited, *Sydney*
Prentice-Hall Canada, Inc., *Toronto*
Prentice-Hall Hispanoamericana, S.A., *Mexico*
Prentice-Hall of India Private Limited, *New Delhi*
Prentice-Hall of Japan, Inc., *Tokyo*
Simon & Schuster Asia Pte. Ltd., *Singapore*
Editora Prentice-Hall do Brasil, Ltda., *Rio de Janeiro*

© 1989 *by*

PRENTICE-HALL, Inc.

Englewood Cliffs, NJ

10   9   8   7   6   5   4   3   2   1

Library of Congress Cataloging-in-Publication Data

Levine, Julius Byron.
  Winning trial advocacy : how to avoid mistakes made by master
trial lawyers / Julius Byron Levine.

        p.   cm.
  Includes index.
  ISBN 0-13-961319-6
  1. Trial practice—United States. I. Title.
KF8915.L485 1989
347.73′7—dc19
[347.3077]   89-31230
                                                         CIP

ISBN 0-13-961319-6

PRENTICE HALL
BUSINESS & PROFESSIONAL DIVISION
A division of Simon & Schuster
Englewood Cliffs, New Jersey 07632

PRINTED IN THE UNITED STATES OF AMERICA

To three great trial lawyers:
G. Joseph Tauro, an eminent jurist whose
teaching insight grew into this book,
Lewis Lester Levine, my initial mentor as
a trial lawyer and my father, and
Frederick E. Levine, my former partner in
trial law and my brother.

And to my three children, Rachel A., Sarah L., and
James G. Levine, who I hope will become
seekers of justice, whether as trial lawyers
or otherwise.

ABOUT THE AUTHOR

Professor Levine was graduated from Harvard College Phi Beta Kappa and Summa Cum Laude and from Harvard Law School Cum Laude. He won a Rhodes Scholarship to Oxford University where he earned a Doctor of Philosophy Degree. His doctoral work led to his book, *Discovery*, published by the Oxford University Press. Immediately following law school Professor Levine observed a variety of trial lawyers and trials when he served as Law Clerk to Judge Edward T. Gignoux of the U.S. District Court. In his own law practice he has both defended and prosecuted criminal charges and tried a wide gamut of civil matters ranging from personal injury to commercial cases. He has continued to try cases since his appointment as a Professor at Boston University School of Law, where his courses include Trial Advocacy and Civil Procedure.

CONTRIBUTORS TO THIS BOOK

Judges

Judge Samuel Adams
Chief Judge Winston E. Arnow
Judge Walter E. Craig
Judge Raymond R. Cross
Judge Albert J. Engel
Judge Francis J. Fazzano
Chief Judge James L. Foreman
Chief Judge Frank H. Freedman
Judge Jacob D. Fuchsberg
Judge Alfred T. Goodwin
Chief Justice John M. Greaney
Judge Anthony Grillo
Judge James T. Healey
Judge Shirley Hufstedler
Judge Samuel P. King
Judge Marie M. Lambert
Judge Henry M. Leen
Judge Jacob Lewiton
Judge Andrew R. Linscott
Judge Thomas J. MacBride
Judge James P. McGuire
Chief Justice Walter H. McLaughlin, Sr.
Judge John J. McNaught
Judge Joseph S. Mitchell, Jr.
Chief Justice Thomas R. Morse
Judge Norris L. O'Neill
Chief Justice G. Joseph Tauro
Judge Roszel C. Thomsen
Judge Homer Thornberry
Judge Fred M. Winner
Judge Alfonso J. Zirpoli

Trial Lawyers

John M. Adams
Hugh Meade Alcorn, Jr.
Frederick W. Allen
F. Lee Bailey

C. R. Beirne

Melvin M. Belli

Jared M. Billings

Robert Button

Ralph W. Campbell

Roy M. Cohn

Al J. Cone

Earle C. Cooley

William P. Cooney

Philip H. Corboy

Mayo A. Darling

Clarence Darrow (by attribution)

Herold Price Fahringer

Frank C. Gorrell

George V. Higgins

Leon Jaworski

Patrick F. Kelly

Leonard A. Kiernan, Jr.

Victor H. Kramer

James Krueger

Ralph I. Lancaster, Jr.

Samuel Langerman

Julius B. Levine

Lewis Lester Levine

B. B. Markham

James McArdle

Professor James W. McElhaney

Beverly C. Moore

John H. Mudd

Michael A. Musmanno

Louis Nizer

John W. Norman

John Lord O'Brian

Albert S. Pergam

Peter Perlman

Stanley A. Prokop

Bernard G. Segal

Harvey A. Silverglate

Lawrence J. Smith

Paul T. Smith

Jacob A. Stein

Richard P. Tinkham

George M. Vetter

Ward Wagner, Jr.

Terry W. West

Edward Bennett Williams

George Williams

Jack I. Zalkind

ACKNOWLEDGMENTS

This book would not have been possible without the contributions of heroes of legal education—the practicing lawyers and judges listed on pages vii-viii, who provided accounts of errors of judgment or tactics which they had committed or observed. As Chief Justice G. Joseph Tauro's Foreword outlines, he began to use mistakes from real trials as one tool to teach his students at Boston University School of Law. After exhausting his own knowledge of mistakes he solicited additional mistakes from a number of trial lawyers. Then he generously shared his innovative, successful teaching tool with me, and together we solicited accounts of actual mistakes from judges and additional trial lawyers. Both the bench and the bar responded splendidly to our solicitations. I am deeply indebted to Chief Justice Tauro and the other contributing judges and lawyers.

I am also indebted to the Boston University School of Law under Dean William Schwartz for financial support of this project. I am grateful to the authors and publishers who have given permission to reprint their materials in this book. They are listed in the reference notes at the end of the chapters. Less tangible but no less real are my debts to the late Professor Richard H. Field and Professor, now Judge, Robert E. Keeton, who jointly taught me Trial Advocacy at Harvard Law School. Professor Keeton's pathfinding book *Trial Tactics and Methods*, which I first read for his course in 1964, has remained a very valuable resource which I have profitably consulted both while trying cases over the years and while writing this book.

Immediately following Professors Field and Keeton's stimulating course, I was privileged to serve as Law Clerk to Judge Edward T. Gignoux. He permitted me to obtain what in effect was a post-graduate trial advocacy course, for he allowed me to be present in the courtroom throughout all trials in his U.S. District Court, even though there may have been legal research to be done on other matters in his Chambers. My detached observations during this period of many lawyers of widely varied backgrounds and styles—ranging from leaders of the Wall Street Bar to sole practitioners from Maine towns—shaped some of my ideas about trial advocacy expressed in this book.

Similarly influential on me have been the growing, excellent literature on trial advocacy, some of which I cite, the three great trial lawyers to whom I have dedicated this book, and the lawyers and judges I have litigated with, against, and before, and have taught trial advocacy with under the auspices of the National Institute for Trial Advocacy, the New England Law Institute, and the Massachusetts Continuing Legal Education, Inc.

I am very grateful also to Attorney Frederick E. Levine, Assistant Dean Barbara Lauren, Attorney and Lecturer in Law Ellen J. Messing, and the trial advocacy faculty of Boston University School of Law for reading and commenting on the manuscript. I must add my most sincere thanks to Georgette Dagher, Catherine Maguire, Valerie Mulholland, and Edith Solomon for their cheerful typing and word processor supervision and to my law students who have also been my research assistants, John W. Guppy, Joanna M. Phillips, Joseph J. Purcell, Scott S. Sinrich, Duncan A. Maio, Daniel F. Markham, Daniel M. Marposon, Sara Lou Lander, and Juliet D. Loebardt.

J. B. L.

FOREWORD

**G. Joseph Tauro, Chief Justice of
Massachusetts Superior and Supreme Judicial Courts
(Retired)**

It was a midwinter day in 1926. As was my usual practice during my law school days, I was at the Boston and Maine Railroad Station, Central Square, Lynn, waiting to take the 8:20 A.M. train to Boston and to Boston University Law School. In my chitchat with some other students at the station I learned of a case being tried at the Essex County Superior Court in Salem. Apparently it was an important case involving several prominent local people. More importantly, Tom Kelly, who was reputed to be the best trial lawyer in the county, represented one of the parties.

I made my decision quickly. Instead of boarding the train to Boston, I took the train going in the opposite direction to Salem.

I was allowed to squeeze into the already crowded courtroom by a sympathetic court officer on the basis of my status as a law student who was cutting some classes to see the great Tom Kelly in action. The fact that Kelly's son happened to be my classmate at Boston University Law School (Class of 1927) was of some help.

A key witness concluded her direct testimony. It was less than helpful to Kelly's client.

My new friend, the court officer, leaned over and whispered, "Hey, Kid—watch Tom pin her ears back."

Before getting up to accept opposing counsel's challenge, "You may cross-examine," lawyer Kelly hesitated for a moment, as though in deep thought.

He walked slowly and deliberately to within a foot or two of the witness stand. I got the feeling that lawyer and witness knew each other quite well. Her smile and relaxed demeanor betrayed no fear or anxiety on her part.

"Mary," he began, in a tone that was a bit sarcastic, "Mary," he repeated, "do you know of any woman in this county who drinks more than you?" There was complete silence in the court. There was no objection by opposing counsel; the Judge said nothing—the jury looked startled.

The witness' smile did not change. She answered, "Yes, Tom—as you well know, your wife does."

The courtroom scene remained frozen for a few moments. Kelly slowly walked to his chair, sat down, and merely said, "No further questions." I realized that I had just witnessed a tactical trial error of significant magnitude by a trial lawyer of great repute.

A court officer informed me that lawyer Kelly had expected that his opponent would object; and, of course, the objection would have been sustained. Thus he would have brought to the attention of the jury his point that the witness was a lush. But the great Kelly had been outsmarted by opposing counsel. As a result, he was hurt rather badly.

In the years that followed I have thought back to that dramatic episode. Those few moments in Salem provided an invaluable lesson in trial advocacy, which ranks in importance with some other lessons I had to spend months or years to learn.

In the chapters that follow Professor Julius B. Levine of Boston University Law School will examine and discuss lawyer Kelly's tactical error and a number of additional tactical errors committed or witnessed by leading trial lawyers and judges throughout the country. Most will be identified by name of counsel or judge. Among them are the errors that F. Lee Bailey admits to committing during his defense of Patricia Hearst. Roy Cohn relates the tactical errors committed by prosecutors in a criminal trial in which he himself was the defendant. Louis Nizer tells of his experience with a tactical error in litigation in which he was counsel. Leon Jaworski and Edward Bennett Williams report common errors. Dozens of other capable and experienced trial lawyers and judges, including former Chief Justice Walter

McLaughlin of the Massachusetts Superior Court, Judge Jacob Fuchsberg of the New York Court of Appeals, and Shirley Hufstedler, formerly a judge of the U.S. Ninth Circuit Court of Appeals and U.S. Secretary of Education, tell of their experiences. They are accompanied by Professor Levine's commentaries which add to their teaching capabilities.

Most of us who have contributed to this volume believe that we learn by our own mistakes. Nowhere is it written that we do not learn by the mistakes of others. There is a tendency not to repeat our mistakes. I believe the same can be said about the mistakes of others.

In 1976 when I reached mandatory retirement age as Chief Justice of the Massachusetts Supreme Judicial Court, I devoted myself for about two years to trial advocacy education at the Boston University School of Law. I noticed that students showed heightened interest when I gave examples of real tactical errors, which I myself had made as a trial lawyer before my appointment to the bench or which I had observed on the Bench of the Massachusetts Superior and Supreme Judicial Courts.

Teaching with examples of real tactical errors, rather than hypothetical or self-laudatory examples, proved to make an important difference to students in the learning process. They accepted the former as more meaningful. My colleague Professor Levine learned of the success I was having with my "real errors" method of teaching and tried it in his own trial advocacy teaching. He was equally successful. This pedagogical approach, of course, is but one of the many tools for educating trial lawyers; but in my view it is an important one.

In order to make real (as opposed to hypothetical) trial tactical errors as one teaching tool available to other trial advocacy teachers, and to make the lessons taught by the tactical errors available to students and practitioners for self-education, Professor Levine has prepared this book of instructive tactical trial errors with appropriate commentaries. As material for this book, many leaders of the judiciary and the American trial bar generously have provided detailed examples of strategic errors they have committed, learned of, or observed. Professor Levine synthesizes and analyzes this material in his book.

I wish to emphasize that Professor Levine is not dealing with reversible legal error, but rather with errors of judgment committed during the trial or in its preparation. As most trial lawyers and judges know, such errors can and do significantly influence the outcome. I repeat my belief that one can learn from another's mistakes as he can from his or her own. In this regard, admission of misjudgment by way of illustration is far more persuasive and meaningful as a teaching device than claims of brilliant tactical trial maneuvers. Many of the latter have already been claimed and published. Professor Levine's book will provide an insight into an important phase of the trial of cases and the operation of our courts not generally available in published form.

Professor Levine has invited me, in view of what he calls my pioneering role in the "real errors" approach to teaching trial advocacy, to initiate the litany of tactical trial errors with one of my own.

Early in my trial practice I was engaged to defend a well known and highly respected doctor against a charge of medical malpractice. These were the facts. The plaintiff had sustained a serious hip fracture in an unrelated accident which, unfortunately, resulted in a permanent disability. The plaintiff discharged the defendant, doctor A, and engaged the services of doctor B, an eminent Boston specialist who was unable to bring about any significant improvement. The plaintiff based her claim on the grounds of improper diagnosis and insufficient and inadequate treatment.

Plaintiff's counsel, as is commonly done in malpractice cases, called the defendant to the witness stand. By the adroit use of hypothetical questions and authoritative medical books, he was able to make out a rather thin jury issue on the questions of proper diagnosis and medical care.

The plaintiff's doctor B testified as to the details of the injury, the treatment rendered, and the fact of a permanent disability. However, in spite of much gentle prodding by plaintiff's counsel (interlaced with my objections) doctor B would not place the onus of malpractice on doctor A.

Counsel concluded his case with the plaintiff as a witness. She detailed her injuries, treatment, alleged lack of treatment, and her permanent incapacity. She made a good impression on the jury. Cross-examination was contraindicated.

"You may cross-examine"—challenged the plaintiff's counsel. At this point the case could have gone either way. The jury was apparently sympathetic to the plaintiff, with the strong suspicion that an insurance company would pay the damages. On the other hand, there was undoubtedly concern for the doctor's reputation. The verdict was a toss-up. The question for my decision was whether to cross-examine and, if so, to what extent. The insurance company's file that had been turned over to me was replete with reports from investigators to the effect that the plaintiff, an elderly woman, although honest, was simple minded.

I decided I could put an end to her case by asking but one question. "Madam, did you hear your own doctor testify under oath that the defendant was not to blame for your unfortunate condition?" I fully expected the answer to be "yes," upon which I would say, "Thank you—no further questions."

But the plaintiff had other ideas. She hesitated for a moment; then she turned to the jury and said with a sweet smile, "That isn't what he told me." Several jurors nodded knowingly to each other and, precisely at that moment, I knew my goose was cooked. A motion to strike plaintiff's answer would have made matters worse. The judge came to my rescue by granting my request for a recess. The case was settled.

As a conclusion to this Foreword, I wish to say that Professor Levine's volume is not just another book on trial advocacy. There are a number already available written by other talented and experienced trial lawyers. Nor is Professor Levine's book intended to be a response to widespread criticism of the quality of the American trial bar. I have set forth my views on this important subject in "Graduate Law School Training in Trial Advocacy; A New Solution to an Old Problem," 56 *Boston University Law Review* 635 (July 1976).

The purpose of this volume is to make available to students and young lawyers the benefit of experiences of others who are willing to share them in the interest of legal education. If one serious tactical error by the reader is thus avoided, Professor Levine's effort in writing this book will have been worthwhile.

PREFACE

THE NATURE OF THIS BOOK

The goal and role of this book have been set forth in the Foreword by Chief Justice G. Joseph Tauro, which you should read in conjuction with this Preface. This book grows out of his confidence and mine, based on our teaching experience, that you will learn very well from the mistakes of others. Hence this book teaches how to try cases with lessons drawn from mistakes made by experienced trial lawyers in real cases. Justice will be better administered, clients will be better served, and as trial lawyers you will improve in your craft as you learn to avoid the kinds of errors of judgment made in the examples from real trials which this book features. Incidentally, inexperienced trial lawyers will be less discouraged by their own mistakes after reading the mistakes by very experienced, leading trial lawyers in this volume. Incidentally, too, even readers who are not trial lawyers will gain insight into the role of errors in our court system. Ninety-eight of the examples from 75 different judges and lawyers are not available anywhere else. Their availability here and my effort to teach the art of trial advocacy with them make this book unique in the trial advocacy literature.

THE NATURE OF THE EXAMPLES OF
MISTAKES

The judges and lawyers who furnished examples were from throughout the United States. All of the lawyers had practiced trial law for more than ten years and were members of the American College of Trial Lawyers except for a few who were recommended by very experienced lawyers. I have culled the examples so as to include in the book only the errors with the greatest pedagogical value.

The examples we received were not evenly distributed among the various trial skills. Those used in this book similarly are not evenly distributed. The disproportion may reflect the fact that more mistakes are made in using some trial skills than in using others.

The examples from actual trials are presented throughout the text with an introductory title which I have added. The name of the contributing lawyer or judge comes under the title. The names that are not preceded by Judge or Chief Judge are those of trial lawyers. I have not added Attorney before the lawyers' names.

The examples remain in the words of the judge or lawyer except for very minor editorial changes. Sometimes the judge or lawyer expressed his view of the lesson taught by his example. I have almost always included his view. Some of the examples have substantially more detail than is necessary for the point of trial advocacy being illustrated. I have not pared them down because they afford you a measure of exposure to the rich texture of real trial practice. That is, they provide you some of the benefit to be derived from apprenticing oneself to a master trial lawyer.

Other examples contain subsidiary lessons on trial practice in addition to the one under discussion at the particular place in the book where they appear. Rather than splinter the examples into two or three different chapters or sections, I have presented the examples in full at one place and occasionally commented there on the subsidiary points they illustrate as well as the principal point. I thus have sacrificed a degree of organizational integrity to preserve the full flavor of the example as a window to the world of real trials.

I use the examples to teach trial advocacy. However, you will notice that some of them, perhaps recounting trials of 60 or more years ago, will seem to presuppose substantive law and laws of evidence, jurisdiction, procedure, or ethics which will appear wrong or questionable or which will differ from that in your own state. You should not rely on the examples for these laws. I have taken as a given whatever the contributing judges or lawyers have presented explicitly or implicitly as the applicable law. My mission in respect to the examples has been only to comment on the trial advocacy lessons they exemplify.

In abstracting trial advocacy principles from the examples, I have written about the likelihood that particular practices will contribute to a winning jury verdict. Likewise, the judges and lawyers in their examples often have advanced their assessment of the effect of what a lawyer did on the jury. All of us who try cases and who teach how to try cases continually hypothesize about the cause and effect relationship between what lawyers do and the verdicts they receive. With very rare exceptions the jurors do not explain what in fact brought about their verdict.

Judges and lawyers make these judgments about the effect of particular practices in the course of litigation on the ultimate verdict based on their long experience. If you see lawyers who give poorly prepared opening statements and closing arguments lose verdicts time and time again, you tend to conclude that neglect of openings and closings bodes ill for the verdict. Thus the judgments about what caused verdicts in this book are informed judgments. They explain the data we have observed as well as we can, although the judgments surely come with no warranty of infallibility. However, they are the same judgments on which lawyers base their own tactics during litigation and their advice to clients. They are also the same judgments with which trial advocacy professors critique their students.

Neither the contributing judges and lawyers nor I often expressly address the likely impact of particular practices on the judge when he rather than a jury is the fact-finder. I have not done so because that impact usually will be the same. Presumably the contributing judges and lawyers feel the same way. On the other hand, we have written in the context of jury trials since they pose additional challenges to the trial lawyer which are not present during bench trials.

Julius B. Levine

September, 1987
Boston, Massachusetts

CONTENTS

Foreword   **xi**
Preface   **xvii**

CHAPTER ONE JURY SELECTION TECHNIQUES   **1**

"Cause" for Challenging a Juror   2

Peremptory Juror Challenges   2

Will Your Efforts to Shape the Composition of the Jury Make a Difference?   **3**

Minority View: Any Juror Will Do   3

Majority View: The Composition of the Jury May Make a Difference   3

Conducting the Voir Dire Examination   **4**

Does the Judge or Counsel Conduct It?   5

How Counsel Should Question Prospective Jurors   5

Five Types of Information to Elicit on Voir Dire   6

Lawyers Usually Must Rely on the Voir Dire Oath, Sometimes to Their Peril   8

Factors to Consider on Whether to Challenge a Juror Peremptorily 9

   Example 1–1: Folklore or Ancedotal Generalizations Do Not Always Prove Reliable (Judge Raymond R. Cross) 10

   Using a Community Network to Find Out About Jurors 10

   Example 1–2: Local Lawyer Is Not Always Favored by the Jury (Richard P. Tinkham) 11

Possible Effects on the Jury of Different Methods of Exercising Challenges 12

   Example 1–3: A Drinker Does Not Lend a Helping Hand to a Fellow Drinker (Lewis Lester Levine) 13

Difficult Judgments of Human Nature Pervade the Decision Making Process 14

   Example 1–4: Keeping an Eye on the Jurors May Answer a Question Before It Is Asked (John M. Adams) 14

Behaving Fairly Should Inspire Juror Trust in You 15

Importance of Juror Eye Contact and Body Language 16

The Persuasion Process Begins, and May Go Far, During Jury Selection 16

   Example 1–5: Do Not Let Your Opponent Steal Your Thunder During Voir Dire (Peter Perlman) 17

Summary 18

CHAPTER TWO   INCREASING THE IMPACT OF YOUR OPENING STATEMENT 21

How to Make the Most of Your Opening Statement 21

   Use Your Opening to Organize the Testimony and Exhibits 21

Capitalizing on Primacy   22

Example of an Appealing Beginning   22

Example 2–1: Usually Leave Humor Out of the Opening, Particularly If It May Irk the Judge (Judge John J. McNaught)   24

Beware of a Directed Verdict Against You on Your Opening   25

Desirable Degree of Detail in Opening   25

Pitfalls of a Detailed Opening   26

Exploit Your Opponent's Failure to Produce Evidence Promised in the Opening   27

Example 2–2: Omitting Evidence from a Detailed Opening (Judge Andrew R. Linscott)   27

How to Use the Opening to Minimize the Effect of Damaging Evidence   28

Turning Weaknesses into Strengths   28

Whether and When to Say That the Opening Statement Is Not Evidence   29

A Straightforward but Persuasive Style Is Best; an Impassioned Opening Is Out of Place   29

Organizing Your Opening to Be Interesting and Lucid   30

An Example of the Self-Dialogue   30

An Example of the Narrative   31

When Should Defendant's Lawyer Make the Opening Statement— Immediately After the Opponent, or After the Opponent Rests?   32

Advantages of Opening Right After Your Opponent   32

Limitations on Your Opening Immediately Following Your Opponent When You Have Not Decided Whether You Will Offer Evidence   33

Avoid Creating a Credibility Gap   34

Example 2–3: A Fatal Credibility Gap (Judge Raymond R. Cross)   34

In Deciding When to Open and What to Say, Consider the Right of a Defendant in a Criminal Case to Choose Late in the Trial Whether to Testify   35

Properly Preparing Witnesses   36

Distinguishing Expected Evidence from Actual Evidence   37

Positive Advantages of Opening After Your Opponent Rests   37

Respond to Your Opponent's Challenge to Open Immediately After Him   38

When to Object During an Opening Statement   39

Two Common Grounds for Objecting Which Justify Interrupting an Opening Statement   40

Summary   42

CHAPTER THREE   PREPARING AND PLANNING THE EVIDENCE   45

Careful Selection and Thorough Preparation of Witnesses   45

Example 3–1: Inadequate Preparation of Evidence (Chief Judge Frank H. Freedman)   46

Subpoena All Witnesses You May Want to Testify   47

Unnecessary and Harmful Witnesses   48

Example 3–2: Make Sure Witnesses Do Not Have Ulterior Motives (An anonymous trial lawyer)   48

Interviewing Witnesses Is Essential to Proper Preparation   49

Example 3–3: Chewing Gum Ruins the Effectiveness of a Witness (Mayo A. Darling)   49

Example 3–4: Beware of the Glitter and Ego of a Materially Injured Client (Judge Samuel P. King)   50

Remember, Your Own Personal Interviews May Be Necessary
52

Advise Your Witness as to Appropriate Dress   53

*Example 3–5: Do Not Depend on an Old Interview (Frank C.
Gorrell)*   54

Filter Out Dispensable Witnesses   55

When Possible, Observe the Witnesses Testify Before Trial
56

Favorable Witnesses May Disappoint You   56

*Example 3–6: The Need to Take Electronic or Written
Statements by Witnesses (Ralph I. Lancaster, Jr.)*   57

Written Statements May Refresh a Witness' Memory   58

*Example 3–7: Cross-Examine Your Own Client Before
Trial (Judge Walter E. Craig)*   60

Interviewing Witnesses in the Presence of Your Client   61

Modern Methods of Discovery Can Avoid Many Surprises at
Trial   62

Cross-Examine Your Own Witnesses   62

*Example 3–8: A Lawyer Is Embarrassed at Having Failed to
Learn of His Key Witness' Criminal Record in an Early
Twentieth Century Informal Trial (Michael A. Musmanno)*
63

*Example 3–9: Interviewing a Hostile Witness in the Face of
Verbal Abuse (Harvey A. Silverglate)*   67

Listen to All a Belligerent Witness Has to Say, However
Unpleasant   69

Prepare Your Witnesses to Testify   70

*Example 3–10: Make Sure That Your Preparation of a
Witness Does Not Lead Him to Forget a Decisive
Detail (Ralph W. Campbell)*   70

Familiarize Your Witnesses with Relevant Legal Fictions
71

Example 3–11: Let the Truth Be Told (John H. Mudd)
72

*Example 3–12: Make Sure That Exhibits Remain in Their
Original Condition (Al J. Cone)*   73

Your Client's Viewpoint Is Not Necessarily What Is Best for Him   74

Inform Witnesses of Courtroom Procedures, Their Role in the Trial, and What to Expect During Direct, Cross, and Redirect Examinations   75

Expert Witnesses   76

Example 3–13: Use Expert Witnesses to Corroborate Your Client's Medical Claims (Paul T. Smith)   76

Example 3–14: Give the Expert All the Facts (Chief Judge Winston E. Arnow)   77

Example 3–15: Be Wary of Live Demonstrations (Chief Justice Thomas R. Morse, Jr.)   78

Plan Live Demonstrations Only When Essential to Your Case   79

Expert Testimony Does Not Always Influence the Jury   80

Example 3–16: Lay Persons May Sometimes Be More Effective Than Experts (William P. Cooney)   80

Cumulative Expert Witnesses on the Same Issue May Undercut Each Other   81

Example 3–17: Two Experts for Defendant Neutralize Each Other (Judge Jacob D. Fuchsberg)   81

Anticipate Cross-Examination Questions When Choosing Witnesses   82

Check for Contradictions Among Potential Cumulative Witnesses   83

Should You Request a View?   83

Example 3–18: No Reasonable Doubt Following a View (Chief Justice Thomas R. Morse, Jr.)   83

Inspect the Area to Be Viewed Before Requesting a View   85

Thorough Preparation of Documentary and Real Evidence   85

Example 3–19: Thorough Examination of Hospital Records Saves a Case (Leonard A. Kiernan, Jr.)   85

Example 3–20: Priority Must Be Given to Investigating Central Issues Before Peripheral Ones (F. Lee Bailey)   86

Example 3–21: You Can't Even Trust a Doctor-Client to Check an Important Record (George M. Vetter, Jr.)   88

In Light of Other Demands on Your Time and in Some Circumstances You Need Not Check All Possible Evidence Yourself   90

Example 3–22: Thoroughly Examine All of Your Client's Documents Before He Testifies (Judge Jacob Lewiton)   91

Example 3–23: If You Miss a Detail as Small as Page Numbering, Do Not Expect the Other Side Will Miss It Too (Hugh Meade Alcorn, Jr.)   92

Inspecting an Adverse Party's Documents   93

Summary   94

CHAPTER FOUR   PRESENTING AND OBJECTING TO EVIDENCE   97

Present Advisable Witnesses Who Are Legally Unnecessary   97

Example 4–1: A Jury Holds the Absence of a Legally Unnecessary Witness Against a Party (Ward Wagner, Jr.)   98

Avoid Jury Misconceptions Resulting from the Absence of a Witness   98

Advisable Witnesses in Criminal Cases   100

You Must Adapt to Unanticipated Developments at Trial   101

Example 4–2: Beware of How Your Client Will Behave on the Stand During a Spontaneous Illustration (F. Lee Bailey)   101

Example 4–3: Failure to Instruct a Witness to Omit an Inadmissible Subject (Judge Francis J. Fazzano)   103

Failure to Object Does Not Always Constitute a Waiver   104

Objecting to Evidence   105

    *Example 4–4: Know Whether an Answer Will Hurt You
    Before Objecting to the Question (Lawrence J. Smith)*
    105

    Negative Jury Reactions to Winning Objections   106

    Try to Avoid Repeatedly Making Losing Offers of Evidence or
    Objections   107

    Familiarity with Documents May Be Necessary to Decide
    Whether to Object   107

    *Example 4–5: Do Not Object to Evidence Before You Know
    What It Is (Judge Jacob Lewiton)*   108

    Be Meticulous and Persistent   109

Presenting Evidence During Trial   109

    *Example 4–6: Double Check Documents Offered in Evidence
    at Trial Even If You Believe You Have Previously Reviewed
    Them (Leonard A. Kiernan, Jr.)*   110

    *Example 4–7: Reading a Document (for the First Time) in
    Front of a Jury (Judge Homer Thornberry)*   112

    Knowledge Is a Better Trial Tactic Than a Hunch   112

    Use Discovery Methods To Avoid Seeing and Evaluating
    Evidence for the First Time at Trial   113

    Organize Your Direct Examination So That Testimony Is
    Understandable and Witnesses Appear Honest and
    Appealing   114

    Do Not Repeat Answered Questions on Direct   114

    *Example 4–8: An Unnecessary Live Demonstration Gives the
    Lie to Satisfactory Preceding Direct Expert Testimony (Chief
    Justice Thomas R. Morse, Jr.)*   114

    *Example 4–9: Know the Answers to Questions Before You
    Ask Them (Judge Alfred T. Goodwin)*   115

    *Example 4–10: Be Content with the Answer "No"; Do Not
    Try to Push on to "Absolutely No" (Judge Thomas J.
    MacBride)*   116

Example 4–11: Do Not Try to Completely Nail Down an Already Solid Case (Judge James T. Healey)   118

Patience Is Essential   119

Summary   119

CHAPTER FIVE   THE KEYS TO SUCCESSFUL CROSS-EXAMINATION   123

Pursue the Primary Purpose of Cross-Examination: Minimize the Damage Done by Direct Testimony   123

Cross-Examination As Perceived by the Public   123

Should Your Style Be Adversarial or Straightforward?   124

Advantages of a Brief, Successful Cross-Examination   124

Summation Supplements Cross-Examination   125

Do Not Invite the Witness to Repeat Direct Testimony   126

Example 5–1: Elusive Understanding (Robert Button)   126

Example 5–2: Do Not Invite a Witness to Expand on Direct Testimony; the Result May Be a Swift Kick (Samuel Langerman)   127

How to Avoid Maximizing the Effect of the Direct Examination   128

Remember: Live Demonstrations Are Always Risky   129

Transitional Statements   129

Damaging Evidence First Presented During Cross-Examination Has a Magnified Impact   130

Do Not Lose Control of the Witness   131

Confine Most Answers to "Yes" or "No"   131

The Cross-Examiner Should Not Answer Questions by Witnesses   132

Should You Use the Foolproof Method of Controlling the Witness—Waive Cross-Examination?   132

> *Example 5–3: An Ideal Time Not to Cross-Examine (Herold Price Fahringer)*   133
>
> *Example 5–4: An Excellent Time Not to Cross-Examine (John Lord O'Brian)*   134
>
> Whether and How to Cross-Examine a Celebrity   135
>
> Do Not Feel Compelled To Cross-Examine or Ask Additional Questions   135
>
> *Example 5–5: If You Have Nothing to Say, Say Nothing (Terry W. West)*   136

Listen for Clues in the Direct Testimony to Subjects for Cross-Examination   136

> *Example 5–6: Be Wary of a Clue Which Turns Out to Be a Trap (Roy M. Cohn)*   137
>
> Prefacing Cross-Examination Questions with, "As You Testified on Direct,..."   139
>
> The Risks of Following a Blind Alley of Cross-Examination   139
>
> If You Have Discredited the Witness, Stop Asking Questions   139
>
> Redirect Examination Makes a Smaller Impact than Cross-Examination, Especially When the Testimony Is Self-Congratulatory to the Redirect Examiner   140
>
> Avoid Open-Ended Questions on Cross-Examination   141
>
> The Court's Instruction to Disregard Evidence May Not Be Obeyed by All the Jurors   142
>
> On Cross-Examination Use Leading Questions and Interrupt Unresponsive, Long Answers   142
>
> Be Wary of Clues for Your Cross-Examination in the Cooperation of the Witness or the Cross-Examinations by Your Co-Parties   143
>
> *Example 5–7: Pursuing a Risky Blind Alley (Beverly C. Moore)*   143

Example 5–8: Distinguish Trial Business from Show Business (George V. Higgins)   145

When You Elicit a Damaging Answer, Stop Rather Than Dig Your Grave Deeper   147

Example 5–9: Stop After the Initial Injurious Answer (Judge Henry M. Leen)   148

After a Helpful Answer, Stop Lest the Favorable Testimony Be Neutralized by the Witness   149

Example 5–10: Stop Questioning After a Favorable Answer (Attributed to Clarence Darrow)   149

Discovery Depositions Invite Similar Errors During Cross-Examination   150

Example 5–11: Quit While You're Ahead! (John W. Norman)   150

Example 5–12: Penny Wise and Pound Foolish (Stanley A. Prokop)   152

Example 5–13: After a Helpful Answer, Do Not Pursue the Subject So That the Testimony Can Be Disavowed by the Witness (Judge James P. McGuire)   153

Dynamic Interaction Among Cross-Examination, Redirect Examination, and Closing Argument   154

Rehabilitating a Witness Through Redirect Examination   154

Example 5–14: Pushing the Limits of an Expert's Self-Deprecation (Chief Judge James L. Foreman)   155

The Redirect Examiner's Dilemma   156

"Why" Questions on Cross-Examination Often Forebode Disaster   156

Example 5–15: Do Not Ask Why an Expert Witness' Opinion Is Adverse to Your Client (Judge Joseph S. Mitchell, Jr.)   157

Example 5–16: Ask for an Explanation and Learn of Your Client's Bizarre Behavior (Chief Justice Walter H. McLaughlin, Sr.)   158

Example 5–17: Asking "Why" Civilly (Judge Fred M. Winner)   159

Example 5–18: An Argumentative Answer May Well Not Be Unresponsive to a "Why" Question (Judge Andrew R. Linscott)   160

Asking Witnesses to Explain Enables Them to Sum Up Their Case   160

Asking Why a Witness Seems Hostile or Biased Against You or Your Client Is Particularly Likely to Boomerang   161

Example 5–19: The Floodgates Open When the Witness Is Asked Why He Hates the Defendant (Victor H. Kramer)   161

Example 5–20: Woe to the Lawyer Who Asks Why a Witness Is Testifying Against the Client (Paul T. Smith)   162

Example 5–21: Don't Ask a Law Enforcement Agent Why He Had Been Tailing the Accused (George V. Higgins)   163

Example 5–22: When the Cross-Examiner Asks Why the Witness Refused to Talk with Him, the Witness Lambastes the Lawyer and the Client (Frank C. Gorrell)   164

"Why" Questions Surrender Your Control over the Witness   166

The "Rule" Against Asking Questions During Cross-Examination to Which You Do Not Know the Answer   167

Example 5–23: Seeing Is Believing (Philip H. Corboy)   167

Example 5–24: Only Time Will Tell (Patrick F. Kelly)   168

Should You Gamble on Long Shot Questions to Which You Do Not Know the Probable Answer?   169

Do Not "Open The Door" to Prejudicial Subjects Which Otherwise Are Inadmissible   169

Example 5–25: When You Have Closed a Door, Don't Be the One Who Forces It Open (F. Lee Bailey)   170

You May Need to Use Redirect to Introduce Previously
Inadmissible Evidence to Which Your Opponent Has Opened
the Door   171

*Example 5–26: The Cross-Examiner Opens the Door to a
Litany of Gory Charges Against the Defendants (Jack I.
Zalkind)*   172

*Example 5–27: Cross-Examination About Delay in Filing a
Criminal Charge Opens the Door to Damaging
Information (Chief Justice G. Joseph Tauro)*   173

*Example 5–28: The Adolescent Girl Had Her Reasons (Judge
Andrew R. Linscott)*   174

**Do Not Cross-Examine Excessively on a Peripheral Subject Which
May Cause the Jury to Attach Undue Importance to the Subject
175**

*Example 5–29: Protracted Cross-Examination on the
Recantation by an Elderly Witness—the Effect on Other
Issues (Judge Albert J. Engel)*   175

**Do Not Appear to Abuse the Witness Lest the Jurors Sympathize
with the Witness   177**

*Example 5–30: Unwise Cross-Examination of a Bereaved
Son About a Most Sympathetic Scene (Edward Bennett
Williams)*   178

*Example 5–31: The Last Vision of a Blind Boy (Frederick W.
Allen)*   179

*Example 5–32: A Cross-Examiner Fails to Foresee That a
Letter, Which Superficially Impeaches a Witness, Will Evoke
Jury Sympathy for the Witness (An anonymous judge)*
180

Cross-Examining a Woman   182

*Example 5–33: Juror Sympathy for an Uneducated
Female (Paul T. Smith)*   183

Effect of an Educated Witness on Jury Sympathy   183

Be Familiar with the Attitudes and Values of the Jurors
184

*Example 5–34: Misplaced Sympathy (An anonymous trial
lawyer)*   184

Do Not Question So Hostilely or Extensively That You Stimulate the Witness to Become a Better Advocate for the Other Side 185

Example 5–35: An Uncooperative Witness Turns Around (Judge Marie M. Lambert) 185

Example 5–36: Do Not Put Blood Back into the Veins of a Dying Adverse Party (C. R. Beirne) 187

Example 5–37: An Expert's Dispassionate Manner Is Transformed When His Qualifications Are Attacked (Judge Norris L. O'Neill) 187

Example 5–38: The Expert Did Not Attend Medical School but Teaches at One Now (Julius B. Levine) 188

Do Not Underestimate the Capability of the Witness 188

Example 5–39: Professional Hierarchies (Judge Fred M. Winner) 189

Example 5–40: A Dual Career Witness (Earle C. Cooley) 189

Example 5–41: The Opposing Plaintiff Gets the Last Laugh (Judge Samuel Adams) 190

Example 5–42: The Expert's Humor Tops the Cross-Examiner's Ridicule (James Krueger) 191

Do Not Word Questions Ambiguously 191

Example 5–43: The Double Meaning of "Handicap" in Golf and in Court (B. B. Markham) 192

Example 5–44: An Innocuous, Ambiguous Question Can Be Devastating (Judge Alfonso J. Zirpoli) 192

Steps to Minimize Ambiguous Questions Which May Result in Injurious Answers 193

Cross-Examination May Be Used Offensively, Although It Is Usually More Risky than Direct Examination of a Witness Whom You Have Selected and Prepared 194

Example 5–45: Asking Too Much of an Adverse Witness (Chief Justice Walter H. McLaughlin, Sr.) 195

Summary 197

CHAPTER SIX   WINNING CLOSING ARGUMENT   203

The Culmination of Your Trial Work: Argue and Tie Together the Evidence   203

  Show the Significance of Your Cross-Examination in Which You Did Not Ask One-Question-Too-Many   204

Four Variables to Adapt to in Planning and Making Speeches   204

  Example 6–1: Watch the Jury's Reaction to Your Argument (Judge Shirley Hufstedler, formerly U.S. Secretary of Education)   205

  Example 6–2: The Judge May Cool Your Zealous Argument (Judge John J. McNaught)   206

  Example 6–3: An Argument Which Puts Tears in Jurors' Eyes Leads to a Sad Result for the Client (Michael A. Musmanno)   207

The Introduction   210

  Set the Mood for Your Argument   211

The Body of the Summation   211

  Use the Judge's Charge on the Law to Organize the Body of Your Argument   211

  The Persuasiveness of Arguing as the Judge Will Instruct   212

  Marshal the Evidence as an Organizational Technique   213

  Recurring Elements in Effective Summations   214

  Minimize the Effect of Weaknesses in Your Case or Defense   216

  Example 6–4: Overdramatizing One Argument May Obscure Others (George Williams and Bernard G. Segal)   218

  Stay Away from Risky Arguments That Enable Your Opponent to Destroy Your Case in Rebuttal   219

  Order of Multiple Arguments   220

Do Not Ignore Your Opponent's Arguments   220

The Chronology of Summations   221

Example 6–5: Strategy, Counter-Strategy, Verdict (Judge Anthony Grillo)   221

Closing Argument Should Rarely Be Waived   223

Comparison with Waiver of Cross-Examination   224

Objections to Closing Argument   224

Objections During Closing Arguments Should Be Sparingly Made   225

The Conclusion   226

Tell the Jury the Exact Verdict You Desire   226

Warn the Jury If You Will Not Have an Opportunity to Refute Your Opponent and Remind Them of Their Promises When Selected   227

Ask the Jury to Find for You, and in Accordance with the Judge's Charge   228

Delivery   228

Example 6–6: Be Yourself (Leon Jaworski)   228

Deliver Your Summation as Conversation Writ Large   229

Example 6–7: Do Not Stand So as to Invade the Jury's Sense of Private Space or Speak Too Long (Mayo A. Darling)   229

How Close to Stand to the Jury   230

Changing Your Position; Eye Contact   231

Example 6–8: The Jury Are Distracted by Inappropriate Delivery (Judge Homer Thornberry)   231

Example 6–9: Superior Substance Prevails over Eloquent Delivery (Judge Roszel C. Thomsen)   232

Summary   232

CHAPTER SEVEN   TRIAL STRATEGY: MISCONCEPTIONS AND MIS-EXECUTIONS   237

Example 7–1: Think Carefully Before Putting Your Defendant's Reputation on the Line in a Counterclaim for Libel (Louis Nizer)   237

Weigh the Consequences of Joining a Defendant or Filing a Counterclaim Even If It Is a Compulsory One   242

Example 7–2: The Beatles as Litigants May Be Just Another Version of the Sue Me, Sue You Blues; But Sue Their Lawyer Personally and You See Speedy Action (Albert S. Pergam)   243

A Double Edged Sword—Protect a Winning Verdict Against Reversible Error in the Record   244

Salvage a Losing Verdict Through Reversible Error in the Record—the Other Edge of the Sword   245

Example 7–3: Do Not Sacrifice an Overarching Strategic Goal for a Lesser One (Jared M. Billings)   246

Keep Your Strategic Priorities Straight   247

Calling an Adverse Party as Your Witness—It May Help, but the Party Can Be Well Prepared for It and the Party's Lawyer Should Adapt Flexibly   248

The Risks in Resting Your Fate on Predictions of the Strategic Moves by Opposing Counsel   250

Example 7–4: Remember to Carry Out Your High Priority Plan (Julius B. Levine)   250

Your Desire for a Bifurcated Trial May Well Turn on Which Side You Represent   254

Summary   255

Index   259

CHAPTER ONE

JURY SELECTION TECHNIQUES

In preparing for trial you must attend to a host of details about the facts in question and the applicable law, as Chap. 3 will amply illustrate. If you do not lose sight of the forest for the trees, you also will concern yourself with who will ultimately decide the case. You may well ask yourself: what good will my dedicated efforts do for my client if, even before the trial begins, the judge or jurors are irreversibly committed to finding against me? The answer is that your efforts will do no good at all. Your predicament would be analogous to a most powerful, technologically advanced computer which may turn out to do its owner no good. The computer cannot do any good unless a human being inputs information of a kind and quality that the computer can work its magic on. "Garbage in, Garbage out" is how commentators lament a state of affairs in which the potential achievement of a computer is not realized.

A similarly lamentable waste of resources might happen to you if, even though you are well prepared, you are faced with an unalterably unreceptive judge or jury. Surely such a judge or jury is unlikely to be encountered, but it could be. In a trial in which the judge is the fact-finder, you will have virtually no influence over the selection of the judge. Occasionally you select the judge in effect when you select a court to use among available state and federal courts. In circuit riding courts, which rotate judges rather than assigning all stages of a case to a single judge, you have a minor influence on who the judge will be through your contribution to the selection of the date for trial. Although you do not have a major voice in selecting the judge, the requirement in many civil cases that a judge give reasons for his decision provides some protection from a prejudiced or close-minded decision.

"Cause" for Challenging a Juror

In a trial in which a jury is the fact-finder you may participate in the selection of the jurors from a larger pool called the venire. In all jurisdictions you may challenge potential jurors for cause or by exercising a limited number of peremptory challenges. "Cause" in this context means a disqualifying status such as age, residence, citizenship, criminal record, or prior jury service, or a relationship or a viewpoint that will prevent the juror from deciding the case impartially and solely on the basis of the evidence admitted at trial and the law presented in the judge's instructions. A juror who is irreversibly committed to the viewpoint that one of the parties should lose is a classic example of a person whom the court will excuse for cause.

Peremptory Juror Challenges

Peremptory challenges are available to strike jurors who are not disqualified by cause. The number allowed is often as limited as three or four per side. You need not give any reason for a peremptory challenge. Nor should you do so lest you alienate remaining members of the venire who may have liked the challenged juror or may disagree with your reason and who yet may wind up on the jury. There is one exception to your right to use peremptory challenges for any reason you choose and without explanation. Under the Equal Protection Clause of the Fourteenth Amendment to the U.S. Constitution, counsel for the government in both federal and state courts may not challenge potential jurors solely on account of their race. A few states have applied the same prohibition to other counsel as well, and the U.S. Supreme Court in 1986 expressly left open the question of whether the prohibition applies to other counsel.

WILL YOUR EFFORTS TO SHAPE THE COMPOSITION OF THE JURY MAKE A DIFFERENCE?

Minority View: Any Juror Will Do

Whether you should make your best effort to shape the composition of the jury by peremptory challenges is a question on which the experienced trial bar disagrees. A minority of trial lawyers are content practically to accept the first twelve or six who are picked for the jury and are not disqualified for cause. They feel that their clients are not likely to wind up with a better verdict if they spend days or weeks questioning and investigating prospective jurors preparatory to deciding which jurors to challenge peremptorily. (And these lawyers know that they would bill their clients for the extra work.) This view draws support from the study by M. Saks and R. Hastie who conclude as follows:

> [D]espite the apparently widely held assumption that the kind of person making a decision affects the decision made, the evidence consistently indicates that a jury's composition is a relatively minor determinant of the verdict....The studies are unanimous in showing that evidence is a substantially more potent determinant of jurors' verdicts than the individual characteristics of jurors.[1]

These social scientists thus are advising lawyers that, except when cause exists, by and large verdicts will be the same whether or not voir dire examination and peremptory challenges are used.

Majority View: The Composition of the Jury May Make a Difference

Other social scientists have pointed out that a voir dire weeding out of potential jurors can affect the verdict in some, even though by no means in most, cases. Zeisel and Diamond, for example, concluded from their experiment "that there are cases in which the jury verdict is seriously affected, if not determined, by the voir dire....Lawyers apparently do win some of their cases,...during or at least with the help of, voir dire."[2]

The importance of the background of the jury often will depend on the nature of the pivotal issue in your trial. If this issue is whether the traffic light was red or green, the profiles of the jurors are much less likely to matter than if this issue is the amount of damages for pain and suffering. Issues of the latter kind which involve value judgments provide far more leeway for the influence of personal preferences.

Most trial lawyers seem to worry that their trial will be one of those in which the composition of the jury may make a diffence in the verdict. They want to diligently gather information about the prospective jurors to use in exercising peremptory challenges. The jurors cannot be investigated much in advance of trial because their names typically are not drawn or made available to counsel until the day of trial. However, the communities from which they are to be summoned are identified in advance by statute or rule of court.

Social science research is occasionally an ingredient in jury selection Since the Harrisburg Seven trial in 1971, lawyers whose clients have had the necessary resources have sometimes engaged sociologists to sample and correlate the attitudes and background characteristics of the population at large in these communities. The sociologist might report, for example, that in the community in question a middle aged female with four years of education after high school typically is lenient on drug abuse, while a male blue-collar worker of any age typically is not lenient. A lawyer who has commissioned such a "scientific" study will make findings like these one factor in his decision on which jurors to peremptorily challenge.

Informal investigation Another factor may be the results of last minute investigation of the particular people who are the prospective jurors, e.g., by interviewing menbers of their community or driving by their homes, although lawyers are prohibited ethically from approaching the jurors themselves and their families.

CONDUCTING THE VOIR DIRE
EXAMINATION

Customarily the bulk of the information about prospective jurors will be gathered by their sworn voir dire examination in court. This examination is not only to assist counsel in exercising peremptory challenges, but also to determine whether any members of the venire should be excused for cause. However, the number of questions necessary to ferret out cause is far smaller than the number that lawyers find helpful in making peremptory challenges. Questions for the latter purpose are geared to enable the lawyers to rank everyone in the pool of prospective jurors from most desirable to least desirable.

Does the Judge or Counsel Conduct It?

Jurisdictions differ widely both on the extent of voir dire interrogation and on who asks the questions. When judges rather than lawyers ask the questions, they tend to generate less information by questioning more succinctly and tending not to follow up relatively ambiguous answers. The least amount of information emerges in the jurisdictions in which the judge alone asks the questions and they are limited to what would constitute cause, such as close relationship to a party or lawyer or a preconceived and unalterable opinion on which side should prevail. The scanty attention to jury selection in these jurisdictions may well reflect Saks and Hastie's view that the verdict usually is not affected by who winds up on the jury. At the other extreme are the jurisdictions where the greatest amount of information is developed. The judge's role here is limited to ruling on objections to questions and challenges for cause, while the lawyers ask all the questions, which may be on any subject that may contribute to the intelligent exercise of peremptory challenges. Between these extremes are (a) jurisdictions in which the judge alone asks the questions but goes beyond those addressing only cause to include either his or her own questions addressing peremptory challenges and/or counsel's, and (b) jurisdictions in which the judge permits counsel to voir dire the venire after he or she has completed his or her own questions.

How Counsel Should Question Prospective Jurors

When counsel themselves are permitted to ask the voir dire questions, those who accept the invitation should seek not only to obtain information but also to act and talk in a way that will create a favorable first impression of their case and themselves. When the people who will constitute the jury are being questioned, either individually or as a group, you are always on stage. According to the theory of primacy, which is discussed in the next chapter, the first impression of a case or defense will be extremely significant. If a juror's impression of you is unfavorable, it may be very difficult for the juror to believe the evidence you present. Hence while asking voir dire questions you must be careful not to offend any prospective jurors. Since the jurors may understandably feel that you are prying into their personal beliefs and background, you should tactfully explain the legitimate purpose of voir dire of working toward an impartial jury, if the judge has not sufficiently done so; and you should interrogate in a conversational, conciliatory style.

Five Types of Information to Elicit on Voir Dire

What kinds of information should you try to elicit by voir dire questions? The kinds that will help you decide which persons are the most likely to hurt your side or help your opponent and so worth using one of your limited number of peremptory strikes on. Aside from the minority of lawyers who accept any juror not disqualified for cause, lawyers who use jury voir dire should be seeking five types of information.

a. *Demographic Background*

The first type is demographic background such as age, religion, education, socioeconomic class, and occupation of the juror and his close relatives and friends. Questionnaires requested by the court in advance of jury service often provide some of this data.

b. *Personality Types*

Second, these lawyers want to discern the jurors' personality types. For example, they try to decide which people tend to be authoritarian like a stereotypical marine sergeant, which tend to be compassionate like the dedicated nurse, and which promise to be persuasive leaders during jury deliberations.

c. *General Attitudes or Values*

The third type of information is the jurors' attitudes or value choices. They can be questioned directly in this vein by asking, for example, in a product liability case what they think about consumer protection or the rising costs of merchandise. Often you may more reliably learn their views by asking about their hobbies, organizations they belong to, magazines they read, and their experiences or relationships, such as whether they or a relative or friend has been employed in investigating personal injury claims.

d. *Reaction to a Particular Awkward Fact*

Either a fourth type of information or a subdivision of the third is the jurors' reaction to an awkward fact that will be revealed at trial but should not affect the jury's decision. For example, I defended a man indicted for murder. He was alleged to have shot a man whom witnesses would testify intruded into his home and bedroom while he was sleeping with the woman with whom he had been living for seven months. I was afraid that some jurors might vote for conviction owing to their disapproval of a couple living together out of wedlock. This factor of course is not one of the elements of the crime of murder, the only crime with which my client was charged. I therefore asked the prospective jurors both what they felt about couples who cohabit out of wedlock and whether in deliberating on the murder charge they would pledge not to hold against my client the fact that he had engaged in unmarried cohabitation. A pledge like this is often extracted during voir dire. If you have done so, then at the very end of the trial during summation you should remind the jurors of their pledge not to use an awkward fact against your client.

e. *Overall Feel for Whether Juror Is Favorably Inclined or Open-Minded*

A fifth type of information is more amorphous than the others and overlaps them. It is an overall feel for whether the juror would be favorably inclined toward the lawyer's side or at least open-minded enough to be persuaded in the end to vote for him. (The latter category is usually more important since alert opposing counsel will peremptorily challenge jurors falling into the former category.) Some lawyers express this criterion in terms of whether they and their clients feel that they relate well to the juror or whether they can communicate on the same wave length with the juror. This kind of information will not emerge if the jurors merely answer "yes" or "no" to leading voir dire questions. You should use open-ended questions so that the jurors will talk enough for you and your client to develop a comparative evaluation of the jurors.

The garrulousness encouraged by open-ended questions will afford the lawyer a better opportunity to judge personality type and attitudes or value choices. Asking a juror what he or she feels about couples who cohabit out of wedlock should shed more light than asking whether he or she agrees that cohabitation out of wedlock is no one's business but the couple's. A final merit of open-ended voir dire questions is that they tend to insulate the lawyer from an adverse effect of an answer that embarrasses a juror under interrogation. If the lawyer asks a leading question to a juror which elicits an embarrassing answer, that juror and other sympathetic potential jurors may react unfavorably to the lawyer. If the juror volunteers an embarrassing answer to an open-ended question, the basis for blaming the lawyer is far less evident.

Lawyers Usually Must Rely on the Voir Dire Oath, Sometimes to Their Peril

Once the voir dire of the venire is completed, you have the data on which you will decide whom, if anyone, to peremptorily challenge. You do not have time to verify the prospective jurors' answers but must assume that they are true. The veracity of the answers are vouched for by the voir dire oath the venire take in which they swear that they will answer the questions truthfully. Nevertheless, the answers are not always true, and your peremptory challenge decisions may be correspondingly sent awry. For example, in criminal trials defense counsel invariably ask the venire, or, to underscore the importance of the question, request the judge to ask the venire, whether they or their close relatives or friends have ever been employed by law enforcement agencies.

An instance involving a part-time policeman In one criminal case I defended I requested and the judge asked just such a voir dire question. Every member of the venire answered in the negative. I used my peremptory challenges in reliance on this answer among others. The jury was empanelled. The trial went forward. The government's chief witness was a policeman. We vigorously contested his credibility. The jury unanimously found my client guilty. Later in the month I tried another criminal case for a different defendant in the same court. The jury was selected from the same venire, which at that time served for a month. I again requested and the judge again asked the same voir dire question calling for revelation of law enforcement employment. This time, to my astonishment, a person who had served on my earlier jury after denying law enforcement employment answered the question in the affirmative and named the police force of which he had been a member. It was the same force to which the chief witness against my first client belonged. The juror had been a part-time member of that force at the time my first client was arrested.

What to do upon discovery of a false answer As soon as my responsibilities to my second client allowed, I filed a motion for a new trial for my first client on the ground of juror misconduct in falsely answering the voir dire question concerning law enforcement employment. My affidavit supporting the motion not only narrated the foregoing scenario but also set forth the fact that I would have used one of my peremptory challenges against the juror in question had I known he had been a colleague of the principal witness against my client. The judge held a hearing on my motion at which he questioned the juror under oath on why he had falsely answered the voir dire question at the first trial. The juror first answered that he did not remember that the law enforcement question had been asked. The judge thereupon showed the part of the court reporter's transcript of that jury voir dire examination containing this question. The juror then replied that he must not have been paying attention at that point. The judge granted the motion. There was a new jury trial at which our evidence and the government's was essentially the same as at the first trial. However, this time the verdict was not guilty.

FACTORS TO CONSIDER ON WHETHER TO CHALLENGE A JUROR PEREMPTORILY

Despite the possibility of bits of false or half-true information lurking in the mass collected by "scientific" sociological studies, informal investigation, or voir dire examination, you must act on the data you have when the judge calls on you to decide whom to peremptorily challenge. Your decision on which jurors are likely to help or hurt your side will be largely based on this data but often not exclusively. You must add to the decision-making process your own judgments of human nature in estimating, for example, a juror's personality type or their attitude on consumer protection. You also have to go beyond the data to reconcile conflicts in it. When a sociological report on the community from which the venire is drawn advises that blue-collar workers of any age are not lenient on drugs, but during voir dire examination a 32-year-old janitor says that he does not find drug use in moderation objectionable, you have to use your judgment in resolving the contradictory signals you have received on this prospective juror.

Finally, you may give weight to generalizations in legal folklore about types of jurors. Trial lawyers from time immemorial have shared their views in speeches and articles that jurors from some ethnic origins, or economic circumstances, or religions tend to be pro criminal defendant and personal injury plaintiff, while jurors from other ethnic origins, economic circumstances, or religions tend to be pro criminal prosecution and personal injury defendant.

Such generalizations may not be reliable.

Example 1–1:

FOLKLORE OR ANCEDOTAL
GENERALIZATIONS DO NOT ALWAYS
PROVE RELIABLE

Judge Raymond R. Cross

Many years ago when I tried one of my first cases as an assistant district attorney for the Northwestern District, I was told by the first assistant to challenge any juror with a red complexion. His reason was that such a juror probably drank and would, therefore, have something in his background that would make him an unfavorable Commonwealth juror.

The case I was to prosecute involved a defendant charged with driving under the influence in Amherst. When the jury selection started, a red faced man from Amherst was seated. Seeing the red complexion, I used a peremptory challenge on him. Subsequently, the jury returned a verdict of not guilty.

The Amherst Police Chief (who was also a court officer) asked my reason for challenging the man. I mentioned that his red complexion was the determinative factor. How wrong I was! The Chief told me that the man was (1) an Amherst Boy Scout leader, (2) a teetotaler, and (3) a person who thinks highly of the Amherst Police Department.

From that time on, I never used a peremptory challenge unless I believed there was a sound reason for its use.

Using a Community Network to Find Out About Jurors

In Judge Cross' trial he may have achieved a better result if, rather than following the instruction of the first assistant district attorney, he had used the "community network" method of investigating prospective jurors. If the prospective jurors had been identified long enough before the lawyers were asked for their challenges, then under this method he would have inquired of a local resident what he knew about his fellow townsman, the prospective juror from Amherst, and which side he would be likely to identify with. Prosecutors have a ready made network of local contacts in local police departments. If Judge Cross had consulted the Amherst Police Chief before the jury was selected rather than after the verdict, he would not have challenged the red complexioned juror.

The folklore about red complexioned jurors is by no means the only one that has proved to be unreliable. Another is that persons of limited education who have not spent time away from their locality will favor the side represented by a well known local attorney over the side represented by an outsider.

Example 1–2:

LOCAL LAWYER IS NOT ALWAYS FAVORED BY THE JURY

Richard P. Tinkham

The incident involves a jury selection by myself in a north woods community known as Phillips, Wisconsin. It was an automobile injuy action in which the plaintiff's attorney came from the north woods area and was very well known. I was concerned about the jurors to be selected, and there were a couple of really tough looking lumberjacks that I decided I had better strike. Immediately after the jury was selected, the toughest looking lumberjack came up to me out in the hall during a recess and said: "It's too bad the plaintiff's lawyer struck me because I knew all about this case and would have held in your favor all the way." Evidently some of the other jurors selected knew as much as he did because they brought in a complete defense verdict.

Mr. Tinkham had expected to find parochial favoritism for his local opponent. Instead one of the prospective jurors he had challenged told him that he would have voted for his client, the defendant; and the actual jurors, some, if not all, of whom presumably were from the same locality as Mr. Tinkham's opponent, turned out in fact to do so. When the challenged juror remarked that he would have voted for the defendant "because I knew all about this case," he seemed to be saying in effect that the evidence would have been the most potent determinant of his vote on the verdict notwithstanding that Mr. Tinkham was not a local lawyer. The challenged juror thus was agreeing with the study by Saks and Hastie referred to previously which shows that evidence is a substantially more potent determinant of a verdict than the characteristics of individual jurors.

POSSIBLE EFFECTS ON THE JURY OF
DIFFERENT METHODS OF
EXERCISING CHALLENGES

The remark by the challenged juror also suggests that Mr. Tinkham was very skillful in the way in which he exercised his peremptory challenge against the lumberjack. The remark makes plain that the juror did not realize that defense counsel Tinkham had challenged him but mistakenly thought that plaintiff's counsel had done so. If the people who wound up serving on the jury likewise did not know that Mr. Tinkham had challenged him, then Mr. Tinkham had achieved a cardinal objective for lawyers using peremptory challenges. This objective is to inform the court of the challenge in such a manner that the remaining jurors do not learn of your decision. Should they do so, there is concern that persons who turn out to be on the jury will be unfavorably disposed to the challenging lawyer because they were, or had recently become, friendly with the challenged juror. The feared reasoning in short is that if the lawyer distrusted our friend, that is grounds for us to distrust the lawyer.

Hence if the exercise of peremptory challenges does not take place out of the presence of the venire and if you plan to challenge, you should request that the challenges be made on a writing that is passed between the opposing lawyers who hold it for an equal length of time. If challenges are made at an oral conference with the court in the presence of the venire and you plan to challenge, you should request that the court require, first, that all opposing lawyers attend even if one or more are not going to use any peremptories and, second, that the statements not be loud enough for the venire to hear. If the court permits the venire to see or hear the process, then as you announce or mark your challenges you should not hesitate lest the people who end up as jurors resent you for hesitating perhaps because you were close to challenging them. The lawyer who does not challenge hopes that the jury will infer that the reason he made no peremptory challenges is his high regard for all of them and his case. The court in most jurisdictions has discretion to determine the method of exercising the challenges.

In Exs. 1–1 and 1–2, folklore generalizations did not prove to be a reliable basis for selecting a jury. The "community network" method would have worked better in Ex. 1–1. Does it always work well?

Example 1–3:

A DRINKER DOES NOT LEND A HELPING HAND TO A FELLOW DRINKER

Lewis Lester Levine

I represented a defendant charged with driving while under the influence of intoxicating liquor. Upon receiving a list of the venire from the clerk of the court a few days before the trial began, I checked on a particular prospective juror with a few people who lived in his hometown. I asked them whether they thought he would make a desirable juror from the defendant's standpoint in a drunken driving case. They all thought that he would be very desirable because he drinks steadily and heavily and drives. I agreed that such a person should be sympathetic to the defendant, who would testify that he had had a couple of beers over an hour before he drove. I did not challenge this prospective juror. Neither did the prosecutor, and he was sworn in as a member of the jury.

The government introduced more than enough evidence to justify a conviction. However, I felt that I presented a better defense than I had in a number of other drunken driving trials in which the jury returned a verdict of not guilty. Hence I was fairly optimistic as the jury deliberated for more than six hours. Finally, the jury signalled that it had reached a verdict.

The bailiff led the jury back to the courtroom, and the Clerk inquired, "Madame Forewoman, have you reached a verdict?" She answered, "We have." The Clerk asked, "What say ye: Is the defendant guilty or not guilty?" The Forewoman, "Guilty."

Several weeks later I met a member of the jury on the sidewalk. He volunteered that many of the jurors early in their deliberations leaned toward a not guilty verdict but that one juror, whom he named and I remembered as the heavy drinker, was very effective in persuading them to change their views and vote for conviction.

In hindsight I concluded that the heavy drinker must have used his jury service as an opportunity vicariously to atone for his own excessive drinking. Persuading his fellow jurors to find my client guilty would tend to deter him (and the heavy drinking juror himself) from driving after drinking. The heavy drinking juror seemed to have decided to salve his guilty conscience rather than extend a sympathetic hand to a fellow drinker.

DIFFICULT JUDGMENTS OF HUMAN
NATURE PERVADE THE DECISION
MAKING PROCESS

In Ex. 1–3, Mr. Levine had obtained accurate information about a prospective juror by the "community network" method. He was in truth a heavy drinker. However, accurately learning that a juror was a heavy drinker was to no avail because he made the reasonable but incorrect assumption that his drinking would lead him to act sympathetically toward a drinking defendant. Example 1–3 illustrates that the judgment about human nature which has to be made in interpreting how a juror's characteristic will influence him as a juror may be a very difficult one indeed.

If all the means for gathering data about a venire are diligently employed—scientific sociological studies, informal invesigation with community networking, and voir dire examination, and if you are fortunate enough to obtain true data and to make what turn out to be correct judgments, you still are not assured that you will not err in the jury selection process.

Example 1–4:

KEEPING AN EYE ON THE JURORS MAY
ANSWER A QUESTION BEFORE IT IS ASKED

John M. Adams

Early in my career, I was defending an action for damages brought against a municipality. Being new at the trial game, I carefully prepared a written voir dire examination of the prospective jury. I was seated at the counsel table with the village engineer, William French.

When the plaintiff's attorney completed his voir dire examination, I proceeded with the examination on behalf of the defendant. Giving my complete attention to my previously written questions and my notes taken during the examination by the plaintiff's attorney, I noticed that the next juror to examine was Mrs. Pauline French. I thought it would be of interest to know whether she was related to the village engineer; therefore, I asked her. My head was brought up from my notes by a burst of laughter from everyone in the room. Upon looking at Mrs. French instead of my notes, I found that she was black

continued

Example 1-4 (cont'd.)

whereas the village engineer was white. I thereupon learned, by the most painful method, to pay less attention to my notes and more attention to the people involved. My blunder was made moot by a directed verdict.

Mr. Adams's blunder may have led the jurors to question how much confidence they could put in him. Their skepticism about him could have proved to be an obstacle to his persuading them to believe his client's defense. To avoid such an obstacle you must adapt to what occurs during jury selection. You should be especially alert not to focus exclusively on your notes during voir dire. Eye contact with the jurors can plant the seed for a positive relationship.

BEHAVING FAIRLY SHOULD INSPIRE JUROR TRUST IN YOU

Mr. Adams's blunder may have led the jurors after the laughter and upon reflection to hold Mr. Adams in enhanced esteem. They may have inferred that he asked the question to avoid an unfair advantage his client might have enjoyed over the plaintiff. He had noticed that the prospective juror had the same last name as the representative of his client who was present with him in court. If they were related, he could anticipate that the juror would favor his side. By asking her whether they were related, he brought this possibility to his opponent's attention. He thus gave his opponent notice to challenge the juror provided that the answer to the question disclosed a relationship.

If the racial difference had not interrupted the question and if the answer had disclosed a close relationship, Mr. Adams would have been well advised to have offered to join in a stipulation excusing the prospective juror. He thus would have demonstrated to the jury that he did not seek to win the case by unfair means. Lawyers are thought to gain even greater confidence from jurors when they voluntarily disclose a relationship of potential bias with a prospective juror which is not obvious from the juror's name. However much Mr. Adams might have gained the trust of the jury by his question in ordinary circumstances, his failure to look at the prospective juror was counterproductive.

IMPORTANCE OF JUROR EYE CONTACT
AND BODY LANGUAGE

The obvious lesson from Ex. 1–4 is not confined to Mr. Adams's particular case. Watching the prospective jurors during voir dire in general is indispensable to securing one of the grounds frequently used to decide which jurors to challenge, namely, an overall feel for whether they would tend to favor your side or at least be open-minded. Their body language, i.e., what they do, may be more revealing than what they say. There are several reasons that may lead them to say what they do not really believe. They may wish to avoid jury service. Or they may wish to be seated on the jury. Furthermore, they may answer voir dire questions less than frankly because they are so in awe or fear of counsel, the solemnity of the courtroom, the uniformed and armed bailiffs, and the black-robed judge that they calculate to answer the way they think counsel or the court desires. Thus what the jurors do with their hands, whether they hang their heads and shuffle their feet, how they look at you, and the quality of their voices may tell more about their opinion on an issue which will arise in the trial than their words.

THE PERSUASION PROCESS BEGINS,
AND MAY GO FAR, DURING JURY
SELECTION

As you watch and listen to the prospective jurors, be mindful that the people who will make up the jury are watching and listening to you and your client. They are beginning to form their impression of you, your client, and to the extent that the nature of the case is referred to, your case. If you think that the process of persuasion does not begin until the opening statements, you are woefully mistaken. Whenever the prospective jurors and the lawyer see each other, whether in the courthouse hallway or parking lot or during voir dire in the court-room, they are taking the measure of each other. In some jurisdictions the persuasion process may be allowed to proceed into high gear during voir dire.

Example 1–5:

DO NOT LET YOUR OPPONENT STEAL
YOUR THUNDER DURING VOIR DIRE

Peter Perlman

On one occasion, I was representing a small girl who had sustained severe and disfiguring burns. During the voir dire proceedings, it was my decision not to discuss the sympathy factor with the jury as I felt that the sympathy element would naturally work in my favor. However, the defense attorney very ably discussed the sympathy aspect of the case with the jury. He told them how many nights he stayed awake thinking about this poor girl's terrible burns and injuries and how he sincerely wished that she could be restored to her former condition. However, he pointed out to the jury that sympathy could have no bearing upon their decision despite all of our natural tendencies to be sympathetic. This was indeed a very serious tactical error on my part, and it permitted the defense attorney to become a "good guy" in the eyes of the jury, while at the same time minimizing one of the strongest points of our lawsuit.

The venire is always given at least a thumbnail sketch of the facts giving rise to the litigation in order to answer questions which may lead to excuses for cause, such as whether they have previous knowledge about the dispute or have already decided what the verdict should be. But many jurisdictions or many judges in their discretion would not allow counsel in voir dire to go so far beyond the unadorned facts as the defense attorney did in Ex. 1–5. While he would be permitted in his summation to amplify his position on sympathy as he did in voir dire, a large number of courts would not even permit him to do so in his opening statement.

Be that as it may, Mr. Perlman is correct that, if the court was going to permit the defense attorney's unbridled argument during voir dire, he too should have spoken during voir dire about the plaintiff's sympathy factor in the course of describing her injuries. As counsel for the plaintiff Mr. Perlman could have done so ahead of the defendant's attorney. Thus the latter would not have stolen the thunder of his sympathy factor from him, and he would have had the force of primacy on his side. Both primacy and stealing an opponent's thunder are discussed in Chap. 2 on the Opening Statement. Most jurisdictions limit references to the merits of the case so narrowly during voir dire that further description of these concepts may await Chap. 2. However, as Mr. Perlman learned, a particular court may permit voir dire to grow from the place where the initial seeds of persuasion are planted to a fully flowering field. When this happens, the lessons about persuasion in opening statements and summations in Chaps. 2 and 6 apply to jury selection as well.

SUMMARY

There are those in the legal profession who believe that the composition of the jury makes no impact on the verdict in a case. Their view is that issues in the courtroom are decided according to the evidence presented and undoubtedly they would agree, according to the skillfulness with which each lawyer presents his or her case. But the majority of lawyers believe that the composition of the jury can influence the verdict. They consider the jury selection process to be an integral part of trying cases. Although the identity of potential jurors ordinarily is not known very long before the jury selection process begins, there are several ways in which you can try to find out whether a particular juror is likely to be favorably disposed to your side, or at least open-minded enough to be persuaded to find for your client. The most common ways are "scientific" sociological studies, informal investigation with community networking, court questionnaires, and voir dire of the venire.

During voir dire the judge and/or the lawyers ask the prospective jurors for information that either bears on whether there is cause to excuse a juror or, in most jurisdictions, helps the lawyers to decide how to use their peremptory challenges. Open-ended questions result in the most information and, therefore are the most productive. They also best insulate against the venire feeling that a lawyer or the judge intended to embarrass a prospective juror.

At the conclusion of the voir dire the lawyers may challenge prospective jurors for cause or peremptorily. A juror will be excused for cause if unable to decide the case impartially and solely on the basis of the evidence and the law. Each side is allowed a number of peremptory challenges.

You may exercise peremptory challenges without stating a reason and for any reason, except that government counsel and perhaps other counsel may not challenge solely on the basis of race. Peremptory challenges must be used with prudence, as each side is often limited to as few as three or four. It is almost always the case that you will not know who your opponent will challenge. It is frequently the case that you will not know who will replace the jurors you have challenged. For these reasons you can end up with more undesirable jurors than the ones you struck in the first place. To try to avoid this and to guide your exercise of peremptory challenges, you should endeavor to learn enough about each potential juror to be able to rank all of them in order of desirableness.

Five types of information about the prospective jurors which you can elicit through voir dire have been discussed in this chapter. Demographic background, personality types and value choices or attitudes may reveal a great deal about how a juror is likely to vote. Sometimes indirect questions about interests and hobbies will point more truthfully to a juror's attitudes and values than direct questions. You also would be well advised to ask potential jurors how they would react to an awkward fact that will surface at trial but should not affect the jury's decision. You might find that a juror, otherwise impartial on the merits of the case, would be unfairly prejudiced against your client because of a collateral circumstance. From the voir dire you should try to get an overall feel about how each potential juror will react to the case. Keep an eye on the venire at all times, for sometimes body language reveals more about people than their answers to questions. It is important to appear fair, friendly, and unthreatening, as you do not want to create an unfavorable first impression with the future jury. Challenges should be made outside the hearing of the venire, lest persons who wind up on the jury feel offended by your decision to challenge a friendly fellow potential juror or by their inference that you considered challenging them.

While well known generalizations in legal folklore may be helpful as guidelines for picking a jury, do not let them lead you down the path to failure. Generalizations are just that. They do not apply to every person who falls in a category. Of course before you decide whether to challenge you should add your knowledge of human nature and apply your good judgment to all the information you have about a prospective juror and about the persons who may replace him or her if challenged.

The voir dire is conducted for the purpose of selecting the members of the jury. Yet it may turn out to have ramifications beyond its purpose. If a member of the jury falsely answers a material question during voir dire, this fact may require a mistrial or a new trial. Furthermore, the persons who ultimately become jurors form their first judgments about you and the case during voir dire. Thus voir dire is the opening bell in the process of persuasion. Some judges permit you to adorn your questions with references to the facts of the case which are nearly indistinguishable from opening statements or even closing arguments. In their courtrooms the process of persuasion is in high gear during voir dire. To represent your client properly during such a voir dire, you must employ the principles applicable to openings and closings set forth in Chaps. 2 and 6.

REFERENCE NOTES

1. M. Saks and R. Hastie, *Social Psychology in Court*, New York: Van Nostrand Reinhold Co., 1978, pp. 66, 68.

2. H. Zeisel and S. Diamond, "The Effect of Peremptory Challenges on Jury and Verdict: An Experiment in a Federal District Court," 30 *Stanford Law Review* 491, 518–519 (1978).

INCREASING THE IMPACT OF YOUR OPENING STATEMENT

HOW TO MAKE THE MOST OF YOUR OPENING STATEMENT

The opening statement is your opportunity to acquaint the jury with your case or defense in general and to outline what you plan to prove. It should preview not only the testimony of witnesses but also the contents of exhibits, and it should prioritize the fact-finder's attention to the evidence by pointing out the testimony or exhibits which you predict will be crucial. There is no single formula for drawing an effective road map for following the expected evidence. However, there is one thing that the opening may not do: it may not argue. Argument is reserved for the closing arguments after both you and your opponent have rested your presentations of evidence in your cases in chief and rebuttals. Even though your opening must be factual and cannot argue, it can be planned, phrased, and delivered in a manner that leaves the jury favorably disposed toward your side. Similar to the statement of facts in an appellate brief, your opening should leave the audience clearly informed of your client's case or defense and disposed to rule for him or her.

Use Your Opening to Organize the Testimony and Exhibits

Because an opening is a preview or an introduction, some lawyers give it scanty attention. They do not prepare it thoroughly and thoughtfully, and they do not deliver it carefully. They are mistaken. The opening is very important. If prepared correctly, you can use your opening to clearly organize the testimony and exhibits to come, which are often introduced in evidence in a disorganized way, since testimony proceeds witness by witness rather than subject by subject. An apt analogy is to the jumbled pieces of a puzzle compared to the picture of the completed puzzle on the box. You should use your opening to show the jury the entire picture of your case before they examine it piece by piece.

Capitalizing on Primacy

Your opening has enormous potential for making a lasting impact on the jury, for they are most attentive at the ouset of a trial when they know very little or nothing about the case. This intuitive rotion has a psychological counterpart, the theory of primacy, which postulates that an audience is most likely to remember and believe in what it hears early in a presentation. Adherents of the theory of primacy believe that jury verdicts almost always turn out to be the same as the impression the jurors form during the openings.

The primacy theory means that the very first part of an opening statement is the most effective. Therefore, a number of trial lawyers begin their opening with an appealing or catchy short statement which symbolizes their case. Professor James W. McElhaney has provided the following example:

EXAMPLE OF AN APPEALING BEGINNING

Assume the case of an injured workman whose back was seriously and painfully hurt when a load of plywood, which had been placed on the roof of a house on which he was working, slipped off and fell on him as he was bending over. Liability is not in serious question. Damages are a difficulty, however, because the plaintiff's new job brings him far more income than he earned as a construction worker. Lost wages, one of the tangible damage issues, is simply not there. Viewing this as one of the most difficult problems, one leading trial lawyer who represented such a plaintiff began his opening statement as follows:

"Ladies and gentlemen: This is a case about a person who is less than a man—and more than a man. Less than a man because for him each day starts and ends with agonizing pain which cannot be made to go away with medication or medical treatment. More than a man

continued

because despite what he suffers from because of another man's carelessness, he is actually able to provide more for his wife and children than before he was injured. This case is about Joe Warren, who used to work, until one fateful day, as a carpenter..."[1]

Avoid starting negatively Even if the facts do not lend themselves to an intriguing or inspiring first few sentences, the theory of primacy teaches that you should be especially careful that the beginning of your opening does not set a negative tone. Too often openings start, "May it please the Court, Ladies and Gentlemen of the Jury: This is a case of..." Such a phrase sounds like, "This is another of many cases of..." It implies that it is a run of the mill case, which is of little importance. It invites the jurors to take a "ho hum" attitude and not pay much attention. It asks them to suppress their natural curiosity which the theory of primacy postulates.

Try to open before your adversary Whatever the theoretical explanation for the importance of the opening statement, experienced trial lawyers often labor hard to obtain the right to open before their adversary. This right belongs to the party with the burden of proof. The allocation of the burden of proof to a party is unlikely to affect the verdict in most civil cases where the burden is not beyond a reasonable doubt or by clear and convincing evidence but merely by a preponderance of the evidence. In the typical civil case you may wish to try to narrow the issues so that the case will be tried only on an issue on which you have the burden of proof.

When to waive your opening statement Your opening statement is so important that you should rarely, if ever, waive it. After all, your opening is the first opportunity for the jury to understand your side and decide tentatively, if not permanently, in your favor. Only in extraordinary circumstances might you correctly choose to waive your opening. One possible reason is that you may not wish to tip your hand by disclosing evidence before actually introducing it. However, there frequently will be so little time between the opening and the introduction of the evidence that the different impact between a surprising opening and the surprising evidence itself will be negligible.

Furthermore, even if advance notice of previously undisclosed evidence in the opening will aid your opponent to adapt to it, your whole opening still ordinarily should not be waived. The surprising evidence should be tantalizingly referred to by only noting that you will present significant additional evidence, and your opening should cover other beneficial topics in the usual way. Only in that rarest of cases when there is nothing else advantageous to cover should you waive your opening on this score.

Another possible reason to waive your opening is if you are unsure of which of several available but inconsistent theories to use. In this age when evidence may be subpoenaed and discovery is readily obtainable except from the defendant in a criminal case, a well-prepared lawyer will practically never be in this predicament. Yet a scenario like the following could happen: Inclement weather might turn out to ground a plane which, at the time you must decide whether to make an opening, is carrying your key witness on a two-hour flight to a one-day trial; the judge does not grant a continuance; and without the witness your case or defense would have to be based on an inconsistent theory. Under extraordinary conditions like these you may wisely decide to waive your opening. But in ordinary circumstances you should not do so because of the advantages of an effective opening and the risk that the jury will interpret the waiver as either a desire to conceal information from them or an admission of lack of a case.

The contribution of an effective opening to reaching a victorious verdict should not needlessly be dissipated by humor.

Example 2–1:

USUALLY LEAVE HUMOR OUT OF THE OPENING, PARTICULARLY IF IT MAY IRK THE JUDGE

Judge John J. McNaught

A dozen or so years ago, I was making an opening statement in Norfolk Superior Court in a personal injury action. I represented the plaintiff in what I knew to be a very heavy damage case and was confident that the liability portion of the case would be a "piece of cake." I was overly confident and somewhat cocky. I rose and acknowledged the court and introduced all counsel inside the bar enclosure, naming each of the attorneys and the parties whom they represented. In an off-hand manner, after giving all the names, I said to the jury something to the effect that there were so many people representing defendants that a score card with names and numbers might be appropriate. The court immediately interjected: "Do you

continued

Example 2-1 (cont'd.)

> want the rest of us to look upon your case as lightly as you do, Mr. McNaught?" That was my last attempt at humor in that case.

Rather than benefiting from primacy while bringing to the jury's attention that the defendants and their counsel grossly outnumbered the plaintiff, Judge McNaught's opening turned out to begin on a negative note indeed. The jury's first and lasting impression may have been that the judge was skeptical about plaintiff's lawyer. If so, it was going to be difficult for him to win their confidence, for jurors by and large follow signals from the judge. A few lawyers believe that when the judge remarks negatively about them, it translates into sympathy for them from the jury. But the odds are far greater that the jury will line their feelings about the lawyer up with the judge's.

BEWARE OF A DIRECTED VERDICT
AGAINST YOU ON YOUR OPENING

Your opening certainly should try to use the theory of primacy to create a favorable first impression. But a good impression can be made by varying presentations ranging from a thumbnail, bare bones sketch of the evidence to a detailed preview. How detailed should your opening statement be? At a minimum it must represent that you have evidence of all the elements of your claim or defense. If it does not, the judge may grant a total or partial directed verdict against you. This is the last thing your client hired you for.

DESIRABLE DEGREE OF
DETAIL IN OPENING

Any trial lawyer would agree that, if you make a brief, general opening in a case in which you will be presenting evidence, you should be sure to state that you will later present evidence to support your generalizations in order to try to prevent the jury from getting the impression that you are not well prepared. However, lawyers disagree on the desirable extent of detailed evidence that should be previewed in the opening. Some favor making the opening as detailed as possible for two reasons. First, they feel that primacy and the superior organizational clarity of the opening make a stronger impact than the actual evidence (the picture of the completed puzzle versus the disjointed separate pieces). In their view, the jurors will believe and remember the evidence as described in the opening far better than when later presented through witnesses and exhibits.

Second, if the witnesses you will call are in the courtroom when a very detailed opening is given, the opening will tend to prevent their testimony from suffering from lapses of memory. Keep in mind that logistical difficulties in assembling the witnesses for the opening or a sequestration order barring witnesses from the courtroom except while testifying may prevent key witnesses from hearing the opening. Moreover, their memories should always be kept fresh by meeting with them to review their testimony shortly before trial. Hence the desirability of a very detailed opening usually rests on the first reason rather than the second.

Pitfalls of a Detailed Opening

Lawyers who counsel against a very detailed opening point to a number of pitfalls in the detailed approach.

a. *Suspicion of Coaching*

If your opening foretells virtually verbatim the testimony a witness gives soon thereafter, the jury may conclude that the witness had been unfairly coached.

b. *Magnification of Contradictory Evidence*

If your opening goes into a detail that turns out to be contradicted by opposing evidence, the effect of the contradiction may well be greater than if the opening had not mentioned the detail.

c. *Enhanced Risk of an Inadvertent Admission*

The more details your opening covers, the more opportunities for you to make a misstatement which may be used against your client as an admission.

d. *Failure to Deliver Promised Evidence*

Finally, the most damaging and likely pitfall will arise if you fail to produce the evidence you promised in your detailed opening. While such a failure occasionally may be excused, for instance, if a witness suddenly became ill, most frequently the jury cannot be expected to excuse the failure since it commonly results from witnesses inexplicably testifying contrary to what they told you in an interview. The stubborn unpredictability of the testimony of some witnesses is illustrated in Chap. 3 in Exs. 3–6 and 3–7. The unexcused failure to deliver the evidence promised in the opening can be devastating, for the jury undoubtedly will feel misled and may even conclude that the client is as dishonest as his or her lawyer. The jury may become so incensed that it will overlook the fact that the undelivered evidence was not essential to the claim or defense.

Exploit Your Opponent's Failure to Produce Evidence Promised in the Opening

To exploit this pitfall in openings, you should take comprehensive notes of the opening statement of your opponent. Then in summation you should bring to the attention of the jury any instances in which the evidence did not keep the promises made in the opening. Even if a credibility gap of this kind does not per se determine the verdict, a reminder to the jury that there was no evidence of a particular point, but only a reference to it in opening, is advisable to combat the effect of primacy, i.e., to try to prevent the jury from confusing an opening with the evidence.

If an opening is rather detailed, evidence that is not mentioned may become conspicuous by omission. If it is unfavorable evidence, it may even be shocking, as in the following example:

Example 2–2:

OMITTING EVIDENCE FROM A DETAILED OPENING

Judge Andrew R. Linscott

In an automobile collision in which the injuries to the driver and passenger were substantial and permanent and which happened on New Year's Eve, the plaintiffs' attorney made a long and detailed opening. He then put the defendant on the stand as his first witness and the next witnesses were police officers and Registry of Motor Vehicles people. The trial lasted about a week. In the middle of the second day of trial the defendant began to develop a very important point—there were about a dozen empty beer cans in the plaintiffs' vehicle at the time of the accident. For the next day and a half, how, why, and under what circumstances the beer cans were present was the chief matter of trial.

continued

Example 2-2 (cont'd.)

> The attorney who made the opening knew about the beer cans. He had seen pictures of them strewn on the front and back seats. In developing his trial strategy, I think he should have prepared the judge and jury for this weakness in his case in his opening. When it was developed by defendant, it came as a shock to the judge and the jury. In the end, the jury was apparently convinced that no one in the plaintiffs' vehicle was under the influence of intoxicating liquor, and the plaintiffs prevailed. Nevertheless, to ignore this important point in the opening seems to me to have been a tactical error.

HOW TO USE THE OPENING
TO MINIMIZE THE EFFECT
OF DAMAGING EVIDENCE

The plaintiffs' attorney should have stolen the thunder from defendant's evidence that there had been beer cans in the automobile. He could have easily done so by including this fact in his opening statement and adding that his clients would explain that none of them had drunk enough to have been under the influence of intoxicating liquor. The place in the opening statement to have referred to this awkward fact would have been an inconspicuous one, certainly not at the beginning where the apologetic effect could engulf the remainder in an aura of weakness. Likewise, the manner of referring to such an awkward fact should be offhand, not prominent.

Turning Weaknesses into Strengths

Attorney Melvin Belli handled a weakness on damages in his opening statement for the plaintiffs in the wrongful death case of *Fisher v. Louisville & Nashville Railroad* in an instructive, skillful way. The damages issue was the amount the victim, a lawyer, would have earned if he had not been killed by defendant's train. At an inconspicuous place in his opening Mr. Belli stated that some years before the collision the victim had had a heart attack but had recovered; and then his recovery was tested by pneumonia and proved to be lasting. Thus Mr. Belli must have seemed honest in the eyes of the jury to have voluntarily disclosed the heart attack and pneumonia. Yet he did so in a way that converted the pneumonia from a factor reducing earning power into a test that confirmed that the heart attack would not reduce earning power.[2]

WHETHER AND WHEN TO SAY
THAT THE OPENING STATEMENT
IS NOT EVIDENCE

The effectiveness of an opening statement is customarily undercut by a disclaimer that what you are about to say is not evidence. A positive value from the disclaimer is that it should dissuade your opponent from charging that in your opening you implied that what you were saying constituted evidence. However, this protection should be achieved through means other than this disclaimer. You need merely and affirmatively say in your opening that you are outlining what the evidence to be presented will show. By once making this declaration you have properly acknowledged the limited role of an opening statement. You then may proceed to present your preview of the evidence without further limitation. Nevertheless, many lawyers preface each reference to expected evidence by repeating, "The evidence will show..., and the evidence will show..., and the evidence will show..., and the evidence will futher show...." Such repetition is distracting, cuts against clarity, and is unnecessary.

If you decide to say that what lawyers say in their opening statements is not evidence, it is usually inadvisable for you to do so at the beginning of your opening, for the disclaimer invites the jury to be inattentive. On the other hand, if you make the disclaimer at the end of your opening, the jury will have already paid attention to you and may become relatively inattentive to your opponent's subsequent opening. Furthermore, if your opening will prove to be far less factual and detailed than your opponent's, you will surely benefit by emphasizing in your opening that what the lawyers say is not evidence. An example of an opening that will be decidedly less factual is that on behalf of the defendant in a criminal case who does not plan to present evidence and whose opening accordingly does no more than stress the presumption of innocence and the government's burden to prove guilt beyond a reasonable doubt.

A STRAIGHTFORWARD BUT
PERSUASIVE STYLE IS BEST;
AN IMPASSIONED OPENING IS
OUT OF PLACE

Thus far I have addressed what the opening statement should say. There remains the subject of how it should be said. In connection with

Examples 6–6 through 6–9 in Chap. 6 on the Closing Argument, which unlike the opening usually is a full-fledged speech, I discuss some principles of oral delivery that apply to openings as well. One of the principles is that beginning a speech at a very high emotional level does not usually carry the ring of sincerity. The same is true of beginning a trial. A passionate opening statement generally is out of place, for at the outset of the trial the lawyers and jurors hardly know each other and do not yet have the shared experience of the testimony and exhibits to get excited about. The opening statement is the first date, the occasion for becoming acquainted. The time for the impassioned proposal of marriage comes much later when the summation is reached.

Accordingly, your style in your opening should be straightforward; your persuasiveness should subtly emanate from the appealing facts of the story you preview and from the words and phrases you select to describe it. For example, instead of defense counsel describing his client's car as "banging into the rear of plaintiff's," he should explain that "because John Smith's properly maintained brakes failed on a sheet of glare ice, his car accidentally contacted plaintiff's." By such indirection an opening statement can leave the jury favorably disposed to your side, which is one of the principal goals of an opening.

ORGANIZING YOUR OPENING TO BE INTERESTING AND LUCID

If the other principal goal—leaving the jury clearly informed of your case of defense—is to be accomplished, your opening must be organized so that it is interesting and lucid. The nature of a particular claim or defense will define the best organization. Attorney Jacob A. Stein has reported that Attorney James McArdle apparently felt that a self-dialogue is frequently the ideal format. Mr. Stein heard Mr. McArdle offer this example.

AN EXAMPLE OF THE SELF-DIALOGUE

Ladies and gentlemen of the jury, you must be asking yourselves who is my client and what does he want. I represent Roger Fry. He is a young man. He is what is called a blue collar worker. He works with

continued

An Example of Self-Dialogue (cont'd.)

his hands. He liked working long hours as a steamfitter. What does he want in this lawsuit? He wants to justify your decision to give him money damages.

Why does he think he's justified in bringing this case before you? The answer to this question takes us back to January 3, 1975. Why that day? Because on that day my client was a healthy, happy man driving through the intersection of Connecticut Avenue and L Street, Northwest, in Washington, D.C. The defendant put an end to his happiness and his health by driving his big Chrysler through a red light and ramming Roger Fry's car. What injuries did Roger suffer when his car was rammed by the defendant's Chrysler? He hit his knee inside the car. The flesh, the ligaments and the knee cap were so badly twisted and torn that the doctors couldn't help him without a complicated operation.

Were there any witnesses to this collision? Well, the police came to the scene and asked that same question. Frank Scott came forth. Who is Frank Scott? He is a young student. He had been in a nearby book store when he stepped outside and saw the defendant's car go right through the red light....

Another organization for holding attention that often is effective and that has stood the test of time is the narrative. Since childhood most people have been intrigued by the invitation to listen to a story. While Chief Justice John M. Greaney was practicing law, he found that usually he could most effectively organize his openings along the following lines:

AN EXAMPLE OF THE NARRATIVE

Your Honor, Madam Forewoman Jordan, ladies and gentlemen of the jury. I am John Greaney, Attorney for the plaintiff Douglas Keene. Doug, who was a pedestrian on a sidewalk, received life-threatening, crippling and very painful injuries when the defendant's car jumped the curb and ran him down. The evidence in the form of witnesses and medical exhibits will show in detail both that defendant's negligent driving caused Doug's injuries and the very serious and permanent nature of his suffering and disabilities. My function in this opening statement is to give you an overview of the evidence to help you follow and piece together the testimony and exhibits as they are introduced in the course of the trial. I think I can do this best in

continued

An Example of Narrative (cont'd.)

story form and by reference to this diagram of College Street in University City. Imagine that we had been standing in front of 84 College Street facing east on August 25, 1963, at noon on a sunny, clear day. We would have watched Doug walking away from the College Chapel and westerly toward us on the south sidewalk. (Mr. Greaney points to the diagram he is using as a visual aid.) As he approaches us he is about sixty yards away. He is walking normally and proceeds about halfway to us. Then, all of a sudden, we would see defendant's car pull out of the driveway at 200 College Street at a high rate of speed, turn west (pointing to the diagram again), weave from north to south, and without the warning of a horn or the screech of brakes jump the curb in front of 110 College Street, and hurtle into Doug on the sidewalk (pointer on the diagram at 110 College Street). We would watch Doug fly through the air 50 feet, land on his head, and bounce 16 feet further, finally coming to a stop at our feet in front of 84 College Street, unconscious....

As the last two examples indicate, there should be no incompatibility between the two principal goals of opening statements—clearly informing the jury and stimulating it to want to return a favorable verdict.

WHEN SHOULD DEFENDANT'S LAWYER MAKE THE OPENING STATEMENT— IMMEDIATELY AFTER THE OPPONENT, OR AFTER THE OPPONENT RESTS?

Advantages of Opening Right After Your Opponent

Beyond the questions of what to say in the opening and how to say it, a third question faces the defendant or the party who does not have the burden of proof. This question is when to make your opening, immediately after your opponent at the outset of the trial or after your opponent presents his or her evidence and rests. There are advantages to opening immediately after your opponent.

a. The jury learns of your side much earlier. You thus have the chance to secure the benefits of primacy.

b. Your very early opening may deny or dull those benefits to your opponent.

c. If opening on the heels of your opponent does not incline the jury to remember and believe in your side, that choice of when to open can at least place first impressions in relative balance and persuade the jury to keep an open mind.

d. By opening right after your opponent you insure that the jury will not be at a loss to fathom where your cross-examination questions are leading.

e. You are guaranteed the opportunity to make an opening statement, which would not occur if you waited until after your opponent rested and then decided not to present any evidence. In that case an opening would not be available to you because you could not fulfill its function, which is to preview the evidence you will present. The upshot is that you would address the jury but once, in closing argument, while your opponent would address the jury twice, in closing argument and in opening statement. Although the opening is a far more limited speech than the closing argument, other things being equal, it is to your disadvantage to make but one speech rather than two in your overall effort to persuade the jury to return a favorable verdict.

Limitations on Your Opening Immediately Following Your Opponent When You Have Not Decided Whether You Will Offer Evidence

If you have not decided whether you will present any evidence, the kind of opening statement you make immediately after your opponent should be considerably different than the typical opening. It should not promise to produce specific testimony or exhibits which you may decide not to produce. Should you make that decision, the jury will feel misled, and the resulting credibility gap may be fatal as Ex. 2–3 will illustrate. Even if you added to your description of possible evidence the candid caveat that you might decide not to present any evidence at all, you would still be courting trouble. The jury might well infer from your indecision that you are poorly prepared and unreliable, unless you can attribute your uncertainty to your skepticism that your opponent will produce the evidence he has promised. Moreover, the judge has discretion to prohibit your opening from describing evidence that may not be introduced because of the danger that during deliberations the jury would misrecall your detailed preview as actual evidence.

In this circumstance what should your opening statement contain? You may say that, after seeing what evidence your opponent actually does introduce, you may present contradictory or explanatory evidence without specifying it in detail. Of course, you must have a good faith basis for this representation as for all representations to the court. In addition, even if you have not decided whether you will present evidence, you will usually be allowed to develop themes which often are part of conventional openings, such as: (a) your opponent has the burden of proof, (b) your cross-examination will test the credibility of his or her witnesses, (c) the jury ultimately must judge their credibility even if uncontradicted, and (d) the jury should keep an open mind until the witnesses have been cross-examined, counsel have made their summations, and the judge has instructed them on the law.

Avoid Creating a Credibility Gap

So much for the advantages of opening immediately after the plaintiff or the party with the burden of proof. There are countervailing advantages if you reserve your opening until your opponent rests. The first is that you can avoid promising witnesses or exhibits that you learn are unavailable during the interval between your opponent's opening and resting. That is, you can avoid a fatal credibility gap such as in the following example.

EXAMPLE 2–3:

A FATAL CREDIBILITY GAP

Judge Raymond R. Cross

Recently in an armed robbery trial in Springfield, the defense attorney requested permission to make an opening immediately following that of the District Attorney. I granted the request. The defense attorney told the jury that the defendant would take the stand and say he was not at the scene of the robbery. The lawyer also said he would expect to produce one or two witnesses who would corroborate what the defendant would tell the jury.

The testimony of the Commonwealth's witnesses then started. It took several days for the Commonwealth to put in its case. After the District Attorney rested, the defendant then rested without taking the stand or producing any witnesses.

The defense attorney in his final argument stressed the duty of the Commonwealth to prove the essential elements of the crime

continued

Example 2-3 (cont'd.)

beyond a reasonable doubt. He proceeded to try and convince the jury the Commonwealth's case was weak and there were adequate grounds for reasonable doubt.

The jury returned a verdict of guilty. I am convinced the defendant's failure to take the stand and to present witnesses was fatal, in view of his opening immediately following the District Attorney's opening in which he promised to do so. The defense attorney told me the defendant changed his mind about testifying and that the witnesses he expected to obtain did not want to become involved. A problem such as this could have been obviated by not making the opening immediately after the District Attorney.

In Judge Cross' view, the jury found the defendant guilty because his attorney made unfulfilled promises in his opening which he made immediately after the prosecutor.

In Deciding When to Open and What to Say, Consider the Right of a Defendant in a Criminal Case to Choose Late in the Trial Whether to Testify

The defense attorney explained to Judge Cross that the defendant did not testify because he had "changed his mind." In the course of a criminal trial it is not unusual for the defendant to vacillate on whether he will testify. He has the opportunity, as well as the right, to vacillate throughout the presentation of the prosecution's case. The Fifth Amendment to the U.S. Constitution prohibits the prosecutor in a criminal case from calling the defendant as a witness. Not until the prosecution rests and his own attorney has no other evidence to present in his case in chief must he finally fish or cut bait. This right of the criminal defendant not to be called as a witness by the government, and the resulting opportunity to change his mind about testifying even after much evidence has been presented, should be taken into account by the criminal defense attorney. It is a factor cutting against opening immediately after the prosecutor or, if he chooses to do so, saying at that point whether the defendant will testify and previewing his testimony in detail. Judge Cross is undoubtedly correct in concluding that in Ex. 2–3 the defense attorney's apparent disregard of this omnipresent factor contributed to the guilty verdict.

Properly Preparing Witnesses

The other contributing factor identified by Judge Cross, the promise in the opening to produce witnesses corroborating the defendant's innocence, also probably was an error by the defense attorney. However, the error does not lie in stating that they would testify, nor in previewing their testimony in detail. The error apparently was in failing to properly prepare the witnesses to testify. The defense attorney told Judge Cross that the witnesses turned out to "not want to become involved." Presumably this means that (a) they would not voluntarily testify or (b) in the interval between the opening and when the prosecution rested they indicated to the defense attorney that they did not remember any helpful information, or that their information would incriminate the defendant.

Proper preparation of these witnesses, which is discussed thoroughly in Chap. 3, Preparing and Planning the Evidence, could have prevented, or minimized the likelihood of, the failure to produce their testimony. One step in proper preparation would have been to subpoena them in advance of the trial. Had this been done, the court would have seen to it that they testified even though they would not voluntarily do so. Proper preparation also would have included obtaining a written statement from them during the pretrial interview when they gave the defense attorney the information on which he based his representation during his opening that they would corroborate the defendant's innocence. The statement might have been used at a conference with them during the trial to refresh their memories or to lead them to reconsider their threats to testify to the contrary.

As Judge Cross concluded in Ex. 2–3, the defense attorney could have avoided the most damaging pitfall of opening statements, namely, creating a credibility gap by promising evidence that is not delivered. He would have done so if he had not elected to make his opening immediately after the prosecutor. Note, however, that since the defense attorney knew by the time the prosecutor rested that the defendant would rest without offering any evidence, the defendant would have wound up not making an opening statement at all if he had not made one right after the prosecutor. Everything he would have been permitted to say in an opening after the government rested he could say in his closing argument, as Judge Cross' report indicates he seems to have done. Although it is not ideal to forego the opening statement, it is far better to do so than to make one that is fatal, as happened in Ex. 2–3.

There is an even better alternative. As explained just before the example, if you do not plan to offer any evidence you may nonetheless make an opening at the start of the trial which is carefully tailored to avoid a fatal credibility gap. This alternative foregoes only part of the potential benefits from an opening statement.

Distinguishing Expected Evidence from Actual Evidence

Another pitfall inherent in opening at the start of the trial which can be avoided by reserving opening until the opposing party rests reflects the difference between expected evidence and actual evidence. Assume that the defendant is being tried for drunken driving under a statute that requires the government to prove the following elements: that the defendant drove while drunk on a public way. As the defendant's lawyer, your investigation indicates that the government will easily prove that the driving was on a public way but will have difficulty proving that the defendant drove or that he was drunk. If you choose to make your opening statement immediately after the government's, it would be sound judgment for you to demonstrate your fairness by conceding in your opening that the driving was on a public way. However, it may turn out that the government's actual evidence omits the expected evidence that the driving was on a public way. When the government rests on this state of the evidence, you would move for a directed verdict. It would probably be denied if your opening conceded the point, whereas if you had not made the concession because you had reserved your opening until the government rested, the directed verdict probably would be granted.

Positive Advantages of Opening After Your Opponent Rests

In addition to avoiding pitfalls inherent in opening immediately after your opponent, reserving the opening statement until after the government or plaintiff rests can produce positive advantages.

a. *More Immediate Refreshing of Memories*
If the opening refreshes the memories of witnesses, their memories will be fresher when they testify soon after it rather than only after your opponent's presentation which may last for days or weeks.

b. *Refutation of Opposing Evidence*
A first-rate opening at this stage pervasively will refute the actual opposing evidence by both content and phraseology, although it still must not be argumentative.

c. *Your Defense Can Meet the Actual Evidence*

You can adapt your statement to the evidence which has actually been presented against your client in contrast to fashioning it to meet merely anticipated evidence. The adaptation in content may be extremely significant. For example, your opponent's actual evidence may differ so drastically from what you had anticipated that your opening may turn out to center on a defense which first surfaced during plaintiff's case in chief. Even if you have used discovery extensively, the stubborn unpredictability of what witnesses will say on the witness stand may bring this scenario about.

Respond to Your Opponent's Challenge to Open Immediately After Him

If the plaintiff's or government's lawyer believes that you will elect not to open until he has rested, he may try to turn this election to his advantage by throwing down the gauntlet. At the end of his opening, he may challenge you by telling the jury that you will have an opportunity to make an opening immediately after him at the beginning of the trial when you can lay all of your cards on the table, just as he has done. Opposing counsel expects that when he sits down and the judge asks you whether you wish to open then or await the close of your opponent's case in chief, you will elect to wait and the jury will infer that you have chosen not to take them into your confidence but to keep your cards close to your chest.

This challenge in your opponent's opening was improper, since it is the function of the judge, not your opponent, to afford you an opportunity to open immediately after him; furthermore, it is not proper for him to have editorialized that if you open at that point you will lay your cards on the table early in the trial. Your exercise of your right to reserve your opening should not be chilled by your opponent's editorialization.

To prevent the jury from drawing an adverse inference against you because you choose to exercise your right to reserve your opening, you should respond to the challenge. Ordinarily when the judge inquires at which point you wish to make your opening, you should answer the question and say no more. However, in this circumstance the challenge by opposing counsel has opened the door for you to say something more. You should say in effect that the challenge to preview your evidence before he has produced any evidence overlooks the fact that the plaintiff or the government has the burden of proof. This means that, unless and until he produces evidence, you need not decide whether to counter with any and, if so, with what evidence. If it is a criminal case, you might add that the presumption of innocence means that there is nothing for you to say until the government produces evidence. In a word, you should deflect the challenge by responding that, under the law of burden of proof, it is premature.

You may decide to follow up your explanation given at the time you announced your election when your opponent has rested and the judge again inquires whether you wish to make an opening. If you have decided not to present any evidence and consequently not to make an opening, the challenge has also opened the door for you to explain that, as you said earlier, you did not have to decide whether to produce any evidence until you heard your opponent's evidence. Now that you have heard it, you would declare that it is obvious that it is unnecessary for you to counter with any testimony or exhibits of your own.

If you have decided to present evidence and make an opening, you may refer back in your opening to your earlier statement that you would have to await your opponent's evidence before deciding what evidence to present in reaction to it. You would go on to say that now you are in a position to outline your contradictory or explanatory evidence. If the plaintiff's evidence diverged from that promised in his opening in a direction favorable to you, you would be well advised to point that out as demonstrating the wisdom of your decision not to open in response to plaintiff's mere opening statement but to reserve your opening until seeing plaintiff's actual evidence.

WHEN TO OBJECT DURING AN
OPENING STATEMENT

I have just suggested responses to an improper part of an opening statement which you can make after, and in part long after, the opening has been completed. Should your response instead be made by an objection which interrupts the opening at the offensive point? Many lawyers would counsel that objections which interrupt an opening statement should be made sparingly. The reason is that a jury, like any audience, will probably consider the interruption of a speaker's train of thought by his adversary to be discourteous and unsportsmanlike. An interrupting objection is especially likely to offend the jury if the judge overrules it, for they may interpret his ruling as confirming their feeling that the lawyer misbehaved by interrupting his opponent's speech.

An interrupting objection should be made if the net benefit from an objection will be significant but cannot be obtained by waiting to make it until the opposing lawyer completes his opening statement, such as when his very prejudicial error will be held to have been waived if not objected to on the spot. Several instances in which an objection should interrupt the speech or should be deferred until the completion of the speech are discussed in connection with Example 6–5 in Chap. 6, Winning Closing Arguments.

If the plaintiff in his opening improperly challenges you to open immediately thereafter rather than reserving your opening until the plaintiff rests, your best response is probably not to object either by interrupting or at the completion of the opening. Exploit the door the plaintiff's challenge has opened by explaining in your own words why you have elected to reserve your opening. Your explanation can be phrased so as to be more readily accepted by the jury than the more arid explanation the judge is likely to give in sustaining the objection and instructing the jury to disregard the plaintiff's challenge.

Two Common Grounds for Objecting Which Justify Interrupting an Opening Statement

Despite the undesirability of interrupting objections in general, two of the most common grounds for objecting to opening statements are usually best remedied by interrupting objections. One pertains to substance and the other to form. The substantive objection is that the opening statement is about to preview evidence which will be held inadmissible. If you anticipate that your opponent might include the objectional evidence in his or her opening, you should try to avoid the jury considering you discourteous by moving in limine, before the opening statement, to exclude this evidence. By the same token, if the opposing lawyer anticipates that the evidence may be successfully objected to, he should try to avoid the jury perceiving him as trying to slip in inadmissible evidence by also moving in limine that the evidence be ruled admissible. But if neither side made a motion in limine, the only way you can prevent the jury from learning of the inadmissible evidence is to interrupt the opening statement by this substantive objection. If you defer this objection until the opening is completed, and if the judge then sustains a motion to strike and instructs the jury to disregard the reference to the evidence, it is realistically very unlikely that the jury will be able to do so. The cat is out of the bag.

Had there been a motion in limine on which the judge ruled, there would have been no excuse for the opening to preview the evidence which had been held inadmissible, or for you to object to a reference to the evidence which had been held admissible. However, the judge may have refused to rule on the motion in limine, as she or he has discretion to do. Usually a judge's refusal to rule at the early limine stage reflects her or his opinion that there will be a better basis to make the correct ruling once the opening statements and some of the evidence are in. The judge's refusal to rule at the limine stage will probably be coupled with an order that the opening statement omit the disputed evidence, at least if the opposing party so requests, since the judge may ultimately rule that the disputed evidence is inadmissible.

The second common ground for objecting to an opening statement, which is usually best remedied by an interrupting objection, pertains to the form of the opening—this common objection is that the opposing lawyer is arguing. Argument is clearly prohibited from an opening statement. What is often unclear, however, is the line between proper opening and improper argument. Most opening statements could contain a spectrum of assertions which would range from one extreme of plainly improper argument to the opposite extreme of plainly proper opening. At the argumentative extreme are a comparison of the credibility of witnesses (although not a statement that the jury will in the end be called on to compare credibility), an assertion of the common sense meaning of the evidence, an exhortation to return a favorable verdict, and the like.

At the opposite extreme is a representation of what a witness is expected to testify or an exhibit is expected to show. Somewhere between these extremes is the line denoting improper argument. If you object to your opponent's opening as argumentative, and the judge overrules you because the judge, in his or her discretion, has drawn the line at a different place, the jury may hold the objection against you for discourteously interrupting your adversary's speech. Therefore, you should not make this objection unless your opponent is plainly being argumentative.

After all, no cat jumps out of the bag if a little argument creeps in. However, if a great deal of argument pervades an opening, a successful motion to strike made after the opening statement ends realistically will be to little or no avail. When jurors' hearts are fired up, their minds probably will not extinguish the blaze. If that fire is to be extinguished, it will have to be nipped in the bud by an interrupting objection.

SUMMARY

The opening statement is a road map of the evidence you will present. It enables you to familiarize the jury with the overall picture of your case so that when the testimony and exhibits are presented in an often inevitably disjointed order, they can follow where you are going. If you avoid the various pitfalls discussed in this chapter and follow its recommendations for planning and delivering your opening, your opening may well turn out to be a major ingredient in winning your case. Jurors are usually most attentive at the beginning of a trial. Hence many successful trial lawyers recognize the opening statement as a priceless opportunity to preview their case in a clear and orderly way and to leave the jury favorably disposed to their side.

Some pitfalls in openings can cause fatal credibility gaps with the jury. If you choose to go into the evidence in detail but omit an unfavorable fact, the jury may well conclude that you had been concealing damaging evidence from them. Similarly, the jury may be offended if your opening promises witnesses or other evidence which fails to materialize. You must be particularly careful not to cause these credibility gaps, for the jury are not the only people who may notice your mistake. Any opposing counsel who is worth his or her salt will take pains in the summation to point out that the gap between the evidence you predicted in your opening and the actual evidence exemplifies the total failure of your case.

If your opponent has the burden of proof and thus the right to open first, you must decide whether to open immediately after your opponent or to wait until he or she presents his or her evidence and rests. If you elect the former, you can minimize the effect your opponent's opening has had on the jury. Opening at this point also should enable the jury to follow where your cross-examination questions are leading.

If you elect to wait until your opponent has rested, you can tailor your opening so that it incidentally discredits the actual evidence that has been presented. At this point your opening will best serve to refresh the memories of your witnesses, if they are present during your opening. On the other hand, if you have decided not to present any evidence, you will have waived your right to give an opening statement and you will wind up addressing the jury but once, during closing argument. Weigh all the advantages and disadvantages of each election when making your decision on when to open.

Objecting during your opponent's opening is very risky because, even if what she or he says is objectionable, the jury might well think you are discourteous or unsportsmanlike to interrupt while your opponent is making a speech. Objections should only be made during the opening, as opposed to at the end of the opening, under two conditions: (a) the damage to your side cannot be substantially avoided by waiting to move to strike until the opening is completed or by exposing the error in your own opening or summation; and (b) the negative effect on the jury by interrupting your opponent promises to be outweighed by the negative effect of what your opponent is telling the jury. Common examples of errors by your opponent which call for interrupting objection are arguing in the opening or previewing inadmissible evidence. When possible, a pretrial motion in limine against inadmissible evidence in the opening is the ideal remedy.

REFERENCE NOTES

1. J. McElhaney, *McElhaney's Trial Notebook*, 2nd ed. © copyright 1987 by American Bar Association and James W. McElhaney, p. 90.

2. M.M. Belli, *The Voice of the Modern Trial Lawyer; An Album of Three Long Play Recordings*, "Opening Statement—Fisher Case." © copyright The Belli Foundation.

CHAPTER THREE

PREPARING AND PLANNING THE EVIDENCE

CAREFUL SELECTION AND THOROUGH PREPARATION OF WITNESSES

Like other artists a trial lawyer usually improves with experience, and experience can only come over time. If the lawyer's inexperience is so extreme that he or she is unable to perform the fundamentals such as opening statement, direct and cross-examination of lay and expert witnesses, objection, introduction of exhibits, and closing argument, then that lawyer is incompetent. When incompetent, the lawyer must insist that his client engage a competent lawyer to try the case alone or with him. A.B.A. Model Rule of Professional Conduct 1.1 (1983); A.B.A. Code of Professional Responsibility DR 6-101 (A)(1) (1980).

If a trial lawyer is competent but inexperienced, the lawyer's inexperience is excusable provided he or she thoroughly prepares for trial. On the other hand, lack of preparation is not excusable, even by the most experienced trial lawyer. That preparation is a sine qua non of proper trial representation, regardless of the experience of the lawyer, is recognized in numerous decisions holding that it is reversible error to be ordered to proceed to trial without a reasonable opportunity to prepare.

You must make the most of your opportunity to prepare for trial. At a minimum you must line up witnesses for each essential element of a claim or defense on which you have the burden of proof or going forward.

Example 3–1:

INADEQUATE PREPARATION OF EVIDENCE

Chief Judge Frank H. Freedman

To show a recent example of an error in a jury-waived criminal trial in my court, a defendant was charged with knowingly and willfully retarding passage of the mail, in violation of Title 18, United States Code, Section 1701.

In order to prove the allegation, the government must prove that the envelope was in the passage of mail, that the act or acts of the defendant obstructed or retarded such passage of mail, and that the defendant committed such acts knowingly and willfully, all beyond a reasonable doubt.

The phrase "passage of mail" means "the transmission of mail matter from the time the same is deposited in a place designated by law or by the rules of the Post Office Department up to the time the same is delivered to the person to whom it is addressed."

In this case, the prosecutor met all elements of the crime but one—a vital one. He had to prove that the letter was in the passage of mail, i.e., that it was mailed and there was an addressee or mailee to whom the letter could have been delivered prior to the time it was retarded. In this case the prosecutor made a significant omission. He introduced as a witness the mailer of the letter from California who testified that he had, in fact, placed the letter in the mailbox. However, although the prosecutor subpoenaed a witness from a distance of about 3000 miles, he failed to subpoena the addressee from Massachusetts who was only about twenty miles from the courthouse to prove the necessary element that there was a real person to whom the letter could have been delivered before being retarded.

This failure to prove the case beyond a reasonable doubt which could only be done by evidence and not by argument alone resulted in my allowing a judgment of acquittal for the defendant.

In any trial, preparation must be carefully analyzed so that the trial lawyer is able and ready to prove his case in all aspects and to leave nothing to conjecture.

The prosecutor may not have prepared to prove the existence of the addressee to whom the letter could have been delivered because he had not done the legal research to learn of this element of the crime. On the other hand, he may have failed to produce this necessary witness even though he knew of this element of the crime. Since the witness was within twenty miles of the courthouse, the prosecutor may have procrastinated about subpoenaing him and then forgot him shortly before trial when intense preparation tends to become very hectic. As the person who lives very close to a meeting place usually is the last to arrive, so the trial preparations which are near at hand are the most likely to fail to be finished. The propensity to procrastinate notwithstanding, you must make all the preparations, those both near and far.

Subpoena All Witnesses You May Want to Testify

Note that Chief Judge Freedman described the prosecutor's error as failing "to subpoena the addressee." Chief Judge Freedman did not describe the error as failing "to request the addressee" to testify, and with good reason. Your process of preparing the witnesses for trial is incomplete until you have subpoenaed them (or the depositions are taken of those beyond the reach of the trial subpoena power); for unless they have been subpoenaed, the trial court will direct that the trial proceed despite the fact that vital witnesses have not appeared. Often witnesses who are favorably disposed to your client will earnestly protest that they will testify voluntarily and need not be subpoenaed; this protest is especially common when the law requires that they be paid a witness fee with the subpoena for it to be enforceable. Indeed, they sometimes will say that they are insulted that you do not trust them to appear voluntarily. You must persevere to serve the subpoena on even the most trustworthy witness, since, if unforeseen forces beyond the witness' control prevent his or her appearance, you are without recourse unless the witness has been subpoenaed. In addition to serving the subpoena, you should assure the witness that there is no mistrust and explain that the service is a customary legal practice and the only way you can shield your client from prejudice in the event that circumstances beyond the witness' control prevent him or her from making it to court on time.

Subpoena enhances credibility of cooperative witnesses If a hypothetical witness existed whom no circumstances could prevent from attending the trial, there still would be an ancillary advantage to subpoenaing that witness, although this advantage may not always outweigh the disadvantage that the witness may become hostile because he or she feels mistrusted. The ancillary advantage materializes if the cross-examiner tries to impeach the witness' credibility by asking, "You voluntarily came to court to testify against my client because you want to do everything you can to hurt my client, isn't that right?" The subpoenaed witness would reply, "No, I was served a subpoena, which left me no choice about testifying."

It is always to your client's advantage to enhance the credibility of his or her witnesses. You must be sensitive to how a jury will react to them, since the jury's impression of the witnesses may well determine their verdict. Whether or not you have subpoenaed a witness may be read by the jury as a clue to the witness' motivation for testifying. When possible, you should avoid calling a witness who is likely to engender a negative jury reaction. Although you must be sure to call all necessary witnesses to prevent the error of Ex. 3–1, you should refrain from calling unnecessary witnesses who may only harm your case.

Unnecessary and Harmful Witnesses

A witness who is not necessary to establish an essential element of your claim or defense can by virtue of his or her demeanor, personality, relationship, or character cause the jury to rule against you on the facts. Consider the son-in-law/mother-in-law relationship in the following example.

Example 3–2:

MAKE SURE WITNESSES DO NOT HAVE ULTERIOR MOTIVES

An Anonymous Trial Lawyer

I have represented a railroad for many years.

A workman on the right-of-way brought a suit alleging serious injuries to his shoulder, resulting from a defective crowbar that slipped out from under the spike he was trying to remove from a crosstie. I pleaded the simple tool doctrine, and that in truth he had long suffered from arthritis in the shoulder joint. I had abundant medical and other evidence of his prior painful condition. His mother-in-law had admitted to our claim agent that plaintiff had indeed suffered from crippling arthritis before this alleged accident. To tie my case tight, I put her on the stand as my last witness. At that point I lost my case. In response to plaintiff's cross-examination she admitted that she and her son-in-law had fought from the day he

continued

Example 3-2 (cont'd.)

> married her daughter, and from her manner it was evident she relished the occasion for evening the score at last.
>
> She lived up to the reputation of mothers-in-law. The jury promptly by their expressions joined in the combat on the side of the son-in-law against this old virago. I was doing fine until I tried to overprove my case with her testimony.

Interviewing Witnesses Is Essential to Proper Preparation

Since the railroad's lawyer had abundant other evidence of his defense that the plaintiff had pre-existing crippling arthritis, he should have foregone the plaintiff's mother-in-law as a witness. If he did not feel that the generalization in our culture that mothers-in-law are inimical to sons-in-law alone would lead the jury to reject the pre-existing arthritis defense, he should have interviewed her before trial probingly to determine whether the cross-examiner could show what he turned out to show, namely, that her particular relationship with her son-in-law was indeed very hostile. In fact it appears from the lawyer's recitation of the incident that he had not interviewed her in this regard but had left the interview to the railroad's claim agent.

If you are sensitive to the impact tangential matters like an in-law relationship can have on a jury, you can interview a prospective witness far more productively than a claims agent or insurance adjuster who has not tried cases. For this reason inter alia, and if resources permit, you should not call a witness to the stand without first personally interviewing him or her or having the benefit of an interview by a trusted associate counsel.

Even if you interview a prospective witness probingly, you may not always succeed in ferreting out a subtle characteristic which may alienate the jury. Other characteristics, however, are not difficult to detect.

Example 3–3:

CHEWING GUM RUINS THE EFFECTIVENESS OF A WITNESS

Mayo A. Darling

In one case I had my so-called "star witness" on the stand, but without having paid too much prior attention to his actions or appearance. His testimony was going in very effectively, I thought,

continued

Example 3-3 (cont'd.)

> until out of a clear blue sky the judge turned to him and asked, "Do you chew gum in church?" I'm afraid that ruined the effectiveness of the witness, and I realized that I should have noticed that he was chewing gum before letting him take the stand.

As motorists are held to see that which is plainly to be seen before them, so you are responsible to look your witnesses over before calling them to the witness stand. Mr. Darling may have perfectly interviewed his "star witness" in advance of trial, but that interview was for nought because he did not notice the witness was chewing gum at the trial.

Failure to look the witness over before calling him to the stand may well have led to loss of the verdict in the next example as well.

Example 3–4:

> ### BEWARE OF THE GLITTER AND EGO OF A
> ### MATERIALLY INJURED CLIENT
>
> #### Judge Samuel P. King
>
> Many years ago, I represented the owner of an automobile which, while in a legal parking space, had been sideswiped by a moving vehicle. The parked car was a Cadillac and was extensively damaged. The owner was not present at the time the damage was inflicted, did not know from personal knowledge what had happened, and carried full coverage which reimbursed him for all costs of repairs.
>
> We sued the driver of the moving vehicle for the property damage and loss of use of the Cadillac. The defense was unavoidable accident because an unidentified vehicle coming from the other direction forced the defendant to veer to the right into my client's Cadillac. There were no other witnesses to this alleged emergency.
>
> I called my client solely for the purpose of testifying to ownership, loss of use, and costs of repairs, all of which could have been established by other means. As soon as I got a good look at him on the stand, I knew I had made a mistake. He was dressed in the flashiest outfit I have ever seen. He wore several rings with huge stones, some diamonds. Questions concerning ownership and bills for repairs went quickly and routinely. Then when I asked him to tell
>
> *continued*

Example 3-4 (cont'd.)

the jury about the loss of use, my client proceeded to tell the jury what an important person he was, how he could not be seen driving anything but another Cadillac, and similar egotistical puffings.

I cut him short, but the defense attorney had gotten the scent and led my client down the rosy path of self-aggrandizement. The jury (demanded by the defense) was completely alienated. Every juror was ready to find for the defense if given an opportunity to do so. They were, and they did.

It is almost needless to add that the defendant appeared in worn clothing and spoke quietly, modestly, sincerely, and apologetically, and that the real law suit was between two insurance companies.

That experience made a believer out of me when I was advised by more experienced trial counsel to beware of open-ended questions even on direct examination.

Open-ended questions—always know what the answer will be before you ask an open-ended question on an important subject

Judge King received sage advice when he was told to beware of open-ended questions even on direct examination. Chapter 5, The Keys to Successful Cross-Examination, deals with their dangers on cross-examination. During direct examination open-ended questions can give a witness free reign to display his egotistical personality in particular and to break or make your case in general. Their opposite number, the leading question, is prohibited on direct examination. Hence as a direct examiner you have no choice but to use relatively open-ended questions. However, you can minimize the danger that when you ask, "Please tell the jury about the loss of use of your car," the witness will froth at the mouth with choices of words and expressions of values which alienate the jury.

The place to minimize this danger is in the pretrial interview. At this point you may ask the open-ended question and learn the witness' answer. When the answer froths with egotistical puffings, you should point out to your witness that whether he is important is not the issue to be tried but is an extraneous topic which may alienate the jury. You should advise your witness to excise the extraneous parts of his answer, and try to answer the question again in a straightforward, factual fashion. If the witness does so successfully, you should remind him to answer the same way at trial and arrange to meet with him again shortly before trial for another dry run. You should know what the answer will be before you ask a very open-ended question on an important subject.

Break down open-ended questions If you conclude that the witness is unlikely to be able to answer an open-ended question satisfactorily, you should try to minimize the potential damage by breaking the question down into relatively less open-ended questions. Ask the witness before trial what his answer will be to each question. For example, instead of asking, "Please tell the jury about the loss of use of your car," you should ask, "Do you use a car in your work?" "What do you do with a car in your work?" "How often per week do you use a car for work?" The answers to these more narrow questions are likely to be free of extraneous, obnoxious remarks because they give your witness far less room to wander.

Opposing counsel might object to less open-ended direct examination questions as leading. However, every question is leading to some degree—it always suggests an answer to a greater degree than if it were not asked. Analytically, the issue is whether the questions objected to are so leading that the judge should exclude them. One factor against the judge excluding these broken down questions is that they do not so directly put the answer in the witness' mouth as they might. Surely the question, "What do you do with a car in your work" is less leading than, "You use your car to transport beauticians between your two beauty shops, according to which is busier, isn't that correct?" Another factor against exclusion which you should bring to the judge's attention is that the witness cannot answer the more open-ended, less leading question without injecting extraneous matters.

Of course the judge would not have been privy to your pretrial interview, but you could describe the witness' response to more open-ended questions. You must do this out of the hearing of the jury so that, as in Ex. 3–4, they will not sense how important your client thinks he is from his statement that he could not be seen driving anything but another Cadillac, and similar egotistical puffings. If the judge is not satisfied with your representation of the witness' answers to the more open-ended questions, you could offer to have the witness himself answer such questions for the judge out of the hearing of the jury.

Remember, Your Own Personal Interviews May Be Necessary

It is possible that Judge King asked the open-ended question which revealed the plaintiff's egotistical personality because an insurance adjuster rather than Judge King himself had interviewed the witness, just as in Ex. 3–2 where only the claims adjuster had interviewed the mother-in-law. This was probably the case; Judge King mentioned that his real client was an insurance company and that he never got a good look at his nominal client until he was on the witness stand. In both examples if an experienced trial lawyer had conducted the witness interviews himself, he would have been more likely to spot the in-law hostility and the egotism.

Advise Your Witness as to Appropriate Dress

Judge King does not indicate that his nominal client's egotistical puffings in response to his open-ended questions were the only factors which did his case in. He feels that his client's flashy manner of dressing contributed to the demise of the case, too. This is undoubtedly correct. The plaintiff's flashy clothes and expensive-looking rings in contrast to the defendant's worn clothing may have led the jury to find for the defendant. If before trial Judge King had interviewed the plaintiff and found him dressed as he was at trial, he would have had the opportunity to recommend that (at trial) he dress more conventionally. At best, unorthodox clothes may only distract the jury from listening to what your witness says. At worst, they can turn the jury irrevocably against your side for calling such a witness.

Even if your witness wears orthodox clothing, it should be clothes that are fitting to his or her station in life. Local customs vary on whether witnesses should dress as though they are going to church or to work. If the latter, it diminishes the credibility of a fireman not to be in uniform while testifying. Civilian clothes are incongruous with what he has testified is his occupation. On the other hand, some courts by rule prohibit police officers from testifying in uniform lest jurors unduly rely on their testimony. Some jurisdictions require male witnesses to wear neckties. Although the latter rule may contribute to the dignity of court proceedings, it is unfortunate, for jurors may be so intrigued to watch a lumberjack squirm at his necktie that they miss parts of his testimony. You should become aware of the rules and customs of the court and prepare your witnesses so that their clothing does not stand out as so different as to make the jury question their reliability.

In Ex. 3–4, the insurance adjuster who interviewed the plaintiff may not have advised him to dress conventionally for trial, as he may have had conventional clothing on at the interview. Regardless of how clothed at the interview, you should always advise your witnesses on dressing for the trial; otherwise they may wind up overdressing as did the plaintiff.

It is also prudent to interview witnesses substantially in advance of trial. The corollary, however, is that you must interview them again close to the time of trial, not only to refresh their recollections but also to learn whether anything significant about them or their expected testimony has changed during the interim.

Example 3–5:

DO NOT DEPEND ON AN OLD INTERVIEW

Frank C. Gorrell

One of the oldest maxims of trial advocacy is never to put a witness on the stand unless you have talked with him in advance. I would like to change that to state, "unless you have talked with him recently." I represented a driver of a tractor-trailer truck that was proceeding down Murfreesboro Road in Nashville, Davidson County, Tennessee. He approached a railroad crossing, but since he neither saw nor heard any warning, he proceeded across the tracks, only to be struck by a locomotive. While the wreck did not harm him personally, it damaged the tractor-trailer truck extensively and so his employer sued the railroad company to collect property damage, alleging that the direct and proximate cause of the accident was the failure of the locomotive to give a warning signal of its approach to the crossing and the failure of the signal bell to function properly. The railroad filed a cross-action alleging that the locomotive did blow its whistle, as required by law, and that the signal bell was in proper working order and was ringing loudly when the truck crossed. The railroad sued for damage to its locomotive.

I represented the owner of the tractor-trailer truck. Before filing the suit, I talked rather extensively to the driver and was convinced from his testimony that the engineer did not blow his whistle as he approached the crossing, and that the bell was not ringing. We prepared for trial on several occasions only to have the case continued for one reason or another. The case actually did not come on for trial until some four years from the date of the accident and some three and a half years after I had initially interviewed the driver. Because I was so familiar with the case and had discussed the details of the accident so many times with the driver, I did not feel that it was necessary for me to talk with him again before the trial, even though it had been a little over a year since I had last talked with him.

continued

Example 3-5 (cont'd.)

> The driver was my first witness and I stood close to him during the initial part of my direct examination in order that I could submit to him several pictures and diagrams which were submitted into evidence.
>
> As I got to the real crux of the case and the main point of my direct examination, I moved to the end of the jury box and in my usual manner and in my usual volume stated: "Now, Sir, as you approached that railroad crossing, did that locomotive blow its whistle and was there any bell ringing?" The driver cupped his hand behind his ear and stated, "Mr. Gorrell, you will have to speak up. I can't hear you." The jury and the judge and everybody in the courtroom burst out laughing and nothing else that transpired thereafter had any bearing on the ultimate outcome of the lawsuit. If I had just talked to my witness one more time, I believe I would have realized that he had grown hard of hearing during the years that had ensued since the accident.

If Mr. Gorrell had re-interviewed the driver near the time of trial, he indubitably would have scrambled to locate evidence, ideally from an expert witness, that his hearing had been normal at the time of the collision. He would have introduced that evidence at trial ahead of a forthright acknowledgment that since that time his hearing had become impaired. Mr. Gorrell never would have allowed his witness' impaired hearing to be revealed at trial in the devastating way it was.

Filter Out Dispensable Witnesses

Despite the driver's defective hearing, Mr. Gorrell had no choice but to use him as a witness. He was apparently the only person who could testify to an essential element of plaintiff's claim, namely, that the locomotive gave no warning signal that it was approaching the crossing. In Ex. 3–2 the defendant's attorney would not have used the plaintiff's mother-in-law as a witness if she had been properly interviewed, for he had abundant other evidence of the pre-existing arthritis. Likewise in Ex. 3–4, Judge King would not have selected the plaintiff as a witness if he had been properly sized up before trial inasmuch as Judge King could have proven all the elements of his case by other means. Obnoxious witnesses simply should not be used when they are not necessary.

When Possible, Observe the Witnesses Testify Before Trial

In Ex. 5–8 in Chap. 5, George V. Higgins, the prosecutor, chose Mrs. Babbitt to be a witness after observing her testify in a different forum. Her brief direct testimony to the effect that the bank robbery did in fact take place could have been elicited from numerous people who were present during the robbery. Mr. Higgins selected Mrs. Babbitt because he had observed her testify before the grand jury, where she displayed the no-nonsense qualities which turned out so crucial in the bank robbery prosecution. It is of immense value for you to be able to observe your prospective witnesses testify in another forum prior to the trial you are preparing. It will help you to decide which of them to call and what subjects to question them on. It will help to gauge the impression they will make on the jury.

By the same token it is of immense value for you to observe the prospective opposing witnesses testify prior to the trial. The way you size up the prospective witnesses on both sides will figure prominently in your ultimate position on compromise settlement or a plea bargain. The most common opportunities for sizing up the impression people make when they are actually on the witness stand are preliminary hearings and grand jury appearances in criminal cases and discovery depositions in civil cases. Indeed, some depositions are taken just to measure how good a witness a person will make. On the other hand, when an opposing party takes your client's deposition, the client often reacts with consternation. In trying to reassure your client, you might want to point out that testifying in a deposition will make him or her a more experienced, and hence effective, witness at trial. Note, however, that the deposition will afford you an opportunity to forecast how your client will present herself or himself as a witness to the jury.

When there is no opportunity to observe your client or witness testify on a real witness stand, you can try to recreate the experience by devices like having the witness "testify" in a vacant courtroom. Of course you should also size up prospective witnesses from interviews with them and whatever you can learn from people who know them. But you can be more confident if you see a person on a real witness stand. There is something about the oath and the formal trappings of a court in session which may uniquely affect the impressions witnesses make.

Favorable Witnesses May Disappoint You

As has been seen there are compelling reasons, such as in-law hostility or general obnoxiousness, to forego calling some witnesses.

But after you have decided that a person will make a good witness and you put him or her on the stand, you may still have difficulty with that person. Even the most thorough initial and follow-up interviews cannot guarantee your witness' performance on the stand.

Example 3–6:

THE NEED TO TAKE ELECTRONIC OR
WRITTEN STATEMENTS BY WITNESSES

Ralph I. Lancaster, Jr.

A car operated by our client was proceeding easterly on a narrow street in a residential area. Snowbanks were piled high on either side of the street. A collision occurred between the left front of our client's vehicle and the left front of a gray Volkswagen operated by a young lady who had her three-year-old daughter as a passenger in the right front seat. Predictably, each driver insisted she was on her own side of the road. Our client stated that when she came around the curve on which the accident occurred, she saw the other driver looking at her child and the other driver's vehicle headed for her. She further testified that, despite evasive action, she could not avoid the collision. The accident occurred at about 8 A.M.

On the day following the collision our client's husband personally reported the accident to his insurance agent. A managing partner of the insurance company told the client's husband, "I bet that's the same woman who ran me off the road." He then said that, at approximately 8 A.M. the preceding morning, he had been at a point about one-quarter of a mile westerly of the accident on the same street when a light colored Volkswagen operated by a woman with a small child as a passenger in the front seat had forced him to drive up into a snowbank. He said when he first saw the car, the woman was looking at the young child and coming straight at him.

My associate interviewed the witness but did not take a written statement, principally because he was friendly with our client.

On the day before trial my associate again interviewed the witness and he again confirmed the story he had originally told our client's husband.

On the second day of the trial, we offered the witness. He had not been contacted by either the investigator or the attorney for the defendant's insurance carrier. Defendant's counsel asked at side bar for a summary of his testimony. We told the court what the witness

continued

Example 3-6 (cont'd.)

had told us. Over vigorous and vehement objection, the court ruled that the testimony was admissible.

The witness then testified as he had previously talked with us in all respects save one: he did not testify that when he first saw the car the woman was looking at the young child. Because he was our witness and we could not lead him, it was not clear whether he was contradicting that statement or whether he had simply forgotten it. His direct testimony concluded the testimony for the day. Defense counsel then moved to strike his testimony and the court indicated that without the testimony that the woman was looking at the child, it would not have admitted the testimony. We thought that ruling wrong then and we think it wrong now, but it was obvious that we were not going to be able to persuade the judge. The judge indicated that he would probably grant a mistrial in the morning, but that he wanted to think about it overnight.

The next morning, faced with the sure prospect of a mistrial, we volunteered to call the witness out of the presence of the jury and ask him the leading question we were prevented from presenting before. The court agreed to this procedure again over objection of defense counsel. The witness was called; however, the court ordered us to interrogate him in front of the jury despite our protestations. We had not discussed the matter with the witness during the recess. When we asked him whether she was looking at the child when he first saw her, he answered "no" and went on to say that he had a clear view of her and she was looking straight ahead. The error was obviously compounded, and of course, the mistrial was granted.

To this day plaintiff's husband and my associate are absolutely sure that the witness told us that the defendant was looking at the young child when he first saw her. To this day the witness denies that he ever told us that.

The moral, if there is one, is: always get a signed witness statement if possible.

Written Statements May Refresh a Witness' Memory

The moral, to get a written or electronically recorded statement from witnesses, is a good one. If Mr. Lancaster's associate had taken one from his witness, he could have shown it to him on the witness stand after he testified that he did not see the woman looking at her child when he first saw her car; and it probably would have refreshed his recollection. But a statement from the witness is not a panacea for all lapsed memories. There are witnesses who read their statements, saying, for example, "When I first saw the Volkswagen, the woman driver was looking at a child beside her," and still insist that they have no such memory. They insist that the statement somehow must be mistaken, although they do seem to find this harder to say when they have written it themselves or when it is an electronic recording of their voice.

Written statements may backfire By and large, however, a witness' statement does refresh his recollection. In the rare case when it does not, it may become a prior inconsistent statement which may be used by opposing counsel to impeach the witness' credibility. For instance, the witness in Ex. 3–6 helped the plaintiff by testifying that a car apparently driven by the defendant had forced him to drive into a snowbank. If the witness had given a statement and denied before the jury the part asserting that the driver had been looking at a child, defendant's counsel could have argued in summation as follows. "Plaintiff is trying to prove that defendant is a negligent driver because the witness testified that she forced him into a snowbank, too. But the witness isn't worthy of belief because he blows hot and cold on what the truth is: remember that a year and a half ago he signed a written statement, which he read over before signing, in which he said that defendant was looking at a child when he first saw her; yet here in court he testified that he never saw defendant looking at a child. How can you give any weight to the testimony of so unreliable a witness?"

The potential benefits from sworn witness statements Despite this possible disadvantage of a statement, Mr. Lancaster is correct that the better practice is to take one. (a) A written statement can help to refresh the memory of your witness. (b) It can help to negotiate a compromise settlement. (c) A statement which is given under oath subject to the penalty of perjury may be used to support or oppose motions for property attachment, summary judgment, and the like. (d) A statement under oath which is inconsistent with your witness' testimony is even admissible to prove the version in the statement under the Federal Rules of Evidence if the statement was given at a "proceeding." F.R. Evidence 801(d)(1)(A)

Beware of the stubborn unpredictability of witnesses: Get it in writing! The witness' inexplicable memory lapse which confronted Mr. Lancaster's associate is not unique. It is a recurring phenomenon which a written statement may deter. It has happened to me. In a boundary dispute, trespass, and conversion case I interviewed a long-time rural resident about a year before trial but did not take a statement from him. The witness told me that, yes, there had been an easily visible chip in the old maple tree and, no, there had not been a stone marker next to the well. When the trial date was fixed, the witness was subpoenaed to appear on the second day of what turned out to be a six-day trial. During the midmorning recess I interviewed the witness again. I told him that I was going to ask him on the witness stand only about the maple tree and stone marker which we had discussed about a year earlier; and I asked him what he remembered about them. The witness answered the same as he had earlier: yes, to the tree; no, to the marker. Not more than five minutes later I called the witness to the stand as the first witness after the recess. After asking his name, address, and how long he had lived in the relevant area, I asked him whether there had been an easily visible chip in what earlier witnesses had called the old maple tree; the answer, "No." Trying not to show disappointment, I next asked whether there had been a stone marker next to the well, and the witness answered, "Yes." To this day I am at a loss to account for the contradictory answers hardly five minutes apart by a witness who had no stake in the outcome of the trial and no known reason to favor either side.

Both Mr. Lancaster's associate and I were disappointed by witnesses who were not our clients. But your own client can subject you to equally rude awakenings.

Example 3–7:

CROSS-EXAMINE YOUR OWN CLIENT
BEFORE TRIAL

Judge Walter E. Craig

As a junior member of a prominent law firm in Phoenix, I was assigned a case by a senior partner involving a prominent automobile dealer, who was my client, against his former sales manager.

According to my client, the sales manager, without authority, had driven a demonstrator to a city one hundred and twenty-five miles distant, at which he disposed of the automobile and took his commission on the sale.

The dealer thought that the sale was made without authority, the price was inadequate, and the manager was not entitled to a commission. The sales manager was fired and brought an action to

continued

Example 3-7 (cont'd.)

recover, not only the commission on that sale, but all other commissions which he asserted he was entitled to under his contract of employment.

In preparation of the trial of the case I thoroughly interrogated my client, his brother-partner, and the head bookkeeper of the automobile agency. In each interview with the partner and the bookkeeper my client was present. I asked if there were any memoranda of the employment contract, or any formal contract, and was advised that there was no agreement, other than an oral one as stated by my client.

We ultimately proceeded to trial. The plaintiff took the stand and recited his several claims. On cross-examination I very "adroitly" pinned the plaintiff down as to each of the claims he asserted as a result of his contract of employment. Having progressed to this point, I came up with the final question that I expected would resolve the case once and for all.

I asked the witness if he had anything to prove his allegations, either in the form of a written contract or memoranda in writing by letter or otherwise; whereupon, the witness responded by reaching into his inside coat pocket and producing a document and stating, "Yes, indeed, Mr. Craig, I have a written document signed by your client and his brother." The signatures on the document were genuine. I, thereupon, asked the court for a recess.

I then showed the contract to my client and asked why he didn't tell me about this. My client said, "I thought the S.O.B. had lost it."

The contract supported in every respect the testimony of the sales manager. I then advised my client to pay off completely under the terms of the contract, which he agreed to do.

The moral, if there is one, is that in the preparation of a case every lawyer, particularly a young lawyer, should not only review the facts of the case with his client, but subject his client to the toughest cross-examination that he can engender. Ultimately the client will be subjected to such a cross-examination in trial.

Happily, after this one lesson, I followed the practice of thorough examination of my client, and had the good fortune of never again being subject to such indignity.

Interviewing Witnesses in the Presence of Your Client

Judge Craig appears to suggest that he might have uncovered his client's fabrication when interviewing his bookkeeper and brother-partner if the client had not been present during their interviews. Certainly the client's presence must have reminded them that he desired them to conceal the fact that there had been a written employment contract. If the client had been absent, they would have been less likely to lie, but they probably still would have lied in compliance with the prior request of the client.

There may, however, be good reasons for you to interview witnesses closely associated with your client on the subject of a case in the presence of the client. (a) The reassuring presence of your client should encourage the witness to be forthcoming to you, for many people feel they should talk guardedly to lawyers even if their boss or partner has asked them to speak openly. (b) What the witnesses tell you may jog the memory of your client which leads to a fruitful line of investigation. (c) Your client may be able to point out why the witnesses are off the track when discussing a topic which will prove irrelevant or otherwise inadmissible. If you suspect that your client is lying to you, then indeed you should interview the witnesses in the absence of the client. Occasionally an order sequestering witnesses will prohibit joint interviews of witnesses. Otherwise, it is not necessarily an inadvisable practice to interview in the presence of the client.

Modern Methods of Discovery Can Avoid Many Surprises at Trial

Judge Craig might have been too critical of himself if he felt that his interviewing method should be blamed for his failure to detect the existence of the employment contract. That failure would not have taken place if documentary discovery had been available at the time this case was litigated. Today one of the first steps that would be taken to defend this suit would be to request that the plaintiff sales manager produce and permit inspection of any alleged written employment contract. See F. R. Civ. Pro. 34. The thoroughness with which Judge Craig interviewed his client, partner, and bookkeeper indicates that he surely would have used documentary discovery if it had been available. Example 3–7 is a case where discovery not only could have made good its claim to save time and expense but also could have spared a thorough lawyer an undeserved indignity.

Cross-examine Your Own Witnesses

Judge Craig learned the hard way that when the client's veracity may be challenged, his lawyer must subject him "to the toughest cross-examination that he can engender." The same is true as to witnesses who appear to be favorable. You should look at your case from the vantage point of the other side, anticipate weaknesses the opposing lawyer may see, and in interviews put questions to your client and witnesses geared to expose and exploit those weaknesses. Then follow the cross-examination questions up with a discussion of the answers. Your interview should cover not only the substantive issues in the case such as whether there was an employment contract but also the bases for impeaching the credibility of witnesses, such as bias or prior criminal convictions.

Example 3–8:

A LAWYER IS EMBARRASSED AT HAVING FAILED TO LEARN OF HIS KEY WITNESS' CRIMINAL RECORD IN AN EARLY TWENTIETH CENTURY INFORMAL TRIAL

Michael A. Musmanno

[A] coal miner asked me to defend his daughter, who had been arrested by Coal and Iron Police. The Coal and Iron Police were private employees, paid and controlled by coal and steel companies but commissioned by the State of Pennsylvania. Many of them were recruited from among thugs, gunmen, ex-convicts, and characters of the shadiest reputation, since their principal function was to terrorize the industrial and mining communities in which they operated. Their concept of entertainment was to jump their horses over children playing in the street, shoot at dogs, and molest miners' wives and daughters. Assault and battery, mayhem, arson, and even murder were not beyond them. From a social-economic point of view, Pennsylvania at this time was at its lowest ebb under an industrial-political-dominated government which permitted this prostitution of the police powers of the state without shock or shame.

My client in the present case was Miss Marian Ludlow, daughter of Johnson Ludlow, president of the United Mine Workers local in the Imperial area. She had been arrested by Coal and Iron Policeman Randall Thompson when, in resisting his attempts at flirtation, she called him a "black-guard" and a few other uncomplimentary names in the presence of many miners, who jeered him. He charged her with disorderly conduct, threw her into a cell in the Coal and Iron

continued

Example 3-8 (cont'd.)

Police barracks, and held her there several hours until her father could obtain bail.

The coal company was...determined to use the arrest of Miss Ludlow...as a means of intimidating her father and his co-miners, who were "getting out of hand." It was an easy matter for the company to take the case before a justice of the peace known to be friendly to its interests. During this era certain industries in Pennsylvania, by liberal subsidies to the dominant political party, could name not only justices of the peace but legislators, mayors, and even governors and judges.

Over three hundred coal miners crowded into Justice of the Peace Rogam's office, which had once been a saloon, to observe and comment on developments. There was little conflict in the testimony as Miss Ludlow admitted she had spoken the words attributed to her by Thompeson. I contended that no words of themselves could constitute disorderly conduct unless they provoked disorder—and there had been no disorder except what Thompeson had himself created.

After the various witnesses had told their story, I stood up and addressed the justice of the peace with as much deference as I would have employed in presenting a case to the Supreme Court: "May it please Your Honor,...the defendant stands charged with disorderly conduct, and while this offense may seem trivial to some people, we know that every infraction of law and order is a serious matter. Particularly is it serious where the majesty of the law itself is involved; that is to say, where the alleged injured party happens to be none other than a police officer.

"The prosecuting witness in this case, Randall Thompeson, wears a uniform, and I have great respect for the uniform. The policeman's uniform is a symbol of security, it is a badge of protection, it is a token of honor, peace, and dignity. The American citizen, as he passes a policeman's uniform on his way home at night, is reassured that his home, which is his castle, will be inviolate and safe from attack and harm. In the blue of a policeman's uniform I see the color of loyalty, in the brass buttons I see intrepidity, in his trim fighting helmet I see courage in the face of every danger."

By this time Thompeson's chest had expanded until the buttons of his jacket were straining at their threads. He had expected to be ridiculed, roasted, and broiled by the seemingly aggressive young attorney for the defendant. Instead, defense counsel had become

continued

Example 3-8 (cont'd.)

philosophical and even complimentary. This was indeed a surprise, a pleasant surprise.

The faces of the assembled coal miners, however, began to mantle with astonishment and rising indignation. They could not believe what their ears were telling them—that a lawyer representing the daughter of a coal miner should be praising Coal and Iron policemen, who symbolized to them the ultimate in Cossack brutality. "And so," I said to the justice of the peace, pitching my voice so as to hold the ire of the miners suspended until I could fire the broadside I had been leading up to, "and so, I respect and admire the policeman's uniform; that is, when *it is occupied by someone who does honor to it.* A uniform can mean all the things I ascribe to it only when it covers a man. You cannot drape a uniform around a horse and say that that makes the horse a policeman. You cannot wrap it around a skunk and say that that will make the skunk a policeman. A skunk will smell through the drapings of a dozen uniforms. You cannot put a uniform on a criminal and expect that the uniform will make the criminal a respecting and respected upholder of the law. Thompeson, standing here, is a *disgrace to his uniform*! He sullies, dishonors, debases, and corrupts—he stains it with his criminality!"

The ex-saloon vibrated as if it had been hit by an exploding bomb. The miners shouted, applauded, laughed, and stamped their feet in thunderous glee. The justice of the peace, startled, rapped for order. Thompeson, his face livid with anger, leaped toward me with clenched fists. The coal company's attorney seized him. "Don't be a fool! Leave this to me. This is a legal proceeding."

"Squire!" the coal company's attorney sang out indignantly. "I must strenuously object to the language employed by Attorney Musmanno. He may not, because he is a lawyer, slander my·client. By what right does he refer to my client as a criminal?"

"Because he is," I replied.

"What proof do you have?

"Here is the proof." I plunged into my brief case and extracted certified copies of court records showing that Thompeson had twice been convicted of aggravated assault and battery. I handed them to my opponent, who glanced at them, gulped in embarrassment, and handed them back. He dropped his current objection and took up another one:

"But why did you call him a skunk?"

"Do you want to defend him on that ground?"

continued

Example 3-8 (cont'd.)

> "Well—ah, er—"He appeared at a loss for words.
>
> "I did not say your client was a skunk," I continued, "but I would be pleased to have you tell me what he is after you read the details of what he has done. You will find that he spurred his horse into a crowd of women and children, inflicting injury on many. I would like to have you inform me what part of the animal kingdom would take him, if you learned that he struck a woman with a babe in her arms. I infer from your protest that he does not belong to the skunk family. I do not think he does so either. The skunk has some pride...."
>
> The former tavern again rocked with cheers and laughter as the miners back-slapped each other in joyous vindication. This is the type of castigation they had been waiting for, and it was particularly sweet to them because a man of the law was administering it.
>
> Justice of the Peace Rogam decided against my client, as I had anticipated, but we appealed to the Allegheny County Courts, where we obtained an easy reversal.[1]

The coal company's attorney did not seem to have interviewed his witness, Policeman Thompeson, on whether he had been convicted of any crimes. Given the criminal backgrounds of many Coal and Iron Policemen, the company's attorney should have anticipated that his witness was likely to carry criminal baggage. This inquiry should have been a standard part of all of his interviews in preparation of testimony by these policemen. Except for the subject of a criminal record, the interview by the company's attorney may have been a model of thoroughness. If Policeman Thompeson was answering his attorney's questions truthfully, the latter only had to ask his witness whether he had a criminal record. Policeman Thompeson's honest answer would have apprised his attorney of the information with no appreciable expenditure of time. In contrast, Mr. Musmanno probably learned of the convictions by the much more arduous route of searching court records.

To say that witnesses should be interviewed searchingly to determine whether their direct testimony will stand up under cross-examination is one particularization of your duty to learn in advance of trial all the facts. You should ordinarily interview all the witnesses, both favorable and unfavorable, either informally or through discovery. In the course of an interview the witness at times will volunteer a clue to trouble which you can fail to follow up only at your peril.

Example 3–9:

INTERVIEWING A HOSTILE WITNESS IN
THE FACE OF VERBAL ABUSE

Harvey A. Silverglate

I was involved in a rather bizarre case in which I attempted to vacate a Federal conviction for stock manipulation. My client had been convicted and sentenced before I arrived on the scene. In fact, his appeal to the Court of Appeals had been turned down before I was retained to file a petition for a writ of certiorari. The petition was denied, but shortly before the client was scheduled to surrender to begin serving his sentence, he got a very lucky break indeed.

It seems that this client was convicted on the virtually uncorroborated word of the architect and chief villain of the stock manipulation scheme here involved. This villain, as is often the case, was given a rather sweet "deal" by the government, and in exchange for his testimony against several people, including my client, he ended up getting a rather short sentence and having numerous serious indictments *nolle prossed*. My client professed innocence, claiming that he was a victim of the stock fraud, and not a co-conspirator. Yet the jury had believed the witness against him.

The *deus ex machina* that entered the picture on the event of surrender was the publication and appearance in bookstores of a book written by the architect/chief villain/chief prosecution witness. In this book, the witness recounted his criminal history, his deals with the government, his continuing criminal activity after the deals were entered into, and numerous other details. Suffice it to say that had the information in the book been available to my client's trial counsel at the time of trial, the verdict probably would have been different. Perhaps most crucial of all were revelations to the effect that the government promised this witness more and assisted him more than was revealed at the time of trial by either the witness or the government. This raised substantial issues involving failure to turn over exculpatory material, among other violations suddenly revealed for the first time.

One of the principal points suggested by the book and raised during the course of a marathon evidentiary hearing held on my client's motion to vacate sentence pursuant to 28 U.S.C. §2255 was

continued

Example 3-9 (cont'd.)

my client's claim that just prior to the date of the witness' surrender to serve his rather brief sentence, the government allowed him to take a trip to Switzerland for several days. This trip was taken notwithstanding the fact that at the time the witness was a convicted and sentenced felon. There was further indication tending to show that the government knew or should have known that the witness had at the time over a quarter of a million dollars "earned" from one of his more recent stock frauds, and that it was likely that he was taking the money to Switzerland to deposit in a secret account. If proven, of course, this favor done by the government for this witness would have impugned the government and the witness, and would have certainly constituted exculpatory information that should have been, but was not, turned over to defense counsel at trial. It would have been a gold mine for cross-examination purposes.

At the evidentiary hearing, it was important to prove that the government aided in this trip, that it knew or should have known that a deposit of funds was a primary purpose of the trip, and that this information was intentionally withheld from defense counsel. It would have been very useful, in this regard, to prove also that the witness in fact did leave the country with $250,000 in cash, for while technically the issue was whether the government knew or should have known of this, the fact that it actually happened could not but help my client's case with the judge who was to find the facts on this matter.

During the course of my investigation prior to the evidentiary hearing, I learned that the witness had a sister who in fact arranged the trip tickets for the witness. I subpoenaed the sister, since I thought I might need her testimony as to dates and as to her brother's itinerary. While her testimony was not crucial, I thought I'd use it anyway.

As soon as the witness' sister received my subpoena she telephoned me very angrily. She said she did not want to testify. I told her she had to testify. She then said, very belligerently, that if I put her on the stand, she would "blow your case sky high." I took this as a threat. However, I knew that most of what she would testify to was documented in writing, and she could not lie. And then I got the "bright" idea that on the witness stand I could bring out her threat to blow my case sky high, thereby raising, I thought, an inference that her brother had gotten to her and asked her to lie for him.

I put the sister on the witness stand at the evidentiary hearing. I asked her some simple questions about the travel plans, and she

continued

Example 3-9 (cont'd.)

answered truthfully. Then, as if about to experience a triumph, I raised my voice indignantly and asked the witness, "Did you not two days ago during a telephone call that you made to me, warn me that if I called you to the witness stand you would blow my case sky high?" Her answer was as follows, "Sure I did, and if you'd given me a chance to explain, I would have told you that while my brother was in Europe, he ran out of money, and I had to telegraph him $500 so he could return home. I figured that this would ruin your theory that he had socked away a quarter of a million dollars in Switzerland."

I was, of course, shattered.

Listen to All a Belligerent Witness Has to Say, However Unpleasant

Mr. Silverglate would not have been shattered if he had not called the sister as a witness. Since he had concluded that she was not a crucial witness, he learned that it can be better to use only crucial witnesses. Nor would Mr. Silverglate have been shattered if he had called the sister as a witness but not asked her whether she had warned him that she would blow his case sky high. He surely would not have asked her that question if he had followed up the warning and learned about the $500 telegram when she had stated the warning over the phone. His reply to the warning should have been, "What do you mean? How can you blow my case sky high?" The fact that the witness had become belligerent at that point in the conversation suggests that she might well have not calmly calculated that she could help her brother more by withholding the information, and indeed she testified that she would have explained the warning to Mr. Silverglate over the phone if he had given her a chance.

If a person speaks belligerently to you in your personal life, you may understandably react in kind and angrily terminate the conversation. But when you are interviewing a potential witness who is not only unfavorably disposed toward your side but also hot-headed about it, you must keep your head and continue to pursue your objective. You must learn all the relevant facts. If the witness spews forth a rapid-fire condemnation of your client brimming with invective, you must listen carefully to detect anything that might be helpful or lead to helpful information. On the other hand, if the witness is reluctant to say anything, it is your job to reassure the witness and coax him or her to reveal what he or she knows. Your role as a trial lawyer in interviewing an opposing witness, who may be as vengeful as a maimed victim, is frequently not a comfortable one. You may have to accept verbal abuse or intrude on another's reluctance. Yet you are under no less an obligation to perform this role than your role to conduct tough preparatory "cross-examinations" of cooperative witnesses.

Prepare Your Witnesses to Testify

After gathering all the facts, you select which witnesses you will call. You must then prepare them to testify. Of course, you may not tell them *what* to testify. They must testify to their honest perceptions. But you may advise them *how* to testify. Unless you place reasonable limits on your advice, however, it can be your undoing, as in the following example.

Example 3–10:

MAKE SURE THAT YOUR PREPARATION OF A WITNESS DOES NOT LEAD HIM TO FORGET A DECISIVE DETAIL

Ralph W. Campbell

A number of years ago as a fairly young trial lawyer I had the privilege of trying a case in which I represented the operator of an automobile in whose vehicle the plaintiff was a passenger. The other two defendants were the owners and operators of large tractor-trailers and both were represented by eminent trial attorneys. The accident occurred when all of the vehicles were leaving McCarter Highway in Newark to enter a viaduct. The problem arose because McCarter Highway is three lanes and the viaduct narrows into two lanes. The key to the case was whether my client was trying to squeeze between the tractor-trailers or the tractor-trailer on the right had to swing into my client's vehicle to get on the viaduct.

Just after making a slight turn to the right there was a large barrier with the words "Do Not Enter." It was obvious to me during the direct examination of the operator of the tractor-trailer on the right that he had been warned by his attorney, if he should be asked to comment on a diagram placed on the blackboard by the investigating police officer, to make sure he placed his tractor-trailer as far to the right as possible. However, he was not called to the blackboard.

continued

Example 3-10 (cont'd.)

On cross-examination I invited him to the blackboard with a request that he draw the path of his trailer in negotiating the jog in the highway. He proceeded to draw the line on the diagram so that it went directly through the barrier. I thought he might be confused. Therefore, I asked the question in a slightly different fashion, and he proceeded to draw a line through the same barrier. When I realized that his attorney's admonition had made such an effect, I asked him to draw another line and again he proceeded in drawing the line right through the barrier. However, he did admit that he did not knock anything down. The barrier was at least 8 feet wide and 5 feet high.

Immediately after the cross-examination was concluded a recess was held and my good friend representing that particular driver grabbed me by the arm as we went out of the court room and said, "Did you ever see a dumber witness in your life?" My only comment to him was: "Don't blame the poor fellow for following your instructions so carefully."

I suppose the moral to the story is that when we prepare witnesses for trial, we should always be mindful not to be over zealous.

Needless to say that particular driver was the one who was found to be the proximate cause of the accident.

The lawyer who prepared the tractor-trailer driver to testify apparently only reminded him that he had said that he had been driving as far to the right as possible. He should have qualified that reminder with the further reminder that as he approached the viaduct he went left around the barrier. The lawyer probably assumed that the driver would remember this without his mentioning it. While he ordinarily would remember, testifying in court is not the ordinary activity of a tractor-trailer driver; and in the excitement or anxiety of appearing as a witness he must have blocked the barrier out of his consciousness.

Familiarize Your Witnesses with Relevant Legal Fictions

Many lawyers take for granted legal fictions such as that a person on trial for a crime who does not testify does not have a criminal record or that a defendant does not have liability insurance. These legal fictions may be very strange to witnesses. When a witness' testimony can be affected by such a legalism, you must very painstakingly and patiently prepare the witness. If the witness has to be prepared hurriedly, beware of the consequences.

Example 3–11:

LET THE TRUTH BE TOLD

John H. Mudd

One example comes to mind where I did not properly prepare the witness. Some eight or nine years ago I was defending a serious automobile case in which my client-driver crossed onto the wrong side of the parkway and crashed headlong into two young dental students. We were defending the case on the fact that our driver had had a sudden and unexpected heart attack.

One key eyewitness was a very young soldier who was flown back from Ft. Bragg to testify. He came from the airport directly to the courthouse, and I only had a couple of minutes during a recess to speak with him. I told him when he took the stand to tell nothing but the truth and not to mention anything about my client having liability insurance. I further said if I ask you on the witness stand on either direct or redirect examination what I suggested you say on the stand, I want you to reply that I told you to tell nothing but the truth, which is what I want you to do.

After rather prolonged direct and cross-examination, in which the credibility and bias of the witness was challenged, I then took the young soldier on redirect and said to the young man that I only want to ask you one additional question and that is what did I tell you to say on the witness stand. To my absolute surprise, he replied, "You told me not to say anything about your client having liability insurance." Needless to say, I wish the floor had opened up so that I could have dropped through it.

Mr. Mudd's instruction to the soldier was too brief on the subjects of liability insurance and the truth. These subjects may have seemed very complex to him. Undoubtedly, Mr. Mudd must have planned a more relaxed, thorough interview, but reality intervened, as it does so frequently. Trial lawyers' schedules are continually buffeted by planes which are delayed, commanding officers who postpone leaves at the last minute, or preceding trials which end two weeks later than expected and just a day or an hour before the next trial begins. You cannot change reality. You must do the best you can to live with it. In Mr. Mudd's case he might have sent the soldier a letter about testifying to the truth and concerning the legal fiction about liability insurance once the case seemed firm for trial. If you often defend for insurers, you would probably find it useful to develop a form letter on the subjects. But a letter received, say, four weeks before trial, would not assure that your witness would remember your instructions about legal fictions and truth. Indeed the letter might only generate questions your witness would need to discuss in person with you, and reality might still limit you to a couple of minutes to confer during a recess before your witness took the stand.

Even when there is time for a full interview in preparation for trial, your client may disregard your advice or may misunderstand things nearly as badly as confusing liability insurance with the truth.

Example 3–12:

MAKE SURE THAT EXHIBITS REMAIN IN THEIR ORIGINAL CONDITION

Al J. Cone

I remember one instance of great embarrassment to me where I was trying a case for an elderly man in Fort Lauderdale. He was a man of considerable pride and dignity and he had a presence that indicated truthfulness in his testimony. Unfortunately, his injuries were of such a nature that there was very little objective evidence of the truth of the sensations that he was having, and the whole case more or less turned on the believability of the witness. He had a low back injury and wore a back brace most of the time. I had a usual pretrial interview with him the week before the trial and told him that I might be asking him to show the brace as he was wearing it at the time of trial to the jury.

Being a man of pride and not wishing to show the jury a worn and somewhat discolored brace, without consultation with me, he went out and bought a brand new brace which he wore to the trial. When the brace was exhibited to the jury, a bright, shiny, new brace that obviously had not been worn at all was exhibited to the jury in contrast to his testimony that he had been wearing a brace every day. This had a devastating effect on the jury verdict, despite my going on to have him testify that this was a brand new, clean brace, not the one he had been wearing for a long time.

I have not yet recovered from my chagrin, but never again will anyone that I am trying a case for wear any kind of new and unworn brace to be exhibited to a jury.

Your Client's Viewpoint Is Not Necessarily What Is Best for Him

The initial adverse impact of the unworn brace on the jury evidently was insuperable. Mr. Cone tried to mitigate the loss by having his client testify that the brace he had exhibited was not the worn and discolored one he had been wearing, but to no avail. If time permitted, and the original brace still existed, Mr. Cone might have retrieved it and exhibited it to the jury also, but it is still doubtful whether this would have undone the damage.

Example 3–12 teaches that when you prepare a witness to display part of his body or a personal article like clothing to the court and jury, you must explicitly explain that they must be in their natural or customary state; and if you have a chance, you should inspect them during a recess at the trial before the display. In a broader sense Ex. 3–12 should teach you that you must manage litigation for your client's good even though it may cause your client some discomfort. However badly Mr. Cone's client would have felt to show the jury a worn and discolored brace, his accumulating anguish from inadequate compensation over the rest of his life must be far worse. In Ex. 6–4, the plaintiff was embarrassed to have the jury see her bald head; however, the dedication of her counsel in removing the bandanna covering her head may well have prevented her from being denied all compensation for the rest of her life.

Your Client Must Know the Truth in Order to Tell the Truth I once represented a client whose interest required that he and his family face a distressing truth. The client was a university student who had sustained a brain injury. My report from the attending neurologist contained the opinion that the client's mental impairments had healed as much as they ever would and that they would be permanent. But, within a few weeks of the date when the trial was to begin, the client's parents told me that at a recent visit to the neurologist he had told them that their son's mental functions had improved and might return to normal. At my pretrial interview with the neurologist, I asked the doctor about the discrepancy between his opinion in his report and his findings at the patient's last visit. The neurologist replied that he stood confidently by his opinion that the mental impairments were permanent and would not show improvement, but he explained his different statement to the client and his parents as aimed to lift their spirits although not grounded in fact. The neurologist's white lie had made the client and his parents happy. However, if they were left in blissful ignorance, their testimony would impeach the neurologist's to the effect that there was permanent impairment, and as a consequence the jury might well withhold damages for permanent impairment over the remainder of the 25-year-old's life.

I arranged a brief meeting before trial between the neurologist and my client and his parents at which the doctor retracted his statement that the young man had improved and might return to normal; the doctor explained that he had made the statement as helpful therapy for the whole family even though it was not so. The client and his parents were bitterly disappointed by this news. But it was necessary to recover adequate damages. Like taking bitter medicine prescribed by a doctor, it was transient pain which was required for the client's long term good. Your witnesses who are unlikely to disappoint you will be those who are informed about both the facts of the case and the procedures of the court.

Inform Witnesses of Courtroom Procedures, Their Role in the Trial, and What to Expect During Direct, Cross, and Redirect Examinations

Thus far our discussion of preparing witnesses, including clients, to testify has not noted a number of fundamentals. Aside from discussing the testimony which will be given, you should familiarize your client and witnesses with the following trial procedures:

- describe the steps in a trial and their order
- convey the prohibition against communication with jurors
- explain the sequestration of witnesses
- sketch where your witness' testimony will fit into the overall trial
- if possible, show the witnesses the courtroom
- to best prepare direct testimony, put your questions to the witnesses exactly as you plan to at trial, and have them answer as though they are actually testifying. This exercise should enable you to fine tune your choice of broad and less open-ended questions.
- prepare your witnesses for cross-examination by simulating trial conditions. Have them answer as though they are on the stand, while you play the role of the opposing cross-examiner.

In addition to providing your witnesses experience with cross-examination, you should give them standard advice about cross-examination such as the following:

1. Answer only what is asked and do not volunteer.
2. Do not quarrel with the cross-examiner.
3. Do not answer so quickly that the jury hears the answer before there is an opportunity to object.
4. Forewarn your witness that trick questions like, "How much will you be paid for your testimony?" or, "Have you talked over your testimony with your lawyer?" may be asked.
5. Be sure that the witnesses know that after they have been cross-examined, you will have a chance on redirect examination to clarify or develop subjects covered in cross-examination.
6. You should stress to every witness you prepare for trial that they should tell the truth.

EXPERT WITNESSES

None of the witnesses whose selection or preparation for trial has been discussed hitherto has been an expert witness. Many of the challenges expert witnesses will pose to you are the same as those posed by lay witnesses, although some are different. In some cases it is essential to locate, prepare, and call expert witnesses.

Example 3–13:

USE EXPERT WITNESSES TO CORROBORATE YOUR CLIENT'S MEDICAL CLAIMS

Paul T. Smith

This is an error which I committed many years ago and has haunted me until today.

I represented a 68-year-old defendant in the U.S. District Court who was charged with assault upon a Federal official. The defendant had been described in the press and on TV (*Anatomy of a Bookie Joint*) as conducting a major gaming operation in Boston. A subpoena had issued for him to appear before a U.S. Grand Jury. Two deputy marshals, knowing that the defendant parked his automobile in a certain parking lot, waited until after dark when the defendant entered his motor vehicle and then ran towards him to serve him with the subpoena. The defendant told me that he saw two men running

continued

Example 3-13 (cont'd.)

towards him; that he was carrying a substantial sum of money and had no idea who they were. Upon discovery, prior to trial, I learned that they were prepared to testify that they shouted "Stop. We are United States Marshals."

The defendant told me he had a hearing problem and did not hear them and drove on, striking one of the marshals. Having learned that he had had no medical treatment, I should have done two things. (1) Gotten an expert otologist. (2) Alerted the defendant that the prosecutor would probably speak to him in a low voice.

To my everlasting regret, I did neither.

During the course of the trial the prosecutor, on cross-examination, turned his back to the defendant and asked him a question, using a well modulated voice.

The defendant responded.

The defendant was found guilty and given a suspended sentence.

That case taught me a bitter lesson.

Half of Mr. Smith's bitter lesson was that he learned to line up an expert witness to corroborate his client on a subject susceptible to expert knowledge. Yet it is not enough for you to engage an expert and put him on the stand to testify. You must also thoroughly prepare him by furnishing him with all the facts that are relevant to the opinion he will testify to. The next example illustrates what happens if he is not given all the facts.

Example 3–14:

GIVE THE EXPERT ALL THE FACTS

Chief Judge Winston E. Arnow

I had a medical malpractice suit tried before me in which counsel for the defendant made a tactical error that proved to be a bad one.

Before trial, counsel for the defendant had submitted a proposed hypothetical question to a doctor whom he wished to use as an expert witness. Based on the information provided in the hypothetical, the doctor was prepared to testify that there was no negligence on the part of the doctor against whom the complaint was made.

continued

Example 3-14 (cont'd.)

> However, at or shortly before trial it became apparent that some facts had been left out of the hypothetical question presented to the witness by the defendant's counsel. Plaintiff's counsel, of course, promptly took advantage of this at trial. The result was that, at trial, the defendant's expert witness, admitting that he had previously stated he believed there was no negligence, but pointing out he was not then apprised of the additional factual matter, reversed his opinion and stated that there was, indeed, negligence on the part of the physician against whom the complaint was made.
>
> The case was being tried before me as a nonjury trial and I never had to reach a decision. Shortly after his testimony came in, the case was settled.
>
> I believe the error in trial preparation in this case points out the necessity for full, thorough and complete trial preparation.

The use of the expert witness before Chief Judge Arnow backfired because the lawyer who had prepared the expert witness had not supplied him all the relevant facts. Even though the lawyer supplied the expert all the relevant facts in the next example, the use of the expert backfired again for a different reason.

Example 3–15:

> ## BE WARY OF LIVE DEMONSTRATIONS
>
> ### Chief Justice Thomas R. Morse, Jr.
>
> Plaintiff brought an action against a bank for injuries sustained when she walked into a glass panel adjacent to the glass door at the entrance. The panel broke and her wrist was badly lacerated by a falling piece of glass.
>
> Part of the theory of liability was that it was negligent for the bank to have plate glass in a panel next to a door because, if it was accidentally broken, it would break into large, jagged pieces. Plaintiff's expert testified that had tempered glass rather than plate glass been used, there would be no injury because tempered glass breaks into small, light, round pieces that would be unlikely to injure anyone.
>
> Plaintiff's expert then went on to demonstrate. The expert spread newspapers on the courtroom floor and laid a piece of
>
> *continued*

Example 3-15 (cont'd.)

tempered glass and a piece of plate glass on the papers. He adorned himself in gloves, coveralls, a heavy overcoat, a football helmet and a clear plastic face mask. He took a heavy hammer and approached the two pieces of glass. The courtroom was hushed, and all eyes were fixed on the witness. The only thing lacking was a drum roll.

The witness knelt next to the plate glass and gave it a mighty whack with the hammer. Nothing happened. He whacked a second time. Nothing. Finally, the plate glass broke into three pieces on the third blow.

Then the witness knelt beside the tempered glass. On the first blow it shattered into hundreds of pieces that flew around the courtroom. Jurors, court officers, and attorneys jumped and hands involuntarily flew to faces.

The jury returned a verdict for the defendant.

Plan Live Demonstrations Only When Essential to Your Case

In Ex. 3–15 the use of the expert witness backfired from overuse. He would have advanced plaintiff's case tremendously if his only role had been to testify to his opinion that plaintiff would not have been injured if the glass in the panel had been tempered rather than plate. As it turned out, the expert ruined plaintiff's case by trying to illustrate his opinion with a live demonstration before the jury. Chief Justice Morse was not in a position to reveal whether plaintiff's lawyer suggested the demonstration or failed to veto the expert's idea to perform it. In either event plaintiff's lawyer erred. A live demonstration is always tricky. The risk of what in fact happened before the jury should not have been taken unless plaintiff had no case without the demonstration. In view of the opinion the expert had testified to, plaintiff plainly did have a case without the demonstration.

The inherent riskiness of a demonstration with pieces of glass which are to be hammered to the breaking point is evident: however many times practice demonstrations may succeed, the demonstration before the jury must be on two pieces of glass that have never been tried before and may fail to behave as expected. Furthermore, even when the object to be demonstrated may be practiced on in advance, a live recreation before the jury may well boomerang, as you will see happened in Ex. 4–8. The only safe demonstration to present to a jury is one which has already succeeded and is introduced into evidence on film or videotape.

Expert Testimony Does Not Always Influence the Jury

If your expert is neither overused/unused nor unprepared, you still cannot always be certain that the jury will give any weight to her testimony.

Example 3–16:

LAY PERSONS MAY SOMETIMES BE MORE EFFECTIVE THAN EXPERTS

William P. Cooney

A very difficult and hotly contested airplane accident case, which took some two months to try, was filled with very extensive and complicated testimony of experts on both sides.

When the question was asked the jury as to how they reached their verdict, they informed us that they had absolutely discarded the testimony of the experts and had resolved it on the testimony of pilots who claimed to have experienced certain conditions in the operation of the aircraft for which they could not account.

In other words, the testimony of lay persons, i.e., the pilots, not as to the technical reasons why the airplane acted in a certain fashion, but rather their own experience as to what they said the airplane did, was the convincing element insofar as the jury was concerned.

In retrospect, we concluded that it was a tactical error to bring in all the design experts and all the government experts and spend two months trying a lawsuit that could have been tried in about two weeks. Hindsight is always better than foresight.

While no one can quarrel with Mr. Cooney's last proposition, you may disagree with his conclusion that experts should not have been used in the trial at all. For one thing, the jury's statement that they "absolutely discarded the testimony of the experts" seems overstated, for they probably needed an explanation by an expert of how the aircraft worked to link what the pilots' experienced to negligence or the absence of negligence. A second reason that it was surely advisable for the trial lawyer to call expert witnesses was that the other side did so. The jury may have disregarded the opposing experts only because the experts called by the other side checkmated them. Lastly, without the benefit of hindsight the lawyer whose side had the burden of proof could anticipate as the sole evidence from lay witnesses "the testimony of pilots who claimed to have experienced certain conditions...for which *they could not account.*" (Emphasis added.) It would be imprudent if you had the burden of proof not to seek expert witnesses who could account for what the lay witnesses could not.

Cumulative Expert Witnesses on the Same Issue May Undercut Each Other

When you find multiple expert witnesses with the opinion your case needs, your work is not done. Next, you must make a judgment on whether to call more than one. The example that follows should help to make that judgment.

Example 3–17:

TWO EXPERTS FOR DEFENDANT NEUTRALIZE EACH OTHER

Judge Jacob D. Fuchsberg

Shallow preparation of an expert—like shallow preparation of any witnesses—may be a boon for one's adversary, especially when it is combined with overtrial of a case by calling too many witnesses, who in the end may contradict one another.

The crucial medical issue in the case I have in mind was whether the plaintiff had sustained a fractured vertebra. The treating physician, a general practitioner, relying on his home-made x-rays, testified simply, and unimpressively, that there was a fracture and proceeded to demonstrate its existence by pointing to a shadow running through the x-ray film. But the defendant's insurance carrier, whose examining physician had previously viewed the plates, insisted there was no break. Moreover, it had decided to call two renowned roentgenologists to prove its contention. No doubt each had assured its counsel that there was no fracture.

The first of these experts was the last witness to testify one trial day. As expected, after stating his impressive qualifications, including the many thousands of spinal cases he had diagnosed, he not only insisted that plaintiff's x-rays revealed no fracture, but that the imperfection pointed out by plaintiff's undistinguished doctor was a common congenital phenomenon without pathological significance.

continued

Example 3-17 (cont'd.)

> Defendant's second expert, equally impressive, testified the following day. He too found no fracture. But, when counsel asked him what the shadow on the film was, with an unhesitant air of equal finality, he told the jury that it was an artifact, that is, an imperfection in the taking of the film rather than any abnormality in the plaintiff's back.
>
> Though defendant's counsel had apparently failed to check each witness' testimony against the other, he earlier had informed the jury that the doctors had each reached an independent opinion. Indeed, they had. So when on cross-examination I asked the second one whether the artifact wasn't in fact a congenital condition, he avowed that anyone who said so was either incompetent or a charlatan.
>
> Later, having to choose between the defendant's two experts, the jury apparently decided to trust plaintiff's unassuming physician in preference to either and brought in a resounding verdict for the plaintiff.

Judge Fuchsberg indicates that the verdict was against the defendant in part because defense counsel apparently failed to check each expert's testimony against the other. Undoubtedly, defense counsel did check the view of each expert on the crucial question which was whether plaintiff had a fractured vertebra; and undoubtedly defense counsel did not check the view of each expert on what the shadow on the x-ray film was, for if he had done so, he would not have called both roentgenologists. It is unclear whether defense counsel's error in pretrial preparation consisted, on the one hand, of failing to determine how each expert would answer any question other than the question of whether the vertebra was fractured or, on the other hand, of failing to determine how each would explain the shadow even though he did determine their answers to many other questions. It does not matter which of the two errors was committed. Each could cause the loss of the trial. Even though some areas of vulnerability are covered in a pretrial interview, the case can be lost unless all areas of vulnerability are covered.

Anticipate Cross-Examination Questions When Choosing Witnesses

A thorough pretrial interview of lay witnesses who are to testify about the same subject is also necessary. The reason is that, although direct examination questions almost always can be limited to those planned in preparation for trial, cross-examination questions are not within your control or ability to predict when you must decide which witnesses to call. Nevertheless, the likelihood that cumulative witnesses will contradict each other is reduced by determining before trial how they will answer all direct examination questions and as many cross-examination questions as can be anticipated.

CHECK FOR CONTRADICTIONS AMONG POTENTIAL CUMULATIVE WITNESSES

Example 3–17 shows that before calling cumulative witnesses, whether expert or lay, you should interview them searchingly to check for a contradiction on a subsidiary point which may cause a jury to disregard them on a crucial point. The example also indicates, however, that despite searching interviews there always will be the risk that such a contradiction will surface at trial. This lesson may lead you in many instances to use only one of multiple available expert or lay witnesses. While something may be lost by foregoing cumulative witnesses, usually emphasis and a display of plural adherents to a position, much more can be lost if they wind up contradicting each other.

SHOULD YOU REQUEST A VIEW?

Up to this point we have dealt with selection and preparation of witnesses for trial. In addition, your trial preparation must include consideration of whether to request a view. What a jury sees on a view is not evidence, but it can have a heavy impact on the jury's evaluation of the evidence.

Example 3–18:

NO REASONABLE DOUBT FOLLOWING A VIEW

Chief Justice Thomas R. Morse, Jr.

A motion for a view occurred during the trial of two defendants on a series of indictments alleging breaking and entering and attempted breaking and entering of a number of different commercial

continued

Example 3-18 (cont'd.)

establishments along Massachusetts Avenue in Cambridge. The commonwealth's principal witness was a police officer who testified as to what he had seen and heard the two defendants do over a period of from about 1:00 A.M. to 2:00 A.M. from various vantage points. Critical to the strength of the commonwealth's case was whether, given the darkness and the positions where the observations were made, the officer's observations were reliable. For example, the officer claimed to have observed one break of a door to a store from a hotel room window at least four hundred feet away. He also claimed to have heard one defendant calling to the other to "come back, come back," from a position behind a store.

The commonwealth relied on an enlarged street map to show the location of the stores involved and the position of the witness when the observations were made, as well as photographs of the doors to the stores. The photographs showed what could be pry marks on the doors of the various establishments. A tire iron, with a sharp end like a screw driver, had been found on the front seat of the car in which the defendants were arrested. The defendants' counsel were not content to rest on their clients' testimony that they had simply been "hanging out" in the area drinking beer and talking to friends. As to a door in which a plastic panel had been broken, one defendant admitted he had been in the doorway relieving himself, and claimed that the panel gave way when he leaned against it. At this point the defendants were in a good posture to argue to the jury that the witness was mistaken and that there was reasonable doubt.

The defendants' counsel insisted on a view. On the view the jury saw the pry marks. They saw that the view from the hotel window was unobstructed. They saw the place where the officer stood when he claimed to have heard one defendant call to the other to "come back," and that it was quite probable that he could have heard what he claimed. The jury saw the street lights which added credibility to the witness' claimed observations. Most important, by going to the scene and seeing the actual stores involved and the places from which the observations were made, any confusion that may have been in the jury's mind was removed.

The jury returned guilty verdicts. The moral of the story may be "look before you leap."

Inspect the Area to Be Viewed Before Requesting a View

Look indeed! Before moving for a view you should visit the scene and scrutinize what the jury will see on a view, compare it with the information the jury will have without the view, and decide which scenario is more likely to result in a victorious verdict.

THOROUGH PREPARATION OF
DOCUMENTARY AND REAL EVIDENCE

Decision on a view and selection and preparation of witnesses do not complete pretrial preparation. Tangible evidence, both real and documentary, must be gathered, selected, and prepared as well. The constant theme running through the examples of witness and view preparation was thoroughness. Attention to documentary and real evidence, however voluminous, must be thorough, too.

Example 3–19:

THOROUGH EXAMINATION OF HOSPITAL
RECORDS SAVES A CASE

Leonard A. Kiernan, Jr.

I was participating in the trial of a case wherein I was defending the plaintiff in a counterclaim. The hospital records were brought in and were quite voluminous. Plaintiff's attorney was going to offer the entire record without reviewing each and every page. I asked him to hold off and to mark them for identification until such time as we could review them at the recess. Reluctantly this was done and, lo and behold, on page three of the hospital record there was a statement that his client smelled strongly of alcohol. Based on the local rules of evidence, we were able to have that particular remark extracted from the record prior to it being submitted for the jury's consideration. The plaintiff received a substantial verdict, and he deserved it.

If Mr. Kiernan had not thoroughly reviewed the voluminous hospital records, the plaintiff may well have been denied the substantial verdict he deserved. Preparation for real evidence, likewise, must be as thorough as circumstances permit.

Example 3–20:

PRIORITY MUST BE GIVEN TO
INVESTIGATING CENTRAL ISSUES BEFORE
PERIPHERAL ONES

F. Lee Bailey

During the cross-examination of Patty Hearst in her bank robbery trial, the prosecutor sought to challenge her assertion that she had been raped by Willie Wolfe, one of her kidnappers. In the course of cross-examination, he obtained from her the answer that although her professed love for this young man (he had been killed in the L.A. shootout) had been broadcast in her own voice after his death, she had been forced to make these assertions and never really cared for him. In a skirmish while cross-examining her, the prosecutor won an admission that she "felt strongly" about Willie Wolfe. Sensing victory close at hand, he asked what that strong feeling consisted of. She destroyed him with a heavy snarl saying, "I couldn't stand him." The prosecutor took the ridicule of the press.

During the trial, our hotel room was a depository for the ideas of every nut who had a new idea about the Hearst case. We tried to block the phones, to screen the calls, but no method was really successful. One morning, as the prosecution was putting in its rebuttal, my wife took a call from an irate mother. She said that her daughter was a schoolmate of the daughter of the prosecutor, and that his daughter claimed that she had been told by her father that the prosecutor had a surprise witness named Mr. McMonkey. I laughed off the information, having by this point become a bit leathered as to "hot tips." Mrs. Bailey, however, thought that the caller was quite sane. She learned that the lady's daughter was in fact a schoolmate of the prosecutor's daughter.

Based upon this information, I went to the prosecutor and demanded to know about the "McMonkey" surprise witness, to avoid a continuance of the proceedings. He became angry, feeling that his own office had leaked the information, and refused to disclose a thing. Under order from the trial judge, he said, "It was something in Patty's pocketbook; if that doesn't help you, that's too bad." We soon learned that the object in question was a small stone artifact given Miss Hearst by Willie Wolfe before his death. It was in fact found in the pocketbook when Patricia was arrested. Part of the prosecution's

continued

Example 3-20 (cont'd.)

rebuttal was proof that after Willie Wolfe's death, Patricia had kept the gift he had given her: the prosecution contended that this demonstrated that she did really care for him. She had a different and perfectly sound explanation for its presence in the pocketbook, but to put her back on the stand in surrebuttal to give that explanation would have led her once more to take a posture of defiance to the court on another subject, namely, a period in her excursion which we felt was beyond inquisition.

This matter, in which it originally appeared that the prosecutor had taken a beating, wound up as a severe wound for the defense. Ironically, until late in the trial neither side had known about the little stone image known as the "Olmec Monkey." An FBI agent had been reading the account in the New Times Magazine by Patty's kidnappers, Emily and William Harris, and had happened across Emily Harris' comment indicating that Miss Hearst had kept the stone symbol. The prosecutor had then been informed, and in a moment of glee in a close case had told his daughter. Thereafter, because of a mother's indignance, it had gotten back to me. By then it was too late to do anything to explain the situation. Had I been more thorough, I would have taken Patricia's pocketbook and asked her to explain every Kleenex and hairpin in it. I was too concerned with central issues to worry about those I thought to be peripheral. What should have been dealt with swiftly and easily on direct examination became a red herring in the case, and a bad one.

Mr. Bailey is correct that he would have learned of the "Olmec Monkey" artifact in time for Ms. Hearst to have explained it during her direct examination in chief, if he had asked her to explain every item in her pocketbook during his interview of her. He also acted correctly by concerning himself with central issues rather than engaging in this peripheral exercise. But given that both sides apparently knew of her publicly broadcast profession of love for Willie Wolfe, the issue of whether she truly loved him was probably a fairly central one. She had been indicted for willingly participating in a bank robbery with her small band of kidnappers. Willie Wolfe had been a member of the closely knit band and one of the bank robbers. If she loved him, it was going to be considerably harder for the jury to accept her position that she participated solely against her will.

To prepare on this rather central issue, Mr. Bailey's interview of Ms. Hearst probably included questions to uncover tangible evidence of the alleged amorous relationship, such as, did you ever write Willie any notes or give him any gifts and did he ever write you or give you anything. If Ms. Hearst had replied that he had given her the "Olmec Monkey," Mr. Bailey certainly would have followed up that answer by asking where it was and how Ms. Hearst could explain receiving the gift and keeping it so long.

If her reply was that she did not remember any gift, as it undoubtedly was, then Mr. Bailey's choice might seem to have been the following: to interview Ms. Hearst about every Kleenex and hairpin in her pocketbook, her dresser and any other place she may have put a gift, or hope for a stroke of good luck, such as that the prosecutor in an unguarded moment before Ms. Hearst completed her testimony in chief would reveal his evidence to his daughter, who in turn would tell a schoolmate whose mother would tell Mrs. Bailey.

However, as Mr. Bailey says, he had another choice, which was to address initially higher priority tasks which were much more likely to pay off. He was right to have made this choice. It would have been a mistake for him to have interviewed his client about every Kleenex and hairpin in her pocketbook and dresser at the expense of working on more central issues. If there are associate counsel, paralegals, investigators or even the client who can work on peripheral issues at the same time, so much the better. If not, the best you can do is to reach the peripheral issues, and less promising areas for investigation, after preparing the central issues and investigating the more promising areas. You will not be able to investigate all possibly relevant areas when your client cannot or chooses not to finance it, or when the court over your objection schedules trial to begin before the investigation can be completed.

When you cannot conduct the investigation yourself and you rely on an investigator, paralegal, or the client, you must be somewhat apprehensive. The next example provides good reason for such apprehension.

Example 3–21:

YOU CAN'T EVEN TRUST A DOCTOR-CLIENT TO CHECK AN IMPORTANT RECORD

George M. Vetter, Jr.

Don't assume a G.D. thing.
This is an iron law of litigation. Trial lawyers who break this law can lose cases.

continued

Example 3-21 (cont'd.)

A number of years ago, the State Public Health Department conducted a mass innoculation campaign. Over a period of several weeks, it held clinics throughout the state. The public would come to a clinic, line up, and be innoculated by one of the participating doctors.

Sometime later, the plaintiff claimed that an innoculation injured the radial nerve in her arm. How so long afterward she identified the defendant doctor as the one administering the innoculation mystified all and sundry. However, as a leading light in the program, he had his picture in the papers.

Plaintiff claimed she had received the innoculation on a certain day in a clinic held in a town which we will call "Twin Mountains." The doctor denied he had been at that clinic.

Since the state sponsored the clinics, it reimbursed participating doctors for travel expenses. The doctor happened to be a state employee. I asked him to check with the state disbursing officer about his reimbursed travel expense for the various clinics he had participated in. Through these records, we could establish the days and the clinics he had worked at.

The doctor said he complied with my request. He reported that the records substantiated his position. He so stated under oath in his deposition.

As his first witness at trial, plaintiff's counsel called the doctor under the adverse witness rule. The doctor testified he had not been at the "Twin Mountains" clinic.

Plaintiff's counsel then called the disbursing officer. The officer produced the doctor's travel voucher to the "Twin Mountains" clinic on the day in question.

The doctor had the following good defenses: plaintiff's suspect identification; improbability that an experienced doctor would give an injection in the wrong part of the arm; weak testimony of causation by the plaintiff's neurologist; and finally, testimony by one of its inventors that the innoculation instrument used by all the clinics could not inject serum deeply enough to reach the radial nerve.

Nonetheless, the jury found for the plaintiff.

At the onset of the trial, plaintiff's counsel had shattered the credibility of the doctor's case. Nothing we did after that could budge the jury from its initial impression.

My mistake. I had assumed that the doctor had checked with the disbursing officer and that he had accurately reported to me. I broke the iron law, "Don't assume a G.D. thing." I also broke the corollary of the iron law, "Check it yourself."

In Light of Other Demands on Your Time and
in Some Circumstances You Need Not Check
All Possible Evidence Yourself

Mr. Vetter considers that it was a mistake for him not to have double checked the investigation of his client into whether there was a record of his reimbursement for travel to "Twin Mountains." Had Mr. Vetter been conducting a "cottage industry" law practice two hundred years ago, he may have had the time to double check his client. Changes in conditions at present, like the need to spend time seeking and giving discovery and the technological innovation of the innoculation instrument used on plaintiff, which Mr. Vetter had to investigate and prepare expert testimony about, leave trial lawyers less time today.

In Mr. Vetter's particular case the subject entrusted to the client was central and promising. If the jury found that the client had not administered injections at "Twin Mountains," the verdict would be swift and sure for defendant; and the jury would not have to reach the other issues. In respect to the factor of centrality of the issue, the investigation should not have been left to the client. On the other hand, Mr. Vetter's client was much better qualified in three respects than most clients would be to conduct the investigation. First, the financial records of a state bureaucracy were to be perused; and because the client was a state employee, he may well have been in a better position to fathom the records than Mr. Vetter. Second, as a doctor, this client was better educated to make a documentary search than many clients. Finally, the plaintiff was charging the doctor with malpractice. Hence his professional pride probably provided him the incentive to do his absolute best in searching the records. In light of these three factors which are peculiar to this case, one might not conclude that Mr. Vetter made an unsound judgment in delegating documentary investigation to his particular client.

Having granted that in exceptional cases like Mr. Vetter's documentary investigation may be delegated properly to the client, it should be emphasized that ordinarily you should examine in advance all documents which may figure in the trial. A judge recounts the disastrous consequences of lawyers failing to examine documents their clients carry with them to the witness stand in the following example.

Example 3–22:

THOROUGHLY EXAMINE ALL OF YOUR CLIENT'S DOCUMENTS BEFORE HE TESTIFIES

Judge Jacob Lewiton

There was a contract case being tried before me in which a plumbing contractor was suing a general contractor for a balance alleged to be due on heating systems which the plumber had installed in eight new houses built by the defendant. One of the crucial issues in the case was the amount of the agreed upon unit price. The plaintiff testified, and he was quite convincing. Then the defendant got on the stand, and he was quite convincing. They were the only persons who were present at the time of the conversation at which the price was agreed upon, and their testimony was sharply divergent.

Counsel for the plaintiff, in cross-examining the defendant, said, "By the way, do you have here the bills that my client sent you?" The defendant said, "Yes, I do." He took a sheaf of papers out of his pocket, fumbled with them, and produced two invoices. Counsel for the plaintiff looked at the face of the invoices, and then very nonchalantly turned them over. He saw some figures on the back of one and said, "Whose writing are these figures in?" The defendant said, "Those are mine." An examination of those figures written by the defendant showed them to be entirely consistent with the testimony of the plaintiff, and entirely inconsistent with the testimony of the defendant in whose possession the paper had been for months.

This turned out to be the decisive bit of evidence in the case, as it affected my appraisal of the credibility of the defendant as to other aspects of the case, too. Needless to say, this episode produced a feeling of consternation and embarrassment in counsel for the defendant. Had he prepared his case thoroughly, by looking at all of his client's documents before trial, he would have seen those papers before stepping into the courtroom, and would not have been taken by surprise but would have settled.

In another case, there was a dispute as to the price which the purchaser of a second-hand automobile had agreed to pay. There again a receipt for the down payment was very innocently produced, and on the back of that receipt was writing in the hand of one of the parties which was inconsistent with his own testimony. It helped me decide which of the parties was not a very reliable witness.

Failure to examine a document very carefully before trial—paying attention to every detail including the page numbering—can be lethal when a witness refers to the document in his direct examination, as illustrated in the next example.

Example 3–23:

IF YOU MISS A DETAIL AS SMALL AS PAGE NUMBERING, DO NOT EXPECT THE OTHER SIDE WILL MISS IT TOO

Hugh Meade Alcorn, Jr.

During my forty-four years as an active trial prosecutor I have seen—and indeed have committed—tactical errors which have had a significant effect upon the outcome of the trial. One that I shall never forget occurred during the trial of a bitterly contested law suit between two large insurance companies concerning responsibility for paying for a very substantial loss caused by an explosion and fire at a chemical plant. Under the policies written by the respective companies, one insurer would be responsible if fire preceded and caused the explosion. The other insurer would be responsible if the explosion occurred first and was followed by fire.

The devastation and wreckage at the chemical plant yielded little physical evidence to provide a clear answer to the question: Which occurred first—explosion or fire? In these circumstances, each insurer relied heavily upon nationally—indeed internationally—known experts who performed tests, did experiments, made models of the plant, etc. I represented one of the insurers. My adversary was a distinguished trial lawyer of considerable renown (and also a member of the American College of Trial Lawyers).

In the presentation of his case, my adversary offered an expert from abroad, a man of international repute. His testimony, if believed, was obviously harmful if not fatal to our case. During his lengthy direct examination, he referred frequently to a notebook which counsel permitted him to use, in order to be precise with respect to certain tests and experiments he had conducted. I assumed that counsel had familiarized himself with that notebook.

At the opening of cross-examination I asked a few questions designed to require reference to the notebook. As I watched the learned doctor thumb through it, I observed that the pages were

continued

Example 3-23 (cont'd.)

numbered but that many pages appeared to be missing. I asked, and obtained permission, over spirited objection, to examine the book. It was a delightful surprise to discover that the pages appeared as "1, 2, 5, 6, 9, 10, 14, 26, etc." Fearful that I might be walking into a booby trap, I delicately explored the question as to why pages were missing and what subject matter they covered. A couple of hours later—after continuing and bitter objections from my adversary—it developed that the expert had indeed performed some tests and done some experiments, the results of which were recorded on the missing pages and which cast doubt upon the opinion he had expressed on direct examination.

The major "explosion" came when the admission was drawn from the witness that those pages had been removed from his notebook in a conference with counsel in his hotel room the preceding evening and had been destroyed in that conference. That insurance company's case exploded with that witness largely through the failure of counsel to observe one of the most elementary rules in the presentation of an expert witness: *Never* invite the witness to use or refer to notes, memos, documents, etc., during his or her testimony unless *you* have personally checked *every* detail—including the page numbering! And don't collaborate in the destruction of part of your expert's notes!

Inspecting an Adverse Party's Documents

Although Mr. Alcorn phrases his rule in terms of an expert witness, Ex. 3–22 has shown that it applies to witnesses in general. Breach of Mr. Alcorn's rule never to allow a witness to refer to documents during his testimony unless the lawyer calling him has checked every detail concerning the documents is especially fraught with danger in jurisdictions such as the federal courts, which give an adverse party the right to inspect and introduce in evidence any document used by a witness while testifying to refresh his memory. F.R. Ev. 612. In some, but by no means all jurisdictions, the adverse party is discouraged from requesting to inspect the document because the request is held to waive any objection to admissibility of the document which the requesting party may have had. Federal Rule 612 does not entail this waiver. Furthermore, Rule 612 provides the adverse party the right in the discretion of the court to inspect and introduce in evidence any document used by a witness to refresh his memory before testifying in addition to those he used while testifying. Thus it is not sufficient when you call a witness to have examined only the documents to be referred to by your witness on the witness stand.

SUMMARY

This chapter has illustrated the importance of thoroughly preparing your case for trial. Many problems that arise during the trial may be avoided through pretrial interviews, investigations, review of documents and real evidence, and dry runs with your client and other witnesses. You may have to disabuse your client of a wrongheaded, but strongly held, idea for advancing her case. Before you call a witness to the stand, whether partial to your side or hostile, you should try to know everything about him: what he will say, what he will wear, how he will act, how his character will come across to the jury. To the extent possible, your witness should know how to respond to his cross-examination. Your witness should be aware of court procedures and be comfortable with what is expected of him.

Personal interviews by you or a trusted associate counsel are the best way to enable you to detect characteristics of a witness, such as his undue suggestibility, which would be detrimental to your case. Once you evaluate your potential witnesses you must select those you will call on the basis of several objectives, such as: (a) producing evidence of each essential element of your case or defense; (b) avoiding cumulative witnesses who may contradict each other; and (c) eschewing unnecessary or obnoxious witnesses. You may decide that the benefit from the testimony by a nonessential witness will be outweighed by the negative impression he will make on the jury, and that it is better not to call him at all. You must be sure emphatically to instruct all witnesses you do select to testify to omit any mention of subjects the law makes taboo under some circumstances, such as the existence of liability insurance coverage of the defendant. To avoid disappointing testimony by a witness, it is in your best interest to take a written or recorded statement beforehand from the witness. The statement in some instances can be helpful to refresh the witness' memory, to negotiate a compromise settlement, and to support or oppose motions such as a summary judgment motion. Patience and meticulousness during interviews can bring out important information, even from hostile witnesses.

Expert witnesses, like a view, may help or hurt your case. A careful determination of whether to use them in a particular case and thorough preparation if you decide to do so are vital. Although live demonstrations may add drama to the courtroom, they can destroy your case if they backfire, which is always possible. Use them only if absolutely essential for your side. Delegating work to associates, paralegals, and investigators is not always a perfect substitute for doing the work yourself. The time saved may free you to focus your attention on more central issues, but you should try personally to examine documents or other tangible evidence which may be offered in evidence.

In setting forth ways to prepare evidence, this chapter has pointed out a number of qualities you should devote to your task, such as persistence, patience, effort, time, and meticulousness. These qualities add up, in a word, to thoroughness. The required thoroughness is often of so consuming a nature as to justify the adage, "The Law is a Jealous Mistress." You should be thorough in every phase of representing your client: factual investigation and legal research, defining the issues in pleadings and at pretrial conferences, and selecting and presenting evidence. Although thoroughness does not dazzle spectators as does a rapier-like cross-examination or a spellbinding summation, thorough and intelligent preparation more often carries the day. Thoroughness is the hallmark of the consummate legal professional.

REFERENCE NOTE

1. Michael A. Musmanno, *Verdict!* pp. 110-113. Copyright © 1958 by Michael A. Musmanno, Reprinted by permission of DOUBLEDAY PUBLISHING a division of Bantam, Doubleday, Bell Publishing Group, Inc.

CHAPTER FOUR

PRESENTING AND OBJECTING TO EVIDENCE

The preparation and presentation of your case are inextricably linked. What you have chosen to prepare and the manner in which you have done so will determine what you are able to convey to the judge and jury. How well you have prepared will determine how smoothly you can present your evidence. Unfortunately, some of the errors or misguided strategies of preparation may not become evident until you are at trial. Fortunately, in some instances there will be ways to recover from these mistakes during your presentation.

PRESENT ADVISABLE WITNESSES WHO ARE LEGALLY UNNECESSARY

Example 4–1 illustrates that incomplete preparation can cause a defeat at trial even when counsel has planned and presented all essential elements of the case. The commentary following the example discusses how to avoid the problem or try to mitigate its consequences.

EXAMPLE 4–1:

A JURY HOLDS THE ABSENCE OF A
LEGALLY UNNECESSARY WITNESS
AGAINST A PARTY

Ward Wagner, Jr.

The case was being tried in Jacksonville, Florida, in state court and involved a rather simple automobile accident with relatively clear liability. The plaintiff's attorney tried his case with testimony of the plaintiff, the defendant, and an eyewitness on the issue of liability. He did not call the investigating officer. To his absolute consternation, shock, and surprise, the jury brought back a verdict for the defendant. He later talked to one of the jurors who stated that it was obvious his client was at fault in some way because plaintiff's counsel did not see fit to call the investigating officer! Of course, at that time Florida was a contributory negligence state where such fault was a complete bar to recovery.

I have always called upon the investigating officer to testify in every case I have tried both before and since this incident was related to me.

Avoid Jury Misconceptions Resulting
from the Absence of a Witness

Prove a witness expected by the jury is unavailable There are many plaintiffs' lawyers who have won automobile accident verdicts without calling the investigating officer. Nevertheless, Mr. Wagner suggests that you should plan to call a witness whose testimony in law is unnecessary to your claim or defense, but whom the jury expects you would always present unless the witness' testimony would be fatal or nearly fatal to your client. If such a witness is unavailable, you should be sure to prove his unavailability to the jury.

Avoid prejudicial inferences through requesting jury instructions If you erred during your preparation for trial by failing to line up such a witness but you realize your mistake during the trial, or if you have appreciated that the jury will expect the witness but you prefer not to present him because, for example, he is obnoxious or would give fatal testimony, all is not lost. You should be able to mitigate the consequence of not calling him by requesting an instruction to the jury on the subject. For instance, in Ex. 4–1, plaintiff's counsel could have told the judge that he understands that local juries in automobile accident cases infer that plaintiffs are at fault unless they call the investigating officer, even though the law does not justify any such inference. He could then have requested the judge to instruct the jury that they are to draw no inference against either party, or concerning what the investigating officer or any other person might have testified had he been a witness, from the fact that the investigating officer or any other person was not called to testify.

The addition of "any other person" to "the investigating officer" in the requested instruction is calculated to avoid singling out the investigating officer with the result that the jury is encouraged to do just what the instruction is intended to prevent. This purpose could be further pursued by generally phrasing the instruction in terms of "any person" and not specifying "the investigating officer." However, a jury, at least the one in Ex. 4–1, might well think that the investigating officer is so special that the general instruction does not cover him. To be more confident of accomplishing the objective of the instruction, the formulation first proposed should be used.

Under one circumstance, the addition of "any other person" to "the investigating officer" would have to be modified. The circumstance is that the jury may infer that a party who has personal knowledge of a subject agrees with the truth of harmful testimony on the subject given in his presence which he does not take the witness stand to deny. In this circumstance the proposed instruction should be modified so that it excludes from the phrase "any other person" the party who is subject to the inference. Elsewhere in the instructions the jury would be informed of the inference they may draw against that party. There is an exception to this inference when the party such as a criminal defendant enjoys the self-incrimination privilege. In such a case the defendant has a constitutional right to be free from an adverse inference that might be drawn because of his decision not to testify.

Two problems with relying on a jury instruction The proposed instruction to the jury not to hold the absence of a witness against either party is a middle course between, on the one hand, not calling a witness and risking the fate of plaintiff's lawyer in Ex. 4–1 and, on the other hand, calling an undesirable witness. This instruction, however, may not solve your problem. The jury may disregard the instruction. Since this is always possible, you should plan before trial to call the witness or, if you have overlooked him in your planning, scramble during trial to locate him if he probably will not be so bad as to ruin your case. Another problem you might face is that the judge may refuse to give the requested instruction. It would surely be within the judge's discretion to do so, for the requested instruction is not part of the law the jury must apply. However, in our age of long docket backlogs, you should try to persuade the judge to give the instruction by pointing out that by doing so a waste of court time as the witness undergoes direct examination, cross-examination, re-direct, recross, etc. will be avoided.

Advisable Witnesses in Criminal Cases

In Ex. 4–1 the jury expected the plaintiff in a civil case to call as a witness the officer who investigated an automobile accident. It is probably more common for the jury in a criminal case to expect that the defendant will be supported at trial by family. Their testimony often in law is unnecessary to the issues making up the defense. Nevertheless, you should try to have them present in court.

For example, if your client has been indicted for rape, you should call his wife as a witness even though she cannot contribute any testimony directly to his defense. She can testify that she is his wife, that they have been happily married for eleven years, and so forth. The judge might exclude testimony like this on the ground that it is immaterial, i.e., that its remoteness from the issues and its waste of time outweigh its slight relevance.

If the wife is not permitted to testify, you should ask her at least to remain in the courtroom whenever the jury is present to the extent possible. Both by testifying and by supporting her husband through her presence, she may prevent the jury from drawing two inferences from her absence: first, that the defendant's wife does not in general stand behind his denial of the charges; and second, that the defendant did commit the rape because he and his wife do not get along well. If you cannot put such jury inferences to rest through the testimony or presence of close family members, you should try to do so by evidence of their unavailability. If you prove that your client's wife and children have been hospitalized throughout the trial, you need not fear that a hard-hearted jury will let these kinds of inferences influence the verdict.

YOU MUST ADAPT TO UNANTICIPATED
DEVELOPMENTS AT TRIAL

You may find that when you and all your witnesses are fully prepared to present your case, new evidence or a new angle comes to light during the trial. To take full advantage of such developments it may sometimes be necessary to wait for or request a recess. Deciding on the spot to exploit an unanticipated opportunity can be very risky.

Example 4–2:

BEWARE OF HOW YOUR CLIENT WILL
BEHAVE ON THE STAND DURING A
SPONTANEOUS ILLUSTRATION

F. Lee Bailey

I was conducting the direct examination of the defendant, Patty Hearst. She had appeared to this point to be, according to her own testimony (the facts of which were producible from no other source) a kidnap victim, forced into her horrendous circumstances. She was physically frail (five feet, 88 pounds), and a persuasive witness. At a point in her testimony she described her apprehension at being in a bank robbery with a weapon in her hands, and how she happened to glance down at it to notice that the bolt was not fully closed. I thought that this was an important point consistent with my thesis that she was a mere pawn on the chessboard of this robbery, who could not have shot her captors if she had wanted to.

To drive the point further home (since the bank robbery film corroborated her by showing her looking down at the bolt of the machine gun) I cocked the weapon (in evidence) that she had used, allowed the bolt to hang up short of full closure (which it would do regularly due to a mechanical defect) and handed it to her with a flair asking, "Is this the condition in which you saw that bolt during the robbery?"

In making this move I had ignored what she had told me; and, more importantly, what she had testified to in open court. A little before, but principally after the robbery for which she was being tried, she had received intensive training in the handling, firing, field-stripping, and combat use of the M-16 machine gun. I should have been more mindful of such training.

continued

Example 4-2 (cont'd.)

> When I handed the weapon to Miss Hearst (I had not fore-warned her that I might do this), she grasped it like a Green Beret, quickly checked it like a munitions expert, and then looked at the almost-closed bolt and said, "Yes." The answer was correct, but the impression left by her reflexive familiarity with the weapon smacked of a female Che Guevara. The fault was mine. In deciding to make a point, I had ignored the pitfalls involved, and left my client in similar ignorance.

Mr. Bailey's fault probably was not one he had much time to avoid. Ms. Hearst may not have remembered that during the robbery the bolt on her weapon was not fully closed until she was testifying at trial. If she had remembered it during Mr. Bailey's interview before trial, he would have had her do a dry run of the part of her direct examination in which he would plan to hand her the weapon (or, during the dry run, one similar to it since the government was probably holding the gun) and ask her the condition of the bolt. The dry run would have exposed her expert, Green Beret-like familiarity with the weapon. Mr. Bailey could then have cautioned his client in no uncertain terms that while testifying she should bridle her extraneous munitions instincts, simply look at the weapon and then answer his question. Otherwise, her reflexive behavior in grasping the weapon and checking it like the SLA guerilla the government charged her to have become could lead more directly to her conviction than any testimony or exhibits which would appear in the court reporter's printed transcript.

However, Mr. Bailey probably did not have an opportunity to put his client through a dry run before trial. Once she actually testified during direct examination that she had noticed that the bolt was not fully closed and Mr. Bailey decided that it would be well to have her identify the bolt in that condition for the jury, he erred by proceeding immediately to hand her the weapon. Since he knew that she had had intensive training with the weapon, he should have tried to have her go through a dry run first during a recess.

Even though the delay for a dry run would have meant that her testimony on this subject would not have been ideally continuous, the opportunity to avoid trouble would have justified the discontinuity. If a regular recess was not expected before the end of the rest of her direct examination, Mr. Bailey should have requested a recess on the ground that he needed to consult with his client briefly about a matter which had just come to his attention. If this request were denied and no recess were available, then he would have had to decide whether to go ahead with the illustration by weighing the value he anticipated from it against the risk that something untoward would result from handing the weapon to his client.

During trial there may be reason to think that a witness will not follow his pretrial instruction to adhere to a legal fiction, which requires him to omit from his testimony a subject he considers very relevant. Preparation of a witness by such an instruction was the subject of Ex. 3–11. To avert a mistrial, the lawyer examining him should repeat the instruction during a recess.

Example 4–3:

FAILURE TO INSTRUCT A WITNESS TO OMIT AN INADMISSIBLE SUBJECT

Judge Francis J. Fazzano

A defendant was being tried before me on the statutory offense of breaking and entering a building in the nighttime with the intent to commit larceny. A police officer of the community in which the offense took place was testifying for the prosecution. He stated that he could see the defendant inside the building in question, that he recognized the defendant, and further that he called on the radio for police reinforcements. The prosecutor then asked the witness why he called for reinforcements. At that point defense counsel objected and requested permission to approach the bench. Permission, of course, was granted.

At the bench, defense counsel stated that he felt the prosecutor was treading on dangerous ground because he was afraid the witness might make reference to the defendant's rather substantial criminal record in giving his reason for calling for reinforcements. I agreed with defense counsel that the matter might well require the granting of a motion for a mistrial. The reason for my fear was that in Rhode Island a defendant's criminal record may be brought out in a trial only if the defendant takes the stand and only for the purpose of affecting his credibility. The prosecutor indicated at the bench that he understood the situation and would withdraw the question.

It is my recollection that counsel both went back to their respective tables and then the prosecutor again asked the identical
continued

Example 4-3 (cont'd.)

question. Defense counsel did not object and as you can imagine the witness said in effect that he knew that the defendant was dangerous and had a criminal record. At that point the defense moved for a mistrial and I had no alternative but to grant it.

The reason that the prosecutor asked the identical question after indicating at the bench that he would withdraw it is difficult to fathom. He is unlikely to have forgotten to omit the question during the brief interval between the bench conference and returning to counsel table. Nor could he plead ignorance of the prohibition against introducing the defendant's criminal record inasmuch as the bench conference had just educated him.

A possible explanation is that after agreeing to withdraw the question the prosecutor had the idea that the police officer's answer would not include the defendant's criminal record as a reason for calling for reinforcements. That idea proved incorrect. But if the prosecutor had had that idea, and in view of Judge Fazzano's warning that he might well grant a mistrial for testimony about defendant's criminal record, the prosecutor's error was in failing to request a short recess before asking the question. During the recess he should have instructed the witness that his answer must not mention the defendant's record, although he could testify to any other reasons for calling reinforcements, such as that he knew the defendant was dangerous.

Lawyers regularly give such an admonition to witnesses before they testify on subjects that may touch topics that are literally or in effect privileged such as the fact that, as in Ex. 3–11, a defendant has liability insurance. Only by explicit, emphatic instructions to witnesses to omit topics the law makes taboo which otherwise would be a natural part of their answers can you avoid mistrials such as that in Ex. 4–3, and the wasteful duplication of subsequent trials.

Failure to Object Does Not Always Constitute a Waiver

Judge Fazzano says that he "had no alternative but to grant" the defense motion for a mistrial. One might think that the fact that "defense counsel did not object" to the repeated question asking the police officer why he called for reinforcements did provide the judge an alternative, namely, to rule that the failure to object waived the prohibition against evidence of a criminal record. However, if one examines the repeated question closely in context, the judge's implicit ruling against waiver is correct. There plainly was no waiver of the rule making criminal records inadmissible because the question was objected to the first time it was asked. In response the prosecutor had indicated at the bench in effect that his next question would not elicit the criminal record. Thus when his next question turned out again to ask "why he called for reinforcements," defense counsel was surely justified in expecting that the answer would not refer to the criminal record but to another explanation for calling for reinforcements. In fact the answer gave one, namely, that the defendant was dangerous. But because the answer also included the inadmissible criminal record, the prosecutor went home without a victory but with a mistrial.

OBJECTING TO EVIDENCE

In learning to object to evidence the initial challenges are to detect the violation of an evidence law and to detect it quickly enough to make the objection before the evidence reaches the jury. The latter challenge arises from the common ineffectiveness on the jury of successful motions to strike.[1] Both challenges are not easy tasks. However, a still more sophisticated challenge is to develop sound judgment on whether or not to object even if the evidence is objectionable.

Example 4–4:

KNOW WHETHER AN ANSWER WILL HURT YOU BEFORE OBJECTING TO THE QUESTION

Lawrence J. Smith

It was a common case of the phantom car pulling in front of a transit authority bus causing it to stop suddenly, throwing my client to the ground. The whole issue was the existence or nonexistence of the phantom car. Most transit authorities have safety records kept on each driver. The driver may be charged or not charged with responsibility for the accident. Whether he is charged or not is generally not admissible in evidence if objected to. I knew that I had a rather pugnacious, hard-driving defense counsel who always objected to everything.

Example 4-4 (cont'd.)

> Accordingly, at the trial, I subpoenaed the driver's supervisor from the bus company. My examination of him consisted of establishing the duties and responsibilities of a station master regarding safety records, safety reports, and whether or not drivers were ever charged with responsibility for accidents.
>
> After establishing that if a driver was at fault he would be charged with responsibility for the accident, I asked the following question.
>
> "Was driver Jones charged with responsibility for this particular accident as a result of the company's investigation?"
>
> Defense Lawyer: "I object, Your Honor. That's not admissible."
>
> Judge: "Sustained."
>
> "No further questions."
>
> I later learned that the company records, as a matter of fact, did not charge the bus driver with responsibility for this particular accident. Nonetheless, the jury returned a substantial verdict for the plaintiff. Later, from talking to three or four of the jurors, I learned that the key point of proof in the case to them, as laymen, was that which they should not have considered at all. They felt that the reason the defense counsel had objected to the question regarding the company records was that the bus driver, in fact, must have been charged with responsibility for the accident.
>
> The lesson to be learned is: Don't object to a question when the answer isn't going to hurt you, even if the objection is a valid legal objection that will be sustained. Despite instructions from the judge to the contrary, often juries consider facts not admitted into evidence.

Negative Jury Reactions to Winning Objections

The lesson with which Mr. Smith concludes this example is certainly an important one. When the answer will not hurt you, you almost never should object to the question even though it is objectionable. The reason is that juries often infer from successful objections that the objecting side is trying to keep from them significant information militating in favor of the other side. The magnetism of the unknown is such that juries tend to assume that the answer they were denied would have been exceedingly harmful to the objecting side.[2]

There is a method of stating objections counsel sometimes use successfully to avoid a negative jury reaction. From Mr. Smith's questions to the bus driver's supervisor about safety records of drivers, defense counsel may have anticipated where Mr. Smith was headed. If so, defense counsel could have requested leave to approach the bench where he would, out of the jury's hearing, make a motion in limine against any reference to whether the bus company charged the driver with responsibility. Even if the judge granted the motion, however, the defendant would not necessarily be spared the negative jury reaction to a winning objection. Some or all of the jurors may have anticipated where Mr. Smith was headed just as early as defense counsel did. Furthermore, they may have interpreted his request for a bench conference followed by Mr. Smith's discontinuance of the line of questioning as action by the defendant to prevent them from learning that the bus company had charged the driver with responsibility. The motion in limine method works only if made before the jury has the scent of the evidence in question. For this reason the motion is usually made in advance of trial.

Try To Avoid Repeatedly Making Losing Offers of Evidence or Objections

An exceptional time when it may be better judgment to make a winning objection, even though the answer will not hurt the objecting side, is when the other side has given, or is well on the way to giving, the jury the impression that it does not play fairly by the rules of the game. If making the objection will significantly contribute to that impression, then the jury is unlikely to infer that the answer would have legitimately helped the other side; instead, the jury is likely to infer that the answer would have been irrelevant or otherwise improper for their consideration. The most common behavior to lead a jury to such an impression is repeated disregard of rulings by the presiding judge, repeated unsuccessful objections, and repeated offers of evidence that are successfully objected to. The coup de grace to bring about this impression by the jury is an expression by the judge in the jury's presence of his or her feeling that the party is not making a good faith effort to try the case according to the rules of law.

Familiarity with Documents May Be Necessary to Decide Whether to Object

There is another lesson underlying the one Mr. Smith articulates at the end of Ex. 4–4. Before trial you must become familiar with all of your client's relevant documents in order to be able to judge whether the answer to an objectionable question will hurt your side. In Ex.

4–4, for instance, the reason defense counsel objected may not have been because he was pugnacious and tended to over-object; he may have objected because he had not done his homework, i.e., he had not checked the transit authority's records before trial and so had not known that the driver had not been charged with responsibility for the accident. If he had prepared for trial by becoming familiar with his client's documents, he would have had the information necessary to make the correct judgment not to object. If he had done so, the bus company supervisor would have answered that its investigation did not charge the driver with responsibility for the accident. In view of what three or four of the jurors told Mr. Smith, the jury undoubtedly would have been markedly influenced against the plaintiff by this answer. Mr. Smith apparently risked this answer owing to his confidence that defense counsel would object to the question. You should keep in mind that taking a risk such as this one does not always pay off, as it did not in the first mistake related by Chief Justice Tauro in the Foreword.

Failure to examine documents is not an error confined to the lawyer for the party possessing the documents as in Ex. 4–4. In the following example the opposing lawyer as well failed to peruse a document before objecting to it.

Example 4–5

DO NOT OBJECT TO EVIDENCE BEFORE YOU KNOW WHAT IT IS

Judge Jacob Lewiton

I recall one contract action that was tried before me in which the defendant's counsel offered a pair of index cards that were stapled together. Plaintiff's counsel objected, without looking at the cards. I overruled his objection and had the cards marked as exhibits. After they were marked, I separated the cards so that I could see all of the writing on both sides of each card.

On the back of the top one, I found notations which were very derogatory to the defendant, whose own counsel had offered the cards in evidence. The notations recited that a collection agency had sent detectives and scouts and everyone else chasing after the defendant, that they had interviewed his wife and she had told them that the defendant was a scoundrel, that he loses all of his money at

continued

Example 4-5 (cont'd.)

race tracks, that he never pays any of his bills, and that he told her that he was not going to pay this particular bill. Counsel for the plaintiff should have been eager to have those cards admitted in evidence, instead of objecting to them. If he had looked at them before objecting he would have realized that his objection was a little bit indiscreet, to say the least, particularly since nothing on the cards was detrimental to his case.

Be Meticulous and Persistent

In Ex. 4–5 both counsel erred. Defendant's counsel should not have offered the documentary exhibit into evidence. Plaintiff's counsel should not have objected to it. The reason for their error appears to be their failure to separate the index cards to see what was written on the back sides. It would have taken far less effort and time to do this than to pore through the voluminous hospital records in Ex. 3–19. All it took was meticulousness. You owe your client all three—time, effort, and meticulousness—if they are called for by the circumstances. You owe your client a fourth quality too, persistence, which played a role in the following case.

In an armed robbery case I prosecuted I was asked if I objected to fourteen "mug shot" photographs that bore on the identification of the defendant. As I was looking them over, the judge asked why I needed time to examine them inasmuch as my assistant had seen them before trial. I replied that my assistant had reported to me on the photographs but had not looked at their backs. The judge remarked that the backs would not show anything. I acknowledged that that probably would be true, but said that with the court's permission I would like to look nevertheless. Then I found on the back of the next to last photograph a recital of an inadmissible criminal record. I brought the fruit of my meticulous persistence to the attention of the judge and opposing counsel, the recital of the record was masked by mutual consent, and a possible mistrial or reversible error was avoided.

PRESENTING EVIDENCE DURING TRIAL

In Ex. 4–5, both counsel failed to examine the index cards thoroughly; defendant's counsel failed to do so before trial in deciding what evidence to present; plaintiff's counsel failed to do so at trial in deciding whether to object. Let us consider another example of failing to look at a document carefully during trial, this time before deciding to facilitate its admission in evidence.

Example 4–6

DOUBLE CHECK DOCUMENTS OFFERED IN EVIDENCE AT TRIAL EVEN IF YOU BELIEVE YOU HAVE PREVIOUSLY REVIEWED THEM

Leonard A. Kiernan, Jr.

Several years ago when I was under the impression that I had mastered the art of trial advocacy, I was engaged in litigation in the Providence Superior Court. The action involved an automobile accident, and the issue of liability was hotly contested. Prior to the commencement of trial, I had obtained a copy of the police report, and of course had it in my file during the trial. I had reviewed the report very carefully and was under the impression that I knew its contents without even a need to refer to the report itself. Opposing counsel at one point was questioning the police officer on the stand and was referring to the report itself. As I have stated, in my former brilliance, I thought that the report was favorable to me and jumped to my feet and dramatically suggested that my opponent submit the report into evidence so that it would be available for everyone to see and review. My opponent then attempted to hand me a copy of the report for my review; however, I cavalierly stated that I had a copy and told him to put it into evidence.

Needless to say, my opponent submitted the police report into evidence and then began to read from the report. When I heard what was being read, I immediately jumped to my feet since this was not in the copy of the report that I had in my possession. Suffice it to say, the information that was being read was absolutely disastrous to my end of the case and after a recess, I discovered there was a third page to the report.

The reason for all of this was very simple. The police department in question had a practice at that time where they would furnish, upon the proper fee being paid, a copy of pages 1 and 2 of the report; however, in those days this particular police department had a third

continued

Example 4-6 (cont'd.)

page that was known as an opinion sheet. This sheet was never furnished unless the entire report was subpoenaed into Superior Court and then the entire report was brought in by the patrolman in question. This is indeed what happened during this trial. My opponent had subpoenaed the policeman and the report that he brought contained all three pages.

I did not know the local practice, but that of course is not the point, and I am sure that a simple review of the particular document which was being offered would have shown me that there was a third sheet. However, under the rules of evidence that were being followed in Superior Court at that time, the third sheet would not have been admissible into evidence, but at my suggestion and without my review, the entire report went into evidence. I do not have to tell you that the jury promptly decided this matter in favor of my opponent based on the opinion of the police officer which was in writing and of course adverse to my client's position.

It was indeed a good lesson, if one can say that, since the error did result in an adverse verdict. I have, hopefully, learned that one never masters the art of trial advocacy and that nothing should go into evidence without being examined very carefully.

In closing I would like to point out a common problem that faces young attorneys who are just beginning to try cases. Many times they fear that they are going to be criticized and looked at with some disfavor if they stand around poring through exhibits while the judge and jury sit idly by. This of course is not necessary with our new modern methods of marking exhibits prior to the trial and exchanging a great deal of information through discovery and pretrial orders. It sometimes happens in a trial that an exhibit or two will be offered that will require some review by the other side; the attorney can simply cure the fear of delay by having the exhibit marked subject to his review at a recess or lunch break at which time he may move to strike whatever he feels is prejudicial. I have found all trial judges most agreeable to this suggestion. They of course do not allow exhibits to be seen by the jury nor commented upon until the attorney has had a chance to review the exhibit to his satisfaction.

Mr. Kiernan has reported the dire consequence to his client in a civil trial of his failure to examine a document carefully. The consequence can be just as dire in a criminal trial.

Example 4–7

READING A DOCUMENT (FOR THE FIRST TIME) IN FRONT OF A JURY

Judge Homer Thornberry

During the time I served as a state prosecutor, I was engaged in prosecuting a murder case. The arresting officer had obtained a confession in which the defendant had made several exculpatory statements that I knew to be false, but rather than undertaking the burden of disproving them after having introduced the statement, I decided that the state could prove the defendant guilty beyond a reasonable doubt without using the statement.

On cross-examination of the arresting officer, defendant's counsel asked the officer if the defendant had made any statement to him at the time of the arrest, whereupon the officer answered that the defendant had given him a written confession. Counsel then asked him for the confession and the officer responded that he had given it to the district attorney, indicating me at the counsel table. Whereupon, defense counsel turned to me and demanded that I produce it. I did not respond, remaining silent. Then, defense counsel turned to the trial judge and demanded that I be compelled to produce it. In his rather vociferous statement to the court, he engaged in a jury speech, criticizing me and my failure to produce it. Apparently, not knowing what was in the confession, an admission that the defendant had committed the act, defense counsel must have thought that the confession contained a denial, but actually the defendant admitted committing the act of killing the victim.

Before the court could respond, I quietly stood and handed the confession to counsel and suggested that he read it to the arresting officer to see if it was the one which had been given. He proceeded to do so in front of the jury, and then introduced it into evidence. This, of course, removed from the state the burden of being the sponsor of the exculpatory statements and proving the legality of the confession. Needless to say, the defendant was convicted.

Knowledge Is a Better Trial Tactic Than a Hunch

Judge Thornberry believes that defendant's counsel read the confession to the jury before reading it himself because he thought that the confession denied the commission of the murder. There may be times at trial when counsel has to act on his mere thought or hunch. This was not such a time. Defendant's counsel could have decided what to do about the confession on the basis of knowledge of its content rather than his hunch. Knowledge is always preferable. He could have gained knowledge of what the confession said simply by reading it to himself. If it was short, he could have read it on the spot when Judge Thornberry handed it to him, and then handed it right back to him. If it was long or he needed time to ponder the implications of what it said or to evaluate whether on balance it would be helpful or harmful, he should have followed Mr. Kiernan's suggestion at the end of Ex. 4–6. That is, when Judge Thornberry handed the confession to him, he should have responded that, rather than delay the proceedings while he reviewed the confession, he would do so at a recess and, with the court's permission, recall the arresting officer for further cross examination if his review of the document so required.

Use Discovery Methods to Avoid Seeing and Evaluating Evidence for the First Time at Trial

Surely Exs. 4–5, 4–6, and 4–7 should teach that when you are confronted by tangible evidence, either documentary or real, for the first time at trial, you must examine it as thoroughly as possible. But the intensive pressure of trial does not provide the ideal condition for evaluating evidence and devising the most desirable reaction to it. It is much better for you to obtain the evidence before trial. In criminal cases today, defense counsel by discovery can inspect and copy a considerable part, if not all, of the government's tangible evidence in advance of trial. Indeed, the prosecutor today is duty-bound *sua sponte* to provide defense counsel before trial all exculpatory evidence similar to that in the confession which is the subject of Ex. 4–7. The prosecutor generally has very little, if any, right to discovery from the defendant.

In civil cases in federal courts and states with similar discovery laws, both sides have wide-ranging opportunities to inspect and copy the real and documentary evidence of all parties before trial. See, e.g., Fed. R. Civ. P. 34. Even the evidence of nonparties, such as the police department's report which is the subject of Ex. 4–6, may be examined before trial in jurisdictions with liberal discovery opportunities. See, e.g., Fed. R. Civ. P. 30, 45 (d) (1). Discovery in civil cases in such jurisdictions also will make it easier to learn whether your tangible evidence will be admitted at trial, for opponents can be requested to admit the genuineness of evidence in advance of trial. See, e.g., Fed. R. Civ. P. 36. The best prepared trials result from inter alia using the opportunities afforded by discovery.[3]

Organize Your Direct Examination So That Testimony Is Understandable and Witnesses Appear Honest and Appealing

Most of the evidence you prepare and ultimately present at trial is usually presented through direct examination of witnesses. You should conduct the direct examination so that the jury both understands the testimony and believes your witness. If, unlike the witness in Ex. 3–4, your witness has an appealing personality and answers questions in a straightforward fashion, use rather open-ended questions so as to project his or her personality. You should select the organization of the examination, whether chronological or topical, according to which method facilitates the communication of the subject at hand.

Do Not Repeat Answered Questions on Direct

Once your witness has given essential testimony, simply be grateful for small favors and restrain yourself from inquiring repetitively. An invitation to your witness to answer substantially the same question again is an invitation to disaster. As the following examples portray, the disaster can strike not only when the witness is hostile but also when the witness is impartial, friendly, or even the client himself.

Example 4–8

AN UNNECESSARY LIVE DEMONSTRATION GIVES THE LIE TO SATISFACTORY PRECEDING DIRECT EXPERT TESTIMONY

Chief Justice Thomas R. Morse, Jr.

The plaintiff brought an action for personal injuries sustained when she was run over by an automobile that rolled down a hill after being parked. The owner was a defendant and testified that he parked the vehicle on the hill and set the emergency brake. He then got out, slammed the driver's door and, as he was walking away, saw

continued

Example 4-8 (cont'd.)

the car start in motion down the hill to the place where the plaintiff was struck. The automobile was a relatively new Dodge. Chrysler Corporation was a codefendant. Chrysler's attorney produced a mock-up of the Dodge, including the frame of the vehicle, wheels, and an emergency brake system. An expert witness testified that it was mechanically impossible for the hand brake to let go if it was set.

Not content with favorable answers to a series of questions reinforcing this testimony and negating the possibility that the slamming of the door could release the brake, the attorney asked one more question. "Are you saying," he asked the expert, "that even if I kicked the side of the car, near the hand brake, that it would not let go?" "That's correct," answered the expert. The attorney then kicked the side of the frame of the mock-up automobile. There was a loud "snap," and the hand brake let go. There was a recess and Chrysler settled the case.

Example 4–9

KNOW THE ANSWERS TO QUESTIONS BEFORE YOU ASK THEM

Judge Alfred T. Goodwin

Anecdotally, I recall a divorce case in which the husband's lawyer on direct examination was trying to show that the mother was unfit to have custody of their child because of her association with another man. His witness had accidentally barged into the house where the lady was entertaining the other man, and the witness told the court (without a jury) that she had stopped at the house to see her friend and found her lying on the bed with no clothes on and a gentleman sitting by her. The lawyer asked, "What was the gentleman doing?" The witness answered: "Joe was sitting there on the bed with one hand on her private parts." The lawyer said, "I see, and where was his other hand?" The witness replied, "Holding a ham sandwich."

Example 4–10

BE CONTENT WITH THE ANSWER "NO"; DO NOT TRY TO PUSH ON TO "ABSOLUTELY NO"

Judge Thomas J. MacBride

This incident involved an alleged bank robber who came on for trial before me in the fall of 1963. He was one of two robbers who, equipped with revolvers, held up a branch of the Bank of America located in a small Nothern California community. Robber No. 1 was apparently in charge of "gathering in the money." Robber No. 2, the man on trial, stood guard at the vault door into which all bank personnel had been herded, holding a gun on the employees, and alternately threatening the few patrons in the bank who had been required to lie on the floor during the robbery.

The robbers successfully made off with their loot and, as I recall, Robber No. 1 was never apprehended. Immediately after the robbery the FBI displayed a spread of pictures of well-known bank robbers suspected of operating in California and three out of four of the bank employees were able to identify the defendant on trial. A Miss Davis, who had been positioned immediately at the bank vault door directly in front of Robber No. 2, was unable to identify the defendant from the picture spread.

Robber No. 2 was arrested and placed in a "line-up" at the local jail. The three bank employees who had identified the defendant from the picture spread were able to immediately pick him out of the line-up. Miss Davis was not asked to participate in the line-up identification for the reason that she had been unable to identify the defendant in the picutre spread. She was not called as a witness.

The government's case against the defendant was overwhelming, and his conviction seemed certain. Just before argument, one of the jurors requested a conference with me in chambers. I granted his request but insisted that both the United States Attorney and the defense attorney be present. The juror advised me that he would be unable to sit in judgment on the defendant for the reason that one of his fellow jurors had been asleep during the trial. I was fairly new on the bench at that time and had been taking copious notes with the result that I had not noticed nor had anyone brought to my attention during the trial that the particular juror had in fact been nodding. I

continued

Example 4-10 (cont'd.)

questioned the alleged errant juror and he "allowed as how" he might have nodded a bit during the trial but he was quite sure that he had heard *most* of it. I asked counsel if they would agree to have the case submitted to an eleven-man jury. Counsel for the defense declined, and under the circumstances I was required to grant a mistrial.

The case was then tried again before my colleague, United States District Judge Sherrill Halbert. The same evidence was presented in his case as had been in mine. Midway in the case one of *his* jurors suddenly awakened to the fact that her son-in-law worked for the Bank of America in another small Northern California community. This was so, notwithstanding the fact that in questioning the jury Judge Halbert had specifically inquired as to whether any of the prospective jurors had ever worked for the Bank of America or had any close relatives who worked for the Bank of America. When this forgetful juror's connection was discussed with defense counsel, he immediately asked for a mistrial, which was granted by Judge Halbert. The case then came back to me for a third trial.

In the third trial the government's case was identical to the evidence that had been put on in the first and second trials. By this time the defendant had a new attorney with a new idea. In the first and second trials the defendant had taken the stand and offered an alibi defense, notwithstanding the very substantial direct and circumstantial evidence that placed him at the scene of the crime. In the third trial, defense counsel decided to buttress the alibi defense by bringing in Miss Davis to testify. After all, she had the best opportunity to see Robber No. 2 for the reason that he had pointed the gun directly at her most of the time as he stood on one side of the entrance to the vault and she on the other. She had been unable to identify him from the picture spread and there was no reason to believe that her failure to identify would not continue during her testimony. Her inability to identify would probably create a reasonable doubt sufficient to produce a hung jury.

Miss Davis was brought to the witness stand by defense counsel. He established that she had an excellent view of Robber No. 2, that because the gun was pointed at her during most of the robbery she was looking straight at him during the entire episode and would never forget his face, and that she would certainly recognize him if she saw him again. Whereupon defense counsel pointed to the defendant and said, "Now, Miss Davis, here is the man that is charged by the government as being Robber No. 2 in the robbery. You had the best

continued

Example 4-10 (cont'd.)

opportunity of anyone in the bank to observe that person. Now, does this man look like Robber No. 2?" Miss Davis then looked intently at the defendant and responded, "No, that is not Robber No. 2."

Defense counsel then said, "Now, Miss Davis, I want you to look very carefully at the defendant. Are you absolutely positive that this is not the person who, as the government claims, is Robber No. 2?" At this point, Miss Davis looked again at the defendant and shook her head negatively. Then she took off her glasses, stared at him even more intently, and then excitedly exclaimed, "Well, I'll be darned— that *is* the man who robbed the bank." Further examination by defense counsel could not shake her from the decision she had made and, of course, government counsel developed it even further. Needless to say, the defendant was convicted.

The obvious lesson to be learned from these experiences is that, once an attorney, either on direct or cross-examination, has obtained a favorable answer there should be no further inquiry. The interrogator who seeks to emphasize or drive home the favorable answer already received runs the risk of a deadly response, or a response that may open an entirely new area for cross or redirect examination which will destroy the witness and possibly the entire case.

If in Ex. 4–10, defense counsel had sat down after getting the answer he wanted, the prosecutor in cross-examination might have let the answer stand for fear of Miss Davis reinforcing her statement. He still had his three positive identifications. On the other hand, there was a good chance that defense counsel now had enough in the record to create a reasonable doubt in the mind of at least one juror. By asking one question too many, he lost the case.

Example 4–11

DO NOT TRY TO COMPLETELY NAIL DOWN AN ALREADY SOLID CASE

Judge James T. Healey

The plaintiff had little knowledge of English and had to testify through an interpreter. The case in chief went in well and the defense was so-so. Plaintiff's attorney decided to nail down his case and in

continued

Example 4-11 (cont'd.)

rebuttal recalled his client. He put a relatively simple question to him and was astonished by a lengthy colloquy between him and the interpreter. Losing patience, he demanded that the interpreter state the answer, which was, "I think we'd better settle." The effect on the jury was predictable.

Patience Is Essential

In the last example the direct examiner destroyed his case in rebuttal. In the lengthy colloquy the interpreter may have been asking the client whether he had really decided to settle. If the lawyer had permitted the colloquy to continue, the answer might not have been so disastrous. However, because the lawyer lost patience, he interrupted the colloquy. He should not have done so, just as a lawyer should not lose patience when interviewing an abusive, hostile potential witness. Trial can be exacting and exasperating, but patience at trial can carry you to a victorious verdict.

SUMMARY

Despite the best preparation possible, the course of a trial may be unavoidably bumpy and winding. A jury in a particular locality may hold against you your failure to call a witness who was not necessary to prove the elements of your claim or defense. A defect in the machine gun used in a bank robbery may be disclosed to you for the first time during trial. And a witness may forget while on the stand not to mention the defendant's prior convictions. When unanticipated events like these occur, you should not panic, but practice damage control. Wait for a recess or request one so that you may decide on your next step in relative deliberateness. The recess will afford an opportunity to review the development with your witness or to draft a mitigating requested instruction by the court to the jury. Try not to be stampeded by the rush of events.

Surely you must take the time to be well informed before responding to what the opposing counsel offers. Examples 4–4 and 4–5 illustrate the dangers in making knee-jerk, ill-prepared objections. Do not object to a question or to documentary or real evidence if the answer or evidence will not hurt your case more than the jury's resentment at your keeping it from them. Jurors seem riveted to the intriguing magnetism of the unheard answer or unseen exhibit. They assume they would have been deleterious to your case. It is very important to review all documents and real evidence offered in evidence, even if you have previously reviewed them. It is possible that the copy of a document that you had seen was not complete, or that some point that first surfaced during trial will modify your appraisal of the significance or admissibility of a document.

Despite the possibility of a variance between the document you are shown before trial and the one offered in evidence at trial, you are at a great disadvantage if you first confront evidence during the hurly burly of trial. The intensive pressure of trial is far from the ideal setting for evaluating evidence and formulating your reaction to it. You should use discovery tools to identify and examine most documents and real evidence before trial. Interrogatories and depositions likewise enable you to obtain the information possessed by the opposing party and his or her witnesses, although your interviews of his or her witnesses may make their depositions, which are costly, unnecessary. These discovery tools can spare you from many surprises at trial.

You should prepare and present the direct testimony of each witness you have selected to testify so that the jury believes the witness and clearly understands what he or she knows. For the jury to believe the witness you must tailor your questions to bring out his or her best qualities. If your witness will strike the jury as obnoxious, break down open-ended questions so that he or she has less room to parade his or her ego, although you must not run afoul of the prohibition against leading questions. On the other hand you may have a witness who is very appealing, in which case you should use more open-ended questions so that the witness talks more freely to the jury.

Examples 4–8 through 4–11 make clear that by repeating a direct examination question, which has been satisfactorily answered, in order to strengthen or reinforce it, you run the risk that your witness will retreat from his or her answer. Be content with the initial good answer. It is not prudent for a lawyer to seek the perfect answer. It is safe for an author or composer to tinker with the manuscript or score in pursuit of perfection. If the tinkering proves fruitless, the initial manuscript or score remains. But the art of the interrogating trial lawyer depends on the answers of the witness, over whom the lawyer does not have full control. When the witness answers a repeated question disappointingly, there is no way to restrict the jury's memory to the initial answer. The lawyer who realistically recognizes his or her limited control over witnesses necessarily is circumspect in presenting evidence.

REFERENCE NOTES

1. See, e.g., "The Jury Will Disregard...," News, 73 American Bar Association Journal 34 (November 1, 1987); W. Thompson, G. Fong, and D. Rosenham, "Inadmissible Evidence and Juror Verdicts," 40 Journal of Personality and Social Psychology 453, 460, 461 (1981); V. Hans and A. Doob, "Section 12 of the Canada Evidence Act and the Deliberations of Simulated Juries," 18 Criminal Law Quarterly 235, 251-252 (1976).

2. R. Keeton, *Trial Tactics and Methods*, 2d ed., Boston: Little Brown and Company, 1973, p. 167.

3. J.B. Levine, *Discovery*, New York: Oxford University Press, 1982.

THE KEYS TO SUCCESSFUL CROSS-EXAMINATION

PURSUE THE PRIMARY PURPOSE OF CROSS-EXAMINATION: MINIMIZE THE DAMAGE DONE BY DIRECT TESTIMONY

Cross examination epitomizes the adversary nature of an Anglo-American trial. In the typical case, one side has presented the direct testimony of a witness who was selected because he could maximize the damage to the other side, and who has just finished doing so. Immediately thereafter the other side may cross-examine the witness. The major purpose of the cross-examination is to minimize the effect of the damaging blow just struck by the direct testimony.

Cross-Examination as Perceived by the Public

You must keep your major purpose constantly in mind. If you do not, you may be thrown off course by portrayals of cross-examination in works of fiction or by actors. The media give the cross-examiner a decidedly adversarial appearance. He uses a hostile demeanor and fire breathing tone as he stalks his prey. The media are correct in assuming that the cross-examiner is working in an adversarial context. But they are incorrect in suggesting that the adversarial style of questioning is always most likely to achieve the purpose of cross-examination, viz., minimization of the damage done by direct examination. The adversarial style telegraphs to the witness that the cross-examiner is hell-bent on destroying him or her, therefore, to be on guard to defend the direct testimony. As a result, the witness may circle the wagons around the campfire of the party who has called him or her to the witness stand. The witness' augmented vigilance may well enhance the difficulty of the cross-examiner's task.

Should Your Style Be Adversarial or Straightforward?

To avoid this drawback of the adversarial style, and perhaps to induce the witness to let his guard down, your style generally should not be adversarial but should be straightforward, fair, and sincere, if not friendly, collaborative, or cajoling. These styles promise to generate more light than heat. Your choice of style for any particular cross-examination, or for any particular part of a cross-examination, cannot be made in advance of knowing all the circumstances. On occasion you should be adversarial. Then you should be careful that your style is one of righteous indignation rather than abrasiveness. You can persuade the jury by the former, but you will alienate it by the latter.

Show adversariness without being abrasive Under the influence of mass media, the jury may be looking forward to some adversariness from the lawyers. If you fail to fit their stereotype, they may hold it against your client. If you decide that adversarial cross-examination of a witness will have an adverse effect on the witness' answers, you are not at a loss to satisfy the jury's appetite for aggressiveness. You may do so (a) by firmly holding your ground in colloquies with the judge within the hearing of the jury concerning objections, (b) by a ringing denunciation of the opposing party in your closing argument, and (c) on cross-examination itself by the order of your questions rather than your style of asking them. Hardly anything is more adversarial than to open cross-examination on the last subject of the direct testimony. It shows that you are eager to meet your opponent's challenge, for you pick up the gauntlet right where it was thrown down.

Advantages of a Brief, Successful Cross-Examination

If your cross-examination on the last subject of direct testimony is successful, you should seriously consider limiting the balance of the examination to the two or three questions that are most likely to be successful. If your next two or three questions turn out to be successful, you can stop. By making the cross-examination brief you avoid boring the jury and, more importantly, you avoid the host of pitfalls in cross-examination that can sink your case and which the remainder of this chapter will illustrate all too vividly. Successful cross-examination questions discredit either the witness' credibility or direct testimony. They minimize the effect of the direct testimony, which is the primary purpose of cross-examination.

Whenever a brief cross-examination achieves its purpose, you should stop. This rule is not limited to cross-examinations that open on the last subject of direct, but applies to all cross-examinations. Being brief not only avoids a host of deadly pitfalls but also may lead the jury to think that you stopped after landing a relatively small number of very devastating blows because you did not want to bloody the witness unmercifully.

Summation Supplements Cross-Examination

When you have cross-examined briefly and succesfully, you may in your closing argument address the subjects in the direct testimony which your cross-examination did not reach; and persuasively ask the jury to give them no weight on the strength of your cross-examination. Since your cross-examination was successful, by definition the witness has been impeached or part of his or her direct testimony has been discredited. Hence you may soundly argue in the summation that the jury should disregard the direct testimony not touched on in cross either because the witness is not worthy of belief, whatever the witness testified to, or because the inaccuracy of part of the testimony makes all of it suspect. An example of this argument would go as follows: if the witness weighed the oranges wrong, can you rely on his or her weighing of the grapefruits?

Cross-examination totally destroys the direct testimony only in fiction Fantastic portrayals of cross-examination in the mass media may mislead you to believe that far from keeping your examinations brief, you should persevere until the witness recants. The fantasy is that the cross-examination will show the lack of merit of the whole of the direct testimony. So thoroughly will the witness be discredited that he or she will recant on the stand. At this point the gallant gladiator will receive the congratulations of everyone in the courtroom except the duly chastised opponent. This fantasy should not be emulated because it cannot be achieved. In reality cross-examination rarely totally demolishes witnesses; and they never, or hardly ever, disavow any of their direct testimony.

Do Not Invite the Witness to Repeat Direct Testimony

In reality, moreover, ill-advised cross-examination often boomerangs to hurt the cross-examiner's case. This will happen if you expressly invite the witness to repeat his or her direct testimony. It also will happen if you indirectly invite the witness to repeat his or her direct testimony by examining it point by point.

Example 5–1:

ELUSIVE UNDERSTANDING

Robert Button

Some years ago there was an automobile collision at one of the main intersections of our small town. Standing on the corner waiting for traffic to clear was the mayor of the town, a civil engineer and surveyor by profession. He was an eye witness to the accident. Subsequently, a law suit developed as a result of this crash and the mayor was called as a witness.

His testimony for the plaintiff was very detailed and complete and very damaging to the defendant. The attorney for the defendant made the mistake of a detailed cross-examination with the result that the testimony of the witness was again detailed in exactly the same manner. Still the attorney for the defendant was not satisfied and started to go over the factual situation again to the obvious annoyance of the witness. Finally, the attorney for the defendant thought he had found some discrepancy in the testimony and started a question by saying, "I don't understand." The witness quickly interrupted and said in effect, "I have told you what happened; only God can give you understanding."

Naturally there was a verdict for the plaintiff.

Plaintiff's counsel had presented the direct testimony because it was helpful; but having the witness repeat it on cross was counterproductive, for repetition only serves to reinforce. Totalitarian regimes are thought to make their Big Lies believable by the masses through sheer repetition. Such cross-examination is a gift to the opposing side of what it cannot confer on itself. If in Ex. 5–1, the plaintiff on direct had tried to have the witness repeat his testimony, the defendant could have thwarted his effort by the objection of repetition.

Worse even than inviting the witness to repeat his or her direct testimony is inviting the witness to expand it. Consider what happened in a trial when the witness accepted the cross-examiner's invitation.

Example 5–2:

DO NOT INVITE A WITNESS TO EXPAND ON DIRECT TESTIMONY; THE RESULT MAY BE A SWIFT KICK

Samuel Langerman

The lawyer was defending a personal injury case and was cross-examining a fine neurosurgeon who had testified that the plaintiff had hyperactive reflexes and that this was, in his opinion, consistent with the residuals that he felt were present as an aftermath of her injury. In cross-examining him, the lawyer established that the reflexes were tested in the manner many of us have seen, to wit, with the doctor taking a little hammer with a rubberized type of material on it and striking the plaintiff somewhere in the area of each knee and seeing the plaintiff's reaction as her leg would then bounce upwards. He indicated that it was a simple test, that there was no question in his mind as to how this lady had responded. The examination continued with the examiner suggesting that all of this was very subjective and that the doctor was describing his impression of what he saw, and that a different doctor might have described the patient's reaction in a different way.

The doctor finally interjected that in this patient's case her reaction was quite extreme and anybody, in his opinion, would have concluded that her reflexes were hyperactive and, for that matter, it is the kind of thing one could demonstrate quite easily in the courtroom. The defense lawyer, feeling trapped, suggested that perhaps the doctor should demonstrate. The doctor seated the lady in the center of the courtroom, supported her leg with his hand, and with the other hand, in effect, gave a kind of mild karate chop to the knee area. The lady was wearing a pump type shoe and, as her leg bounced up in the air, the shoe flew all the way across the courtroom.

continued

Example 5-2 (cont'd.)

> When the jury stopped laughing, the defense lawyer attempted to continue with his cross-examination, stalling for time until he could reach a recess period when he could settle his case.

How to Avoid Maximizing the Effect of the Direct Examination

The consequence of the cross-examiner's invitation to the neurosurgeon to demonstrate the basis for his direct testimony was to maximize the effect of the direct. Yet the principal purpose of cross-examination is to minimize the effect of the direct. The response of the defense lawyer to the neurosurgeon's assertion that he could demonstrate the plaintiff's hyperactive reflexes easily in the courtroom was the worse of two alternatives. The better alternative was to reply to the neurosurgeon that plaintiff's lawyer was in charge of trying to prove the injury; and if he had desired to have the alleged hyperactive reflexes demonstrated, he would have asked the neurosurgeon to do so in direct examination. The defense lawyer then would ask a question on another subject. However, he would have to await redirect examination of the neurosurgeon before learning the consequence of the better way out of the trap.

If during redirect plaintiff's lawyer did not ask the neurosurgeon to perform the demonstration, the defense lawyer would have escaped from the trap unscathed. In addition, defense counsel would have acquired a basis for impeachment of the neurosurgeon. He could argue in his summation that the jury should not give full weight to the neurosurgeon's testimony because he had been overzealously trying to help plaintiff win exaggerated damages. The defense lawyer could charge that the neurosurgeon left his proper role as a detached, scientific doctor and tried to take on the role of fervent advocate for the plaintiff. As evidence of the neurosurgeon's overzealousness, the defense lawyer would point out that the neurosurgeon had wanted to go so far as to try to demonstrate the hyperactive reflexes in front of the jury, when even plaintiff's lawyer would not try to do so. The effect of this attack on the neurosurgeon should not be overstated, for plaintiff's lawyer could respond in argument that he did not ask for the demonstration because it was unnecessary in view of the overwhelming evidence of hyperactive reflexes. Plaintiff's lawyer's argument could include the suggestion that the neurosurgeon had to have been very confident about the plaintiff's reflexes to have volunteered to demonstrate them in front of the jury and, therefore, the jury should credit his testimony very highly indeed.

Remember: Live Demonstrations Are Always Risky

Plaintiff's lawyer would have been using good judgment if he decided against asking the neurosurgeon to perform the demonstration on redirect examination. The reason is that live demonstrations before the jury, as contrasted with video-taped demonstrations, are always risky. Recall Exs. 3–15 and 4–8 in Chaps. 3 and 4 in which demonstrations backfired. When the neurosurgeon struck the knee, plaintiff's leg might not have bounced up in the air, especially because he apparently did not have a rubberized hammer with him but had to use his hand. If plaintiff's leg did not react as expected, her case would have sustained a terrible, perhaps lethal, blow.

You should not present a demonstration unless the witness has all necessary implements such as the hammer, unless the witness has sufficiently practiced under conditions similar to those in the courtroom, and unless you are prepared by consultation with the witness who will present the demonstration to lay the foundation for its admissibility. Since in Ex. 5–2 none of these conditions was true, and since plaintiff's lawyer was not in the predicament of desperately needing evidence, the wiser course for plaintiff's lawyer would have been for him not to ask for the demonstration on redirect. Indeed, even if all the conditions are true, a live demonstration is always risky, as pointed out in the discussion of Ex. 3–15.

If plaintiff's lawyer nevertheless had asked the neurosurgeon to do the demonstration on redirect, the defense lawyer might have objected on several grounds; but his objections would have been unsuccessful. The objection that the demonstration was repetitive and cumulative of the direct testimony probably would be overruled owing to the qualitative difference between the doctor testifying on direct about his observation of the leg reflex and his testing the leg on redirect so that the jury itself could observe the reflex. The defense lawyer might also object that the demonstration was improper redirect because it was outside the scope of cross-examination. This objection probably would lose as well, for the defense lawyer opened the door for the neurosurgeon's offer to demonstrate by in effect challenging him on cross-examination to produce more evidence of hyperactive reflexes. The cross-examination questions summarized in Ex. 5–2 would seem to have made the demonstration plainly admissible on redirect.

Transitional Statements

I hypothesized that if the defense lawyer had declined the doctor's offer to demonstrate and moved to a different subject on cross-examination, the defense lawyer would explain that plaintiff's lawyer is in charge of trying to prove the injury. Such a transitional statement adds to the already high likelihood that the court would rule that the cross-examination opened the door to the demonstration on redirect. For this reason this transition carries a small disadvantage. However, it carries advantages over reacting to the witness' offer to demonstrate by either failing to respond but moving abruptly to another question or by a neutral transition, such as saying that the question did not call for a demonstration and it will be appreciated if the witness will kindly answer the next question. An advantage of the hypothesized transition is that the defense lawyer avoids appearing timid about what the result of the demonstration would be; after all, the reason he declines the demonstration is that fixed rules of court make it plaintiff's burden to prove the injury, not his. Another advantage is that it sounds a theme to impeach the neurosurgeon which the defense lawyer will amplify in summation if plaintiff's lawyer does not use the demonstration during redirect. This basis for impeachment has been referred to above.

Damaging Evidence First Presented During Cross-Examination Has a Magnified Impact

The consequence of the defense lawyer taking the better way out of the trap when his opposing counsel chooses to have the neurosurgeon do the demonstration during redirect obviously depends on the outcome of the demonstration. If the demonstration did not show a hyperactive reflex, the consequence would be a triumph for the defendant. On the other hand, if the demonstration during redirect showed, as it did in Ex. 5–2, so hyperactive a reflex that not only did plaintiff's leg bounce up but also her shoe flew all the way across the courtroom, the defendant would be seriously hurt. As great as this damage would be to the defense, it would not be so bad as the damage done by the same demonstration during cross-examination at the invitation of the defense lawyer.

A successful demonstration makes a greater impact during cross-examination because of the adversary setting. Jurors expect witnesses on direct and redirect examination to say and do what helps the party who has selected them to testify. By the same token jurors do not expect the opposing lawyer on cross-examination to present evidence which helps his adversary. If you do so, as in Ex. 5–2, the jurors will sit up and take particular notice because it is so unexpected. They will also be more impressed with cross-examination when it puts to rest a charge that you are in the process of leveling at the witness.

In Ex. 5–2, the cross-examiner had been hammering away at the witness owing to the subjective character of his impression of the plaintiff's reflex. A demonstration refuting the charge is more devastating the greater its proximity to the charge, i.e., during cross-examination itself rather than during redirect. Keep in mind that jurors who are not lawyers identify with the witness who is not a lawyer and visualize him during cross-examination as compelled to match wits with the cross-examining lawyer. They figuratively cheer and hug him as a member of their own team when he scores decisively in the game of wits, as in Ex. 5–2. Following the neurosurgeon's demonstration during cross-examination, the erring defense lawyer did not overreact by deciding to settle rather than fight further.

DO NOT LOSE CONTROL OF
THE WITNESS

In Ex. 5–2, the cross-examiner invited the witness to expand and improve his direct testimony. That invitation amounted to a surrender of control over the witness. Usually witnesses are able to, and often they want to, hurt the cross-examiner's side of the case. Indeed they have almost always been selected to give direct testimony because they can do just that. When the direct examiner turns the witness over for cross-examination, it is often as though a hostile nation has placed a subversive operative in the disguise of a diplomat on the territory of its arch enemy. The enemy like you must watch the operative like a hawk and keep him on a short leash. When you do this well, you will keep the witness under control. The result of keeping the witness under control during cross-examination usually is success in the sense that the effect of the direct examination is minimized.

Confine Most Answers to "Yes" or "No"

There are many ways for you to keep the witness under your control. One is to limit the content of each question to a single fact. For example, "Did you feel terrified?" Such questions provide the witness no pretext for answering with a lengthy and harmful speech. Nor do they enable him plausibly to defend an unresponsive answer on the ground that he misunderstood the question. You can also control the witness by making the form of the question very leading indeed. For example, "You felt terrified, right?" The witness almost always can answer "yes" or "no." If he tries to expand and you object that the question calls for only a "yes" or "no" answer, you stand a much better chance of a favorable ruling since you had used the leading form than if you had used an open-ended question.

It is very important to confine many cross-examination answers to "yes" or "no." Unlike the direct examiner the cross-examiner customarily has not thoroughly interviewed the witness to prepare his or her testimony. Hence you frequently do not know how the witness will answer. When the answer turns out to be unfavorable to you, you will almost always be hurt less by a one word "yes" or "no" answer than by a long answer containing the reasons underlying the "yes" or "no."

The Cross-Examiner Should Not Answer Questions by Witnesses

Another way to keep the witness on a short leash arises if the witness turns the tables by asking you a question. For example, "Wouldn't you have felt terrified if you had been in my circumstances?" If you answer the question, you may open the door for the witness to set forth the reasons for his disagreement with you; these reasons may well enhance the injury to your case. Instead of answering the question, you should reply that the rules of court procedure call for the lawyers to ask the questions and the witnesses to answer them. An answer along these lines not only prevents the witness from enhancing the injury but also informs the jury that, if the witness persists in asking you questions, the witness is acting improperly.

SHOULD YOU USE THE FOOLPROOF METHOD OF CONTROLLING THE WITNESS— WAIVE CROSS-EXAMINATION?

Most errors in cross-examination fall under the general heading of failure to keep the witness under control. This is true of the examples of errors which will follow in this chapter, although they shall be described by the particular subdivision of surrender of control which they illustrate. The only foolproof way of keeping the witness under control is not to cross-examine at all. The decision not to cross-examine is an easy one to make if the witness' direct examination either has helped the cross-examiner's case or has not hurt it. Under this condition the raison d'être for cross-examination does not exist. There is no harmful effect of the direct to minimize.

Example 5–3:

AN IDEAL TIME NOT TO CROSS-EXAMINE

Herold Price Fahringer

The error that I remember most vividly occurred during the course of a conspiracy trial in Buffalo, New York, where five public officers were on trial, in Federal Court, for conspiring to accept kickbacks on the construction of a public building, the City Hall.

A witness for the government had identified three of the men at a meeting at a supplier's place of business. He did not identify my client or one of the other co-defendants. On cross-examination the young attorney for what we will call "Co-defendant D" arose from his chair and in one dramatic moment asked, "You didn't see my client at that meeting, did you?"

You can imagine that lawyer's surprise when the witness then stated, "Now that you mention it, I do remember—he was there!"

As it turned out, that was the only piece of evidence connecting that defendant with the conspiracy. Had he not asked that question, a motion to dismiss the indictment against his client might well have been granted. As it turned out, he was forced to go to the jury with the rest of us.

I am happy to report that all the defendants were acquitted; but that tactical error could have been one that the young lawyer might have had to ruefully remember for the rest of his life.

When unlike in this example the direct has harmed your case, the decision of whether to cross-examine is by no means always easy. A factor pointing against cross-examination is that you may lose control of the witness who will harm your case even more than he did on direct. A factor pointing in favor of cross-examination is the need to minimize the harm done by the direct examination. Occasionally the harm can be minimized without cross-examination but through introducing an exhibit or calling or cross-examining other witnesses whose testimony will question the accuracy of the direct or impeach the credibility of the witness.

In practice the choices you face are not as pure as in theory. For instance, before your witness will be permitted to impeach the opposing witness, cross-examination may be necessary to elicit information that will identify the opposing witness as the person the impeachment applies to. Furthermore, a particular state's evidence law may not allow impeaching testimony by another witness unless the witness to be impeached first had been cross-examined on the impeaching subject. In calculating whether to cross-examine, you should anticipate that the opposing lawyer may argue in summation that the lack of cross-examination bespeaks acknowledgment of the unshakable truthfulness of the direct testimony. On the other hand you could argue either that the witness(es) you called in rebuttal of the opposing witness thoroughly discredited him or her or that the direct testimony was so plainly harmless that it would have wasted the time of the court and jury to have cross-examined the witness.

Peculiarity of particular litigation may signal that a witness should not be cross-examined.

Example 5–4:

AN EXCELLENT TIME NOT TO CROSS-EXAMINE

John Lord O'Brian

Some of Mr. O'Brian's partners in the Washington, D.C., law firm of Covington & Burling recall one of his decisions not to cross-examine. Electric utilities were litigating against the Tennessee Valley Authority, which Mr. O'Brian was defending. A star witness for the utilities was Wendell Wilkie, the Republican Presidential candidate in 1940. His direct testimony consisted of generalities and was brief. Mr. O'Brian felt that Mr. Wilkie planned to throw in his main points when cross-examined. Mr. O'Brian also knew that Mr. Wilkie was a very appealing figure to the fact-finder. Hence at the close of his direct testimony Mr. O'Brian said simply, "No questions."

This decision not to cross-examine was wise because Mr. O'Brian viewed the goal of the cross-examiner as to minimize the harmful effect of the testimony of the witness, whether coming from direct or cross. Mr. Wilkie never put his main points against the TVA into evidence because he was not cross-examined.

Whether and How to Cross-Examine a Celebrity

The decision on whether to cross-examine a popular figure such as Mr. Wilkie must take into account the special effect he is likely to have on the jury. He may be so popular that the jury misinterprets any cross-examination of him at all, even though in fact on the merits of the case, as an attack on his integrity and reputation. Such a jury also may proceed to misconceive their function as to return a verdict which vindicates their hero rather than decides the issues in the case. Popular public figures, especially pillars of the community, frequently are selected to testify as character witnesses. Since such testimony does not usually concern the central issues on the merits, and since it is possible that the jury will misinterpret cross-examination as quarreling with the integrity of the witness, character witnesses who are popular figures are usually best left not cross-examined.

Even when celebrities testify substantively, the likelihood of jury endearment toward them means two things for you. First, there is a thumb on the scale toward no cross-examination when weighing whether to cross-examine at all. Second, if you decide to cross-examine the popular figure, you should do so with kid gloves and with the utmost deference. By an obeisant attitude toward the witness, you can convey to the jury that, far from attacking the integrity of their hero, you salute it, as they do. You should try to convey to the jury that, to help them do justice, the hero simply is being given the opportunity on cross-examination to supplement his testimony beyond the questions opposing counsel chose to ask on direct examination.

Do Not Feel Compelled to Cross-Examine or Ask Additional Questions

Some inexperienced cross-examiners would use the foolproof method of controlling the witness, viz., waiver of cross-examination, except for one concern. They are concerned that they will be thought to be ineffective if they do not cross-examine. A similar concern has led neophyte lawyers to ask cross-examination questions without a good reason to do so. One lawyer who lacked the confidence not to question in his first trial has confessed as follows.

Example 5–5:

IF YOU HAVE NOTHING TO SAY,
SAY NOTHING

Terry W. West

I recall one very brief episode which occurred in the very first matter I handled and which made an indelible impression and verified my theory that one should not ask a question of a witness simply to be having something to say. At that time I recall asking the Deputy Sheriff if he had been acquainted with my client prior to arresting him. There was no real reason to ask the question but I felt something should be said. He immediately responded with, "Oh yes, I have arrested him several times before."

In Ex. 5–5 the cross-examiner's question, which he asked because he had not thought of anything else to ask, informed the jury of his client's former arrests, one of the things a criminal defense lawyer should be most vigilant to prevent the jury from learning.

LISTEN FOR CLUES IN THE
DIRECT TESTIMONY TO SUBJECTS
FOR CROSS-EXAMINATION

On the spectrum of cross-examination questions ranked by their riskiness, the question in Ex. 5–5 is near the most risky end. Near the safest end is where one would expect that a cross-examination question following up an offhand, potentially favorable remark during direct testimony would fall. Indeed you should listen carefully to the direct testimony for clues to fertile subjects for cross-examination. However, when you detect a clue, you must be cautious, if not skeptical, about pursuing the subject on cross. The clue may be a skillfully placed bait to trap you. Cross-examination following up the clue may turn out to be disastrous. Roy M. Cohn, famous since the Army–Senator Joe McCarthy hearings, and a trial lawyer, recounts just such a trap in a trial in which he had a personal as well as professional interest.

Example 5–6:

BE WARY OF A CLUE WHICH TURNS
OUT TO BE A TRAP

Roy M. Cohn

I was a defendant in a criminal trial that lasted over two months, and resulted in my acquittal on all counts on December 16, 1969. My attorney, the late Joseph E. Brill, sustained a coronary attack just before the close of the prosecution's case. My law partner Thomas A. Bolan took over presentation of our case—and I summed up to the jury in my own behalf. The case turned largely on whether a certain meeting between me and the Corporation Counsel of New York City had in fact occurred—as we contended—and if so, on what date. We argued an earlier date than the prosecution contended—and this was crucial. Fortunately for us, the meeting had taken place at the home of William Cassidy, the retired editor of "The Tablet," the publication of the Brooklyn Diocese. Bill Cassidy—unlike me—is meticulous. When the indictment was handed up, he phoned Tom Bolan to say he kept exact diary entries, and had the date and hour of my meeting with the Corporation Counsel at his home carefully and contemporaneously recorded. It destroyed the government's theory. Mr. Cassidy's appearance on the stand was a turning point in the case.

He was advanced in years, and had just had a cataract operation. He was led to the stand. Tom Bolan conducted the direct examination. He elicited Mr. Cassidy's career and retirement. He then carefully asked: "Since your retirement, have you done any work for compensation?" Mr. Cassidy replied: "Yes, I have done some work for a couple of law firms in New York." Mr. Bolan dropped this line at that point. Out of the corner of my eye, I saw the young prosecutor busily making a note—which I knew must be a firm reminder to destroy Mr. Cassidy's credibility by bringing out on cross that one of the law firms that paid him was Tom Bolan's and mine— with the inference that he was therefore biased. If not so, why would Bolan have deliberately refrained from having Cassidy name the firms that paid him? The diary went into evidence, and the prosecutor took over on cross.

His first mistake was to belabor the damaging date entry in the diary. As he pressed Mr. Cassidy on it, Mr. Cassidy had to be helped

continued

Example 5-6 (cont'd.)

from the witness stand to a place right next to the jury box, where the lighting was better, and supplied with a magnifying glass. As he carefully reread out loud the diary entries, the jurors leaned forward, and hung on every word. Finally, as the prosecutor realized this was accomplishing nothing but indelibly emphasizing evidence damaging to his case, he dropped this area.

He then turned to what he believed would be a devastating denouement. He had Mr. Cassidy repeat that he had indeed been paid for work by a couple of New York law firms. I should mention at this point that there were a number of Catholics on the jury. The prosecutor drew back, and asked: "Mr. Cassidy, could one of those law firms which pays you be Saxe, Bacon—in which the defendant and his counsel, Mr. Bolan, are partners?" Mr. Cassidy unhesitatingly responded: "Yes, sir." "And how much did they pay you?" "$500 per month." "And you're not even a lawyer?" "No, sir, I did research." "Research for what?" Then came the devastation. Cassidy slowly and dramatically replied: "Sir, Mr. Cohn and Mr. Bolan represent the Cardinal and the Archdiocese on such matters as restoration of right to prayer in schools and discrimination against Catholic teachers. Although they refuse to accept any compensation for their services from the Church, they have insisted on compensating me for my time and expenses in doing the research for them."

The prosecutor shriveled under the glares from the jury box. Later, he was frank enough to tell me: "You just heard one of the dumbest questions asked in an American courtroom." He concluded the cross with another equally disastrous tack. He asked Cassidy, who by this time had obviously won the respect of the jury: "Mr. Cassidy, isn't it a fact that Mr. Bolan is a good friend of yours?" Cassidy replied: "Tom Bolan is not only a good friend of mine, but he is one of the finest, most honorable men I have known in my lifetime." In a last gasp, the prosecutor asked: "And I suppose you'd say the same about the defendant, Mr. Cohn?" Cassidy hesitated, and said: "No, I can't. I do not know Mr. Cohn as well as I know Mr. Bolan. But I can say that in my observations of Mr. Cohn, he is a person of integrity and dedication." When the jury retired to deliberate, Mr. Cassidy's diary was requested by them. An acquittal followed shortly. What a perfect situation for the prosecutor to have said "No questions."

Prefacing Cross-Examination Questions with, "As You Testified on Direct,..."

Mr. Cohn's account of Ex. 5–6 does not reveal how the prosecutor phrased his initial question to Mr. Cassidy concerning his direct testimony that he had been doing work for a couple of New York law firms. The prosecutor wanted Mr. Cassidy to confirm his direct testimony so that he could build from it to the conclusion of a financial connection between the witness and Mr. Cohn and his counsel, Mr. Bolan. Hence it would have been well for the prosecutor to have prefaced his initial question of this topic with, "As you testified on direct,..." This preface warns the witness being cross-examined that he will be caught in a prior inconsistent statement if his cross-examination answer diverges from his direct answer. Conversely, when the goal of the cross-examiner is not to reinforce direct testimony but to reverse or dispute it, he should studiously avoid reminding the witness of his direct testimony by using any preface such as, "As you testified on direct,..."

The Risks of Following a Blind Alley of Cross-Examination

The prosecution was sorely injured by the defense's trap. There was no foolproof way the prosecutor could have distinguished Mr. Cassidy's matter-of-fact reference to his work for a couple of New York law firms as baiting a trap rather than a clue to decisive impeachment of the key defense witness. If the prosecutor reckoned that he had a good chance to win without this decisive impeachment of Mr. Cassidy, he erred in pursuing it. But if he needed this impeachment to snatch victory from the jaws of defeat, his judgment to risk proceeding up a blind alley of cross-examination was correct. Any cross-examination question is risky if you are not prepared to offer evidence rebutting a harmful answer, as is discussed in connection with Exs. 5–23 and 5–24. Sometimes the risk is worth taking. What the prosecutor learned in Ex. 5–6 is that the risk at times is encased in an offhand indication in direct examination of a promising topic for cross-examination.

If You Have Discredited the Witness, Stop Asking Questions

Once the prosecutor took the bait, he could not have avoided injury. But he could have managed to have been injured less than he was. His first four or five questions in unbroken sequence succeeded in impeaching Mr. Cassidy. They informed the jury that the law firm of defendant and his counsel had been paying Mr. Cassidy, who is not a lawyer, $500 a month for what they called research. If the prosecutor had stopped this topic of cross-examination here, he would have suffered no injury whatsoever at the cross-examination stage. But he had to ask one-question-too-many, "Research for what?"; and with Mr. Cassidy's answer the roof fell in on the prosecution's case. In failing to rest on the laurels of the impeachment he had achieved without asking the one-question-too-many, the prosecutor is not alone. We shall encounter in this chapter many fellow-travelling cross-examiners who are first-rate, although fallible, trial lawyers.

To be sure, if the prosecutor had stopped short of the one-question-too-many, his achievement of impeachment would have been short-lived. On redirect examination Mr. Bolan undoubtedly would have asked Mr. Cassidy what research he had been doing for his law firm. Mr. Cassidy undoubtedly would have given the same answer he gave on cross-examination to the effect that he had been researching cases for the Archdiocese and the Cardinal, whom Attorneys Cohn and Bolan represent; and that they insist on providing the legal representation without compensation. Yet this revelation during re-direct would have inflicted less injury than did the same revelation during cross.

Redirect Examination Makes a Smaller Impact than Cross-Examination, Especially When the Testimony Is Self-Congratulatory to the Redirect Examiner

One reason for the smaller impact during redirect is the more adversary setting of cross-examination, as is spelled out on pages 130-31. Another reason arises from the unusual coincidence that Mr. Cassidy's revelation is not only that the defendant works for the Catholic Church free of charge but also that his counsel Mr. Bolan does so as well. Had Mr. Bolan's redirect question elicited this self-congratulatory fact, Mr. Bolan would have been seen as singing his own praises. Jurors, just as people at large, tend to distrust or resent a person who blows his own horn. Distrust of defense counsel spills over into distrust of the defendant. To avoid a resentful reaction by the audience, skillful public speakers are very careful to arrange in advance that the moderator recite their accomplishments in introduc-ing them. They know that they will appear arrogant if they do so themselves. At the same time they want the audience to learn of their pedigree so that the audience will be more receptive to them. Similarly, Mr. Bolan wanted the jury to learn that he and his client donate their services to the Church. He also must have preferred that they learn it from the prosecutor rather than himself. The prosecutor obliged by asking the one-question-too-many, "Research for what?"

Avoid Open-Ended Questions on Cross-Examination

Most of Mr. Cassidy's answer to this question was responsive. The question asked for the nature of the research Mr. Cassidy did for the two lawyers. A strictly responsive answer would have been that he researched matters of concern to the Catholic Church such as restoration of prayer in public schools and discrimination against Catholic teachers. The responsive part of Mr. Cassidy's actual answer was to this effect, although he expressed it by saying that the lawyers represent the Church on these matters and he did research on them. The lawyers' representation of the Church is implicit in the strictly responsive answer when the preceding questions and answers are taken into account. Mr. Cassidy's actual answer made the representation explicit. The open-ended character of the prosecutor's cross-examination question, "Research for what?" allowed the witness to answer responsively and yet expressly inform a jury with Catholics on it that the Cardinal had selected the defendant and his counsel to represent the Church.

Open-ended questions often result in unresponsive answers Despite the open-ended character of the question, the most damaging part of Mr. Cassidy's answer, namely, that "they [Mr. Cohn and Mr. Bolan] refuse to accept any compensation for their services from the Church," was indisputably unresponsive. The fee arrangement between the lawyers and the Church had nothing whatsoever to do with the nature of the research Mr. Cassidy did for the lawyers. Nor was his reference to the lawyers' fee arrangement justified on the ground of a tenuous relationship to his fee for research. His answer to an earlier cross-examination question had already disclosed his $500 monthly fee. By no stretch of the wording of the question under discussion did it call for any reference to fees. The prosecutor did not object to or interrupt the indisputably unresponsive part of the answer. He had every right to do so. He could have done so as soon as Mr. Cassidy revealed that he was saying that the lawyers "refuse to accept any compensation...."

The Court's Instruction to Disregard Evidence
May Not Be Obeyed by All the Jurors

The prosecutor was wise not to have made this objection. Mr. Cassidy volunteered without prior warning that the lawyers do not charge the Church for their services. By the time the prosecutor heard it, the jury had already heard it too. Technically it was too late to object, and a motion to strike was the correct mechanism. But if the prosecutor had interrupted to object or move to strike, he would have dramatized the most damning testimony against him of the whole trial. If the judge denied the motion to strike, the accreditation of the defendant from donating his services to the Church might well seem to the jurors to gain the imprimatur of the court. If the judge granted the motion to strike and instructed the jurors to disregard the unresponsive testimony, some of them probably would not have been able to do so. Recall the reaction of the jurors to an objection referred to in Chap. 4, Ex. 4–4.[1] In fact, to single out testimony by a motion to strike and ruling from the judge is to render it harder to forget than testimony not given this treatment.

On Cross-Examination Use Leading Questions and
Interrupt Unresponsive, Long Answers

The prosecutor's open-ended one-question-too-many gave Mr. Cassidy wide freedom to answer responsively. The prosecutor surrendered considerable control over Mr. Cassidy. In another question the prosecutor used a very leading question, which promises tight control over the witness. He asked, "Mr. Cassidy, isn't it a fact that Mr. Bolan is a good friend of yours?" The answer was, "Tom Bolan is not only a good friend of mine, but he is one of the finest, most honorable men I have known in my lifetime." The prosecutor should have interrupted the witness as soon as he proceeded past the first comma. Up to that point the answer was entirely favorable, and Mr. Cassidy had answered the question fully. Everything he said after that point was unfavorable and unresponsive.

The interruption did not have to go through the judge in the form of an objection or motion to strike. The cross-examiner might have cut off the witness by saying courteously but firmly, "Thank you. That answers the question." Then he would ask his next question. If the witness persisted in praising Mr. Bolan, the prosecutor should ask the judge to admonish the witness to confine his answers to the questions. Such an admonition may well be interpreted by the jurors to diminish the reliability of the witness. The extremely leading question asked by the prosecutor would have entitled him to the admonition and to cut the witness off as soon as his answer strayed into unresponsiveness. The prosecutor's failure to do so deprived him of the control over the witness which the excellent form of his question made possible. The possibility is not realized unless you follow through by interrupting the witness.

Be Wary of Clues for Your Cross-Examination in the Cooperation of the Witness or the Cross-Examinations by Your Co-Parties

A clue to promising cross-examination that backfires may come from direct testimony, as it did in Ex. 5–6. It may also come from a witness whose cooperation and malleability on a subject on which you need to question her embolden you to examine her on a subject on which you have no need to question her.

Example 5–7:

PURSUING A RISKY BLIND ALLEY

Beverly C. Moore

Defending for an insurance company, I had a case where the plaintiff contended she purchased a bottle of soft drink which contained some foreign substance, which she unknowingly imbibed, and which made her very ill. She sued both the bottler and the retailer. Her only special damages, as she was not employed, was the medical bill of $10.00 which she paid to the family physician who came to her home for the purpose of treating her. At that time the law of North Carolina was to the effect that in such a suit a plaintiff had to show either negligence or similar occurrences.

Before the case was set for trial I thought it best to take the deposition of the plaintiff to stake her out in advance on the issue of negligence. I knew that there were no instances of similar circumstances because I had inquired of the local bottler and the grocer from whom the bottle was purchased who reported that they knew of no similar occurrences.

On direct examination, which was of course a cross-examination because the plaintiff was adverse and we were permitted under our law to put questions as if on cross-examination, I had to

continued

Example 5-7 (cont'd.)

decide whether plaintiff had any evidence of negligence on the part of the defendants, and on this I succeeded because she could not testify as to any negligence. She made such a good witness for me that I decided to proceed and enlarge the scope of my inquiry. I then asked her if she knew of any similar occurrences; that is, did she know of any individuals who had purchased the soft drink with a foreign substance in the capped bottle. She quickly responded in the affirmative and went further to state that three of her neighbors had purchased bottles within about two to three weeks of the time of her purchase, and that they all became very ill. Plaintiff's attorney made much of this and asked for the addresses of the individuals. I of course went no further and closed the deposition.

Not more than a week elapsed before the insurance company forwarded to me the summons and complaints in three new actions. The plaintiffs were the three individuals named by the plaintiff in the deposition. The same attorney who represented the plaintiff in the first action also represented the others, and he merely copied the first complaint in the other three cases. I immediately went to work to settle all four of the claims, and I was very fortunate in settling all four of the cases for very nominal sums indeed inasmuch as the only special damages were medical expenses, as I recall, in two of the cases.

I am afraid my client, the insurance company, was the loser by my bad judgment in getting into the similar occurrences issue, because I doubt that the particular attorney for the plaintiff who was involved could have made out a case at trial otherwise.

The idea or encouragement for subjects for cross-examination which backfired came from the opposing side in Exs. 5–6 and 5–7, but such an idea can come from your own side too, as in the following example.

Example 5–8:

DISTINGUISH TRIAL BUSINESS
FROM SHOW BUSINESS

George V. Higgins

In 1973, I prosecuted six men and a woman who had robbed the same bank on two different occasions. Only three of the men actually entered the bank; the others stole and operated the getaway and switch cars. Two of the actual robbers pleaded guilty, and were available at the trials of the rest, as witnesses for the government. The third robber had selected the one place in the bank that was not covered by the automatic surveillance cameras. I had no picture of him in the act.

When trial commenced before Judge Garrity in the Boston Federal court, my first witness was one of the tellers from the bank. Her name was Sylvia Babbitt. She was, I should say, as fit at 55 as most people are at 20, a tough, smart, no-nonsense lady, who took no guff from anyone. I had been impressed by her performance before the grand jury, and was perfectly confident of her ability to hold her own on the witness stand.

What I did not know was whether she could select the third robber from the five defendants seated at the bar to be tried. The FBI had bagged them separately, so we never had a line-up. I did have mug shots, but the Supreme Court had not, by then, clarified the rules on photographic show-ups. Since I had two accomplices ready to testify, I decided to avoid the possibility of tainting my case with reversible error by displaying the photograhs to her, in obedience to the rule that one should not try to prove too much.

Her direct testimony, therefore, was brief. She established that the bank existed, that she worked in it, and that three men robbed it on the date in question. Counsel (I have some decency, and will not report his true name—we will call him Wilson) for Plante, the third robber, cross-examined briefly, eliciting some innocuous stuff, and sat down. Counsel for each of the four remaining defendants, none of whom to my knowledge had ever entered the bank, then seriatim ordered the defendant he represented to stand. Each obtained the response that Mrs. Babbitt had never seen his client before in her life. When everyone had had the opportunity to examine Mrs. Babbitt, she had identified no one.

continued

Example 5-8 (cont'd.)

Wilson was not content with this state of affairs. I believe he was mistakenly convinced, whether by his client lying to him, or by failure to consult with other counsel for the defense, that Plante was innocent. Whatever the reason, he demanded the right to recross-examine Mrs. Babbitt, and the Judge, over my objection (I had no idea what the devil Wilson wanted, but followed the grouchy rule of objecting when you don't know what the fellow's up to), allowed it.

"Mr. Plante," Wilson said, "will you stand up, please."

Plante stood.

Now, with triumphant anticipation in his voice, Wilson said: "Mrs. Babbitt, I ask you if you have ever seen this man before?"

"I certainly have," she said. "He was the one over by the door, the one with the shotgun. It looked about this long, and he was pointing it right at me."

That, of course, would have been a good time for learned counsel to experience a genuine cardiac arrest, slump to the floor, and lie there until he had thought up some ethical way to get a mistrial. Or at least to shut up. But we are egotistical sorts, and I believe the failure of some to keep their faces straight provoked him into a desperate effort to try to recoup.

"You're sure of that?" he said.

"I certainly am," she said. "He didn't have the beard and the moustache then, but that's him, all right."

"You saw him that one day, and you can say that?"

"One *day?*" she said. "That Plante. He's had an account at the bank ever since he was fifteen years old. I've waited on him many times myself. I've seen him dozens of times. He was standing over there by the door, and I simply couldn't get over it, that here was the Plante boy coming in with a shotgun and pointing it at me and robbing the bank. I just couldn't get over it."

At a bench conference, a few minutes later, Judge Garrity ruled on another point. Then, as we turned to take our places, he paused: "Well, Mr. Wilson," he said, "you've learned something today: there are two kinds of business—show business, and trial business. The trouble is, you seem to have gotten them confused."

A major lesson from Ex. 5–8 is that it surely behooves the trial lawyer not to confuse trial business with show business. Grandstanding by Attorney Wilson in reopening his cross-examination, so that he could dramatically confront the witness with his client, dashed his client's hope for an acquittal.

WHEN YOU ELICIT A DAMAGING ANSWER, STOP RATHER THAN DIG YOUR GRAVE DEEPER

In both Exs. 5–6 and 5–8, the cross-examiners initially elicited harmful testimony. They could have minimized their losses by stopping at that point. Instead they made a mistake by going on so that Mr. Cassidy and Mrs. Babbitt could enlarge and deepen the harm. After Mr. Cassidy had repeated his direct testimony about the crucial date, the prosecutor was harmed by his inquiry about Mr. Cassidy's research work for Roy Cohn's law firm; and Mr. Cassidy enlarged even that tremendous harm when the prosecutor went on to inquire about his friendship with Mr. Cohn's counsel and his regard for Mr. Cohn himself.

Attorney Wilson's recross-examination of Mrs. Babbitt opened with the show business flourish of having his client Mr. Plante stand, asking Mrs. Babbitt if she had ever seen him before, and her show business flop of an answer, namely, "I certainly have. He was the...[robber] over by the door, the one with the shotgun. It looked about this long, and he was pointing it right at me." Attorney Wilson did not stop but enabled Mrs. Babbitt to deepen the harm she was doing to Mr. Plante by going on to ask her whether she was sure about her identification in view of the fact that she had only seen him that one day. Her answers mightily supported her damning testimony by informing the jury that Mr. Plante had been a bank customer for many years, that she had waited on him or seen him dozens of times, and that during the robbery she could not get over the fact that a customer was one of the robbers.

Exs. 5–6 and 5–8 were criminal cases. In the following civil case a cross-examiner who received harmful testimony likewise did not cut his losses but proceeded until the witness deepened the harm.

Example 5–9:

STOP AFTER THE INITIAL INJURIOUS ANSWER

Judge Henry M. Leen

The following is my best memory of an incident which took place quite a few years ago in a will contest in which I was engaged. The issue was that of testamentary capacity. It was the position of the contestants that at the time of the execution of the will the testator's mental condition was such that he did not appreciate the nature and extent of his property and the natural objects of his bounty.

The testator was a man of approximately 70 years, who up to the time of his death conducted a successful business in the Boston area. He died by suicide a short time—weeks or a few months—after the execution of the will. The proponent and principal beneficiary of the will was the testator's second wife from whom he had been estranged for several months prior to the making of the will. The contestants were two daughters of the testator by a prior marriage.

At the trial held before a probate judge, without a jury, there was considerable psychiatric testimony, and also testimony from a number of people who knew the testator and/or did business with him. One of these latter witnesses, called by the contestants, testified that he had known and done business with the testator for several years up to the time of his death. He liked the testator and did not want to "hurt" him. He was reluctant to testify, but responded to a subpoena and did testify on direct examination. He testified that the testator at or about the time of the making of the will was upset, disturbed, and worried about his affairs.

On cross-examination, counsel for the proponent of the will questioned whether there really was anything abnormal or unusual in the testator's behavior. The witness, while reluctant, adhered to the testimony he had given on direct examination. Counsel became somewhat exasperated with the witness, although it did not appear up to that point that his testimony had been especially critical.

Finally, counsel asked this question: "You say he was nervous and worried. You didn't expect him to commit suicide did you?" The witness replied: "I certainly did—I wasn't surprised when I heard of it," (or words to that effect).

continued

Example 5-9 (cont'd.)

This answer was, of course, very damaging to the proponent's case. As I recall, the judge in making his findings in which he disallowed the will referred to this testimony. The question of counsel was certainly a tactical error, for it gave to the testimony of the witness an emphasis that it couldn't otherwise have had. I have always thought this was a good example of going too far with a witness—especially one who didn't want to testify in the first place.

In Exs. 5–6, 5–8, and 5–9, the cross-examiners went too far. They should have stopped their lines of inquiry when the witness provided injurious answers. Instead they sought, and received, additional harmful answers. If they had stopped after the first answers, they would have spared their clients the additional injury.

AFTER A HELPFUL ANSWER STOP, LEST THE FAVORABLE TESTIMONY BE NEUTRALIZED BY THE WITNESS

As a cross-examiner you must aspire to spare your client the initial injury as well. One opportunity to do so arises when a witness gives the cross-examiner favorable testimony on a subject. When this happens, you usually should stop examining on this subject. If you fail to stop but go on, you enable the witness to disavow or neutralize his favorable testimony. Consider the following classic example.

Example 5–10:

STOP QUESTIONING AFTER A FAVORABLE ANSWER

Attributed to Clarence Darrow

The defendant was being tried for the crime of mayhem. The State alleged that in the course of a fight the defendant bit the victim's ear off. The defendant sharply disputed this allegation. The State called a disinterested bystander as a witness. Her direct testimony said that the defendant had bitten off the victim's ear. On cross-examination the defendant's lawyer asked the witness, "Did you see

continued

Example 5-10 (cont'd.)

the defendant bite off the victim's ear?" The witness replied, "No." Then came the fateful one-question-too-many, "Then how can you say that defendant bit off his ear?" The witness answered, "Because I saw him spit it out."

Discovery Depositions Invite Similar Errors During Cross-Examination

The lesson graphically illustrated by the last example, namely, do not at trial continue to cross-examine on a subject after you have successfully dealt with it, is applicable as well to a deposition upon oral examination. The deposition is one of the pretrial discovery tools. However, the record of a deposition also is admissible in evidence at trial under a number of circumstances. See, e.g., Federal Rule of Civil Procedure 32. A common circumstance is when the deponent, whether a party or a witness, is unavailable to testify at the trial in person. Hence when you participate in a deposition, you must be mindful that the testimony may wind up before the jury on videotape or through a reading of the transcript. You must conduct yourself accordingly. For example, you should be content with a favorable cross-examination answer and not question the witness further on the subject, unlike what happened at the following two depositions.

Example 5–11:

QUIT WHILE YOU'RE AHEAD!

John W. Norman

Defense counsel, representing the airplane manufacturer in a products liability aircraft accident case, was cross-examining plaintiff's witness on deposition. Plaintiff's theory of the case was that an air vent into the fuel cell had become obstructed and (due to defective design) created a vacuum in the fuel cell which prohibited flow of available fuel to the aircraft engine, resulting in engine fuel starvation and the consequent crash. The lay witness, a squirrel hunter in the mountains where the plane crashed, had assisted the

continued

Example 5-11 (cont'd.)

FAA investigator in conducting the crash investigation. During the investigation, he testified that he had lifted the wing tip from the ground and placed a post under it, so that the FAA investigator could observe the vent line.

During the witness'deposition, which was to be read at the trial, defense counsel was doing what he could to bolster his defense that the plaintiff had simply exhausted all of the available fuel in the aircraft, i.e., run out of gas. Defense counsel asked the witness a series of questions which went something as follows:

Q: When you raised the wing tip, what did you hear?

A: Nothing

Q: Alright, as I understand it, you raised the wing tip to fit the post under it, and that would have been about three feet?

A: Right.

Q: And you heard nothing?

A: No.

Q: Did you raise it slowly or swiftly?

A: Well about average I guess.

Q: Alright, so as you were raising this three feet, at average speed, you heard nothing in the wing (where the fuel cell is located)?

A: No, nothing.

Q: Nothing at all?

A: No, nothing other than just that gas sloshing in there.

Defense counsel, if he had stopped at the first, second, or even third question, would have done a great deal to the settlement value of that case. His enthusiasm in his discovery overcame him. By not leaving everything alone, with that final question, he destroyed everything that he had gained. Had he left it alone, I, as plaintiff's counsel, would have been afraid to have gone into it on redirect, so that the testimony in all probability would have stood, and defense counsel could have argued it in closing argument. The case was settled without trial.

Example 5–12:

PENNY WISE AND POUND FOOLISH

Stanley A. Prokop

Plaintiff was the widow of a man who died when he was crushed between his cabin cruiser and a dock on the Columbia River. The eye witnesses' accounts of the event indicated that he was thrown from his craft into the water between the boat and the dock because of a very large wake, in violation of the "no wake law" under the State and Federal boat safety acts.

The eye witnesses indicated that there were two large cruisers on the river immediately prior to the incident. The main eye witness was an elderly woman who was fishing in the area.

We represented one boat called the "Catapult" which was a forty-five foot Chris Craft. The other party defendant was the owner of a fifty-seven-foot Chris Craft Constellation cruiser called the "Marachino."

Although both boats were on the river at the same time, plaintiff had the burden of proving that each boat or one of them caused the wake which resulted in the plaintiff's decedent's death.

Counsel for the codefendant's boat discussed the matter with the elderly woman witness before her deposition was taken, and she informed him that all she knew was that the boat that caused the wake was a large white boat. She was not good at identifying makes of boats or various exotic features about them.

Counsel for the Marachino noticed the deposition of the elderly woman and prior to her deposition engaged the services of a professional photographer to visit a local yacht club and take a dozen pictures of large white boats which all looked substantially the same.

His tactic was evidently to make the witness go through a "line-up" procedure and indicate that she could not identify either of the boats as the one that caused the wake.

At her deposition, the witness again reiterated that she could not tell one large white boat from another and that she would not be able to identify the exact boat which caused the wake.

Evidently, counsel for the Marachino felt that, having made a substantial investment in photographic expenses, he should make use of the pictures that his client had paid for.

continued

Example 5-12 (cont'd.)

He then displayed the twelve photographs to the witness, asking her if she could identify the boat that caused the wake. After indicating that she doubted that she could do so, the witness began looking more closely at the pictures and promptly discarded about eight of them. She then looked at the four that were remaining and then discarded three of them, leaving one boat which she said was the boat that caused the wake. Unfortunately for counsel for the Marachino, she had identified the Marachino.

This incident would seem to be a good illustration that counsel should be careful not to use "overkill" since once you have a good answer, you can do nothing but ruin that by continuing further.

Examples 5–10 through 5–12 have pertained to a potentially decisive witness. When you find that a decisive witness has given testimony which promises to bring you victory, you must be wary of cross-examining him by questions that lead him to neutralize or reverse his testimony. But you must not relax your wariness even when questioning less central witnesses or when questioning on subjects which are not the central issues. Injuries inflicted by relatively peripheral witnesses or on peripheral subjects cumulatively may mean defeat. A judge who had presided over a criminal trial has noted the failure to stop after a cross-examiner had successfully impeached one of a number of witnesses.

Example 5–13:

AFTER A HELPFUL ANSWER, DO NOT PURSUE THE SUBJECT SO THAT THE TESTIMONY CAN BE DISAVOWED BY THE WITNESS

Judge James P. McGuire

Counsel for a defendant tried to show that a witness for the prosecution was drunk. He finally elicited an answer that the witness was intoxicated. He had made a strong point for his defense at this time, but instead of leaving it there, in an effort to improve upon that which was very good, he proceeded further, and then, as always happens, the roof fell in on him. The witness recanted and said, yes, he had been intoxicated several hours before, but at the time in question he was completely in control of himself and had a clear recollection of that which had happened.

DYNAMIC INTERACTION AMONG CROSS-EXAMINATION, REDIRECT EXAMINATION, AND CLOSING ARGUMENT

In the last four examples, the cross-examiners would have had trenchant points to make in summation, if (a) they had not asked the witnesses one-too-many-questions on cross-examination and (b) their opposing counsel did not on redirect examination elicit the rehabilitating testimony. In all of these examples except 5–12, redirect examination undoubtedly could have developed the neutralizing or disavowing testimony, provided opposing counsel were alert enough to realize the damage done by cross-examination and decided to try to rehabilitate the witnesses on redirect. Example 5–12 is exceptional since rehabilitation seemed to require a group of "line-up" boat photographs that opposing counsel had not thought to use. Of course, if opposing counsel did not try to rehabilitate the witnesses, the cross-examiners' points would be intact for summation. Moreover, if opposing counsel did do so, the rehabilitation of the point might well not be so persuasive as if it had occurred during cross-examination for the reasons discussed on pages 130–31.

Rehabilitating a Witness Through Redirect Examination

If you ask the one-question-too-many you remove the burden of deciding whether to try to rehabilitate the witness from the redirect examiner. The redirect examiner will hesitate to ask a rehabilitating question if he or she has not gone over it with the witness in preparation for his or her testimony. Either insufficient preparation or failure to anticipate cross-examination subjects may have left the redirect examiner in the unsettling position of not knowing how the witness will answer. For all one knows, the answer to the redirect question will embellish the summation point which has emerged in cross-examination.

Let us consider the choices open to the redirect examiner after the cross-examination in the following example.

EXAMPLE 5–14:

PUSHING THE LIMITS OF AN EXPERT'S
SELF-DEPRECATION

Chief Judge James L. Foreman

In a jury trial, the defendant was charged with the crime of forging an endorsement on a United States Treasury check stolen from the mail. The government had called as one of its witnesses a handwriting expert who gave his opinion that the signature on the endorsement of the Treasury check when compared with known exemplars of defendant's handwriting was made by one and the same person.

Upon cross-examination, the attorney for the defendant did a particularly good job in getting the handwriting expert to agree that the whole field of handwriting identification was an inexact science, based upon one's opinion after some formal study along with practical experience. He was able to futher elicit from the witness that in the past he had made mistakes in identification of handwritings and some other expert in the field might have an opinion contrary to his in a given case.

The attorney, not willing to settle for the already created doubt as to defendant's signature through the admission that a mistake may have been made, went further. Apparently wanting to prove his client innocent (a mistake often made by defense counsel), he asked one final question. "Since the science of handwriting identification is based on opinion and you have testified you may have made mistakes in the past, then you may have made a mistake in this case?" The witness replied, "I may have made mistakes in other cases, but I have made no mistake in this one, and there is no question in my mind but that the signature on the back of the check in question is that of your client." Obviously, this was a totally unexpected answer, very disarming to the attorney for the defendant and no further questions were asked. Needless to say the defendant was convicted.

Plainly the cross-examiner should have stopped rather than asking the one-question-too-many. Let us assume he had stopped. Let us also assume that the handwriting expert had not advised the redirect examiner in advance how he would answer the one-question-too-many, namely, "Since the science of handwriting identification is based on opinion and you...may have made mistakes in the past, then you may have made a mistake in this case?" The choices facing the redirect examiner would be to ask the expert the substance of this question or to leave the subject as it stood.

The Redirect Examiner's Dilemma

These choices place the redirect examiner in a dilemma. If the question is asked on redirect and the answer is that the expert may be mistaken, the blow to the case may be lethal. If the redirect examiner does not ask the question, the cross-examiner in summation may administer a lethal blow by adroitly pointing out that the government had the burden to prove its case beyond a reasonable doubt, and that the only evidence of forgery was by an alleged expert who admitted that handwriting identification is an inexact science, that he had made mistaken identifications in the past, and that other experts might disagree with him in this case. How much better off the cross-examiner would have been had he or she stopped and been able to make this argument rather than going on to allow the expert to testify, in effect, that he may have made mistakes in the past but that the present case was different and free from error!

Furthermore, the cross-examiner's error in asking one-question-too-many after eliciting helpful testimony insulates the redirect examiner from the difficult dilemma. On the other hand, there is only one way for the redirect examiner to be sure to be spared the dilemma, namely, to be confident of the answer to rehabilitating questions as the result of thorough advance preparation of the witness for anticipated subjects of cross and redirect examinations as well as for direct examination.

"WHY" QUESTIONS ON CROSS-EXAMINATION OFTEN FOREBODE DISASTER

A common subclass of the ill-advised one-question-too-many is "why" questions or questions asking the witness under cross-examination to explain something.

EXAMPLE 5–15:

DO NOT ASK WHY AN EXPERT WITNESS' OPINION IS ADVERSE TO YOUR CLIENT

Judge Joseph S. Mitchell, Jr.

As a young Assistant United States Attorney I was given a case for criminal prosecution involving an alleged securities fraud by a corporation and its president. In particular, the indictment alleged that a registration statement and prospectus used for the sale of the company's common stock were deliberately falsified by stating that the net profits of the corporation for three successive years had increased from 4.1 percent to 5.2 percent to 6.1 percent of total sales. The case was of an extremely technical nature and largely based on the opinion of accountants from the Securities and Exchange Commission that the statements were false. However, it was incumbent on the prosecution to prove beyond a reasonable doubt that the president of the corporation knew that the statements were false.

It was my intention to do this by reasonable inferences to be drawn from the nature of the false statements and his knowledge of the contents of the registration statement and prospectus. These inferences were weak proof at best since the burden of proof was so high. But unforeseen help came in the form of cross-examination of one of the prosecution witnesses. To show to the jury how the questionable percentages were prepared, an accountant who had been employed by the company testified for the government. From books and records in evidence he testified on direct examination what the actual net profit figures were for the years in question and that the percentage increases shown in the prospectus did not accurately reflect these figures.

Now came the cross-examination. Experienced and most talented counsel for the defendants led the witness back through the figures pointing out adjustments that could be legitimately made to make the percentages in the prospectus consistent with the book figures. Just as he was about to finish his cross-examination, he asked the witness the fatal question, "Now then why do you say these percentages are false?" The witness snapped back without hesitation, "Those figures were false then and are false now." There was a noticeable reaction from the jury. The verdict came back guilty.

The cross-examiner had succeeded in neutralizing the accountant's harmful direct testimony until he asked a "why" question which was one-question-too-many. It enabled the accountant to drain the success from the cross-examination by answering in effect that in fact the adjustments were not applicable.

The harm from asking for an explanation after eliciting successful cross-examination can be illustrated by a more common criminal case than stock fraud.

EXAMPLE 5–16:

ASK FOR AN EXPLANATION AND LEARN OF YOUR CLIENT'S BIZARRE BEHAVIOR

Chief Justice Walter H. McLaughlin, Sr.

While waiting to begin a trial, I observed the following. The desk sergeant, who was not on duty at the time the defendant was booked, testified that in his opinion the defendant was drunk. He was charged with driving under the influence of liquor and drunkenness.

The defendant's lawyer started to cross-examine. The format as I remember was as follows:

Q: Sergeant, you weren't on duty when the defendant was booked were you?

A: No.

Q: So you didn't have an opportunity to talk to him?

A: No.

Q: And you didn't talk to him when he was in the cell?

A: No.

Q: So you have no idea, Sergeant, whether his speech was coherent or incoherent?

A: No.

Q: You don't know whether his walk was steady or unsteady, do you?

A: No.

Q: How close did you get to him that night?

A: About 30 feet.

Q: Did you hear him talk during that period of time?

A: No.

Q: Where were you when you saw him 30 feet away?

A: At the top of the stairs leading to the cell area.

Q: Where was he?

A: In his cell.

continued

Example 5-16 (cont'd.)

Q: Do you mean to tell the court that this man was drunk when you didn't see him walk, you didn't hear him talk, and the only time you observed him was when he was 30 feet away?

A: Yes I do.

Q: Sergeant, how can you form that opinion under these circumstances and have it credible?

A: Because he had defecated in the middle of his cell and he was sitting in the middle of it waving his hands; I thought he was drunk.

The last question destroyed the gains in discrediting the sergeant's opinion which had been achieved and generated graphic evidence that the defendant had been drunk.

Examples 5–15 and 5–16 which illustrate the danger of asking for explanations of cross-examination are both criminal cases. The danger is just as acute in civil cases.

EXAMPLE 5–17:

ASKING "WHY" CIVILLY

Judge Fred M. Winner

In the course of a three-way donnybrook over the way a very large apartment complex was constructed, the owner accused the contractor, the contractor accused the architect, and the architect didn't care who was to blame just so long as the judge didn't blame him for the many frailties in the building.

One of the complaints had to do with the cement finish on the balconies. The owner's expert testified to his examination of the balconies and to the horrible finish of the cement. Representing the contractor, I brought out that the expert had examined only about half the balconies, although the owner was claiming damage for poor cement finishing on all of them. I asked the fatal question, "Why didn't you examine all of the balconies?" and I got the horrible answer, "I couldn't open the doors which led out to the other balconies. They were installed out of line and wouldn't slide.

Judge Winner's cross-examination had given him the right to argue in summation that the expert had examined only about half of the balconies. The judge lost that right by asking the expert why he had not examined the rest.

The cross-examiner in another civil case also weakened the summation by asking for an explanation.

EXAMPLE 5–18:

AN ARGUMENTATIVE ANSWER MAY WELL NOT BE UNRESPONSIVE TO A "WHY" QUESTION

Judge Andrew R. Linscott

In an automobile tort trial, the plaintiff testified to the before and after value of his car to show damages. Waving a copy of the repair bill, defendant's attorney brought out that it cost only $1,800 to fix the car, yet the plaintiff, in giving before and after value, was claiming $2,900.

Rather than leave the matter for argument, defendant's attorney said to the plaintiff, "Kindly explain to the jury why you are claiming so much more than the acutal cost of fixing your car."

The plaintiff started to talk. He said, among other things, that anybody should realize that repairs were never successful; that his car never ran as smoothly after the accident as it had before; that no matter what the repair people did they could not make the vehicle the car it had been. The defendant's attorney moved to strike. The judge pointed out that, in view of the broad question, the answer was responsive and could stand. The plaintiff got the $2,900.

Asking Witnesses To Explain Enables Them To Sum Up Their Case

As a result of asking the plaintiff to explain, the cross-examiner's summation pointing out that the car was repaired for only $1800 would be significantly weakened. The plaintiff's argumentative answer under oath probably was more persuasive to the jury than his lawyer's summation to the same effect would have been. This should not be surprising in light of the tendency of jurors to identify with witnesses in contrast to lawyers. A disadvantage of asking witnesses to explain on cross-examination is that it enables them to argue or sum up their cases. Although in Example 5–6 Mr. Cohn, who was the defendant, did not directly say that he benefited from giving the summation in his own behalf, the very fact that he mentioned it in relating Example 5–6 suggests that he gave his self-summation a prominent place when he reflected back on the significant parts of the trial.

Asking Why a Witness Seems Hostile or Biased Against You or Your Client Is Particularly Likely to Boomerang

Questions asking for one particular kind of explanation are especially likely to boomerang. When a cross-examiner asks why a witness seems hostile or biased against him or her or the client, the answer is likely to be a barrage of prejudicial statements which otherwise would have been inadmissible.

EXAMPLE 5–19:

THE FLOODGATES OPEN WHEN THE WITNESS IS ASKED WHY HE HATES THE DEFENDANT

Victor H. Kramer

A California financier was on trial for some offense, the nature of which I have forgotten. The defendant had done many bad things in his life, and the prosecutor tried to bring them out in the course of his case. Judge St. Sure regularly sustained objections by counsel for defendant to any line of inquiry based on other offenses.

Finally, the prosecutor put on a government financial witness (perhaps IRS or FBI) whose testimony was damaging to the defendant. Counsel for defendant was exasperated and said finally in the course of his cross-examination: "You hate the defendant, don't you?" The answer was, "No, I don't hate him; I despise him." In a fit of rage the defendant's lawyer said, "Why do you despise him?" The witness then was able to testify at length concerning the other offenses of the defendant. The testimony lasted over two court days and all of the erstwhile excluded evidence got into the record, despite repeated objections from the defense which were always overruled by Judge St. Sure with comments such as these, "You asked him the question, and so I am going to let him answer it."

Once the defendant's counsel succeeded in having the witness admit that he despised the defendant, he should have stopped. A circumspect cross-examiner would not have gone on to ask the witness why he despised the defendant. Instead he or she would have made a note to remind the jury in summation that the witness had departed from his role as an objective financial witness and had let his personal feelings against the defendant govern. In summation counsel could have argued that the witness lacked the impartiality that makes a witness reliable. Counsel relinquished this argument by asking, "Why?"

Another cross-examiner asked a similar question, and received a similar answer.

EXAMPLE 5–20:

WOE TO THE LAWYER WHO ASKS WHY A WITNESS IS TESTIFYING AGAINST THE CLIENT

Paul T. Smith

I am reminded of a case that was tried in the United States District Court for the Southern District of New York where Judge Murphy was the Presiding Justice. The defendant was charged with some serious crimes involving extortion arising from loan shark activities. He was represented by his brother, who was a lawyer.

When the victim got through testifying, the defense counsel attacked the alleged victim's credibility by showing that he had been convicted of various crimes in the past and further attacked his credibility by attempting to show that the victim had entered into a plea bargaining arrangement with the prosecutor whereby he was to be immunized from conviction for certain crimes. The cross-examiner then went on to ask "whether it was a fact that the only reason *why* the witness was so testifying was because he had made a 'deal' with the prosecutor." The witness answered that that was not the fact. The cross-examiner then said "Then, tell us *why* you are testifying for the government?"

Judge Murphy turned to the cross-examiner and said, "Do you really want to know *why*?" The cross-examiner said, "I'm entitled as a constitutional right to pursue this line of inquiry." The judge, lowering his eye glasses, turned to the witness and said, "All right, tell him 'why'." The witness then went on to testify that the real reason he was testifying was that the defendant had threatened to bomb his house, kill his children, and maim his wife. The judge then turned to the lawyer and said: "Now, do you know *why*?"

Listen to the judge's comments It is hard to imagine a more pointed warning against asking why a witness opposes one's client than that by Judge Murphy. Yet this cross-examiner determinedly ignored the warning and blithely walked right over a waiting cliff. He failed to recognize that a judge's comments may be generously motivated to help counsel. Judge Murphy may have heard that the witness had been saying that the defendant had been threatening him. The judge, therefore, may well have been anticipating the witness' reply when, without objection but on his own, he reacted to the "why" question by asking whether the cross-examiner really wanted to have the question answered. The cross-examiner's response that he had a constitutional right to the question suggests the rigid mind-set of an overly zealous advocate who fights for his question without considering that the judge may be trying to suggest that the answer will be catastrophic to him.

Asking even the most innocuous-looking witness why he has been hostile to one's client can be devastating.

EXAMPLE 5–21:

DON'T ASK A LAW ENFORCEMENT AGENT WHY HE HAD BEEN TAILING THE ACCUSED

George V. Higgins

It was a firearms case, and the treasury agent was a particularly shrewd man, who benefited greatly in his work from his appearance, which was that of an amiable dolt. People were always underestimating him, none to more devastating misfortune than the lawyer who demanded to know *why* he had been tailing the poor lad charged with bartering heroin for stolen weapons. To this day, I don't know what he expected to get, but I remember vividly what he actually received. "Well," the agent said, settling back comfortably for a long recitation, "we started to get reports on this guy about three years ago, I think it was. The local police told us they suspected him of pushing heroin to junior high school kids, but they couldn't seem to get anything on him. Then there was a very bad battery that we knew was drug-related, but the victim refused to testify against him, so we couldn't make a case. The victim later changed his mind, and came in—this was after he got out of the hospital—but then he changed it

continued

Example 5-21 (cont'd.)

> back again, because he said the defendant had gotten wind of it and threatened to kill him if he testified." It went on like that, for a good five minutes, in the midst of which counsel for the defense objected unsuccessfully to his own question, then moved unsuccessfully to strike the answer.

The judge correctly ruled that the cross-examiner was stuck with the answer to the ill-advised question he had asked. Despite the witness' innocuous appearance, the question never should have been asked. The cross-examiner could not reasonably have expected that a law enforcement officer would admit that he had been tailing the defendant out of an improper motive. The cross-examiner should have expected an answer like the spine chilling one he received.

Examples 5–19 through 5–21 illustrate the danger of asking a witness why he or she is hostile to the cross-examiner's client. It is likewise very ominous to ask a witness why the hostility extends to the cross-examiner too. If the answer does not cause personal embarrassment to the lawyer, it may nevertheless cause damage to the client's case.

EXAMPLE 5-22:

> ### WHEN THE CROSS-EXAMINER ASKS WHY THE WITNESS REFUSED TO TALK WITH HIM, THE WITNESS LAMBASTES THE LAWYER AND THE CLIENT
>
> **Frank C. Gorrell**
>
> I have always been cautioned never to ask, on cross-examination, a witness a "why" question. It simply gives him an opportunity to make a speech, and if he is clever, he may fully capitalize on this opportunity.
>
> I witnessed a perfect example of a violation of this principle. I was trying a lawsuit defending a company that had been accused of hiring away some of its competitor's employees, who, allegedly, brought with them certain trade secrets, including plans and specifications for a newly designed piece of machinery. The chief engineer for my client had quit my client's employment and had been working
>
> *continued*

Example 5-22 (cont'd.)

for another company for a long period of time prior to the trial of my case.

I used this engineer as one of my chief witnesses and his direct testimony was superb. The attorney for the plaintiff eagerly began his cross-examination, and it was quite evident that he believed that he could substantially weaken the impact of this witness' testimony.

He started out by asking the engineer if he now had any interest whatsoever in the lawsuit, which, of course, the witness denied. He asked the witness if he had anything to hide, and again the witness answered no. He continued by asking whether or not the engineer had talked with me, the defendant's attorney, several times during the period from the time the lawsuit was filed to the present. The witness stated that he had talked with defendant's attorney on many occasions about the facts to which he had just testified.

Plaintiff's attorney then, with finger pointing and voice rising, demanded, "Then tell me, Mr. Dunn, if you have no interest in this lawsuit and if you have nothing to hide, why did you refuse to talk with me when I called you last week?" Mr. Dunn then, in reply, asked the attorney if he really wanted him to respond to that question. The lawyer, ignoring the warning, and with back to the witness but face to the jury, responded in a very stern and sanctimonious voice, "I most assuredly do." Thereupon, the witness responded as follows: "Because this lawsuit is totally without merit. I am the one person that could have told you that and explained, I feel to your complete satisfaction, why it is without merit if you had simply taken the time to talk with me during the three years that this suit has been pending. But you chose not to talk with me, but rather harassed this defendant and these individual defendants by depositions, interrogatories, motions, etc., all of which could have been avoided by a simple interview with me.

"You chose not to call me and ask me what I knew until one week before this case was to be tried. During these three years you have never bothered to call me, you did not take my deposition, nor did you ever attempt to find out what I knew about the facts. I have known the president of your company for ten years; I personally know that he knows this lawsuit is without merit, and he is merely using this courtroom for the purpose of harassment and out of spite in order to explain his own failures and to seek revenge upon this defendant because it has succeeded while he has failed. Since you chose not to talk with me until a week before this trial, I felt that you

continued

Example 5-22 (cont'd.)

could just wait to hear what I said from the witness stand. That is the reason why I would not talk with you when you called."

The cross-examining attorney never recovered from the shock of listening to that speech, and his loss of composure was evident as he struggled through the rest of an ineffectual cross-examination.

"Why" Questions Surrender Your Control over the Witness

The cross-examination questions in Exs. 5–15 through 5–22 all produced harmful answers. The cross-examiners would have been better off to have stopped without asking them. This is easy to see in hindsight, to be sure. But it is also not hard to foresee that these questions would produce harmful answers. Consider their form:

"*Why* do you say these percentages are false?"

"*[H]ow* can you form that opinion [of drunkenness]?"

"*Why* didn't you examine all of the balconies?"

"Kindly explain to the jury *why* you are claiming so much more than the actual cost of fixing your car."

"*Why* do you despise him?"

"[T]ell us *why* you are testifying for the government?"

"*[W]hy* [have you] been tailing the poor lad...?"

"*[W]hy* did you refuse to talk with me when I called last week?"

The form of all the questions is very open-ended. They surrender the control which the cross-examiner should exercise over the witness. The "Why" questions enable the witness on cross to continue to testify for the same ultimate purpose of defeating the cross-examiner for which the direct examiner put him or her on the witness stand in the first place. These broad questions hand the forum over to the witness' side for explanation when the objective of his or her side is to hurt the cross-examiner. Little wonder that the explanations do indeed hurt the cross-examiner.

To keep witnesses under control during cross-examination very open-ended questions should not be asked at all. If you are determined to venture into the witnesses' explanations, you should use some of the suggestions for keeping witnesses relatively under control (see pages 131–32, 142–43) such as limiting each question to a single fact or making the questions so leading that they call for a "yes" or "no" answer. It is far less dangerous to ask, "You have testified that in your opinion defendant was drunk because you want to support your fellow officer, correct?" than to ask, "How did you form your opinion that defendant was drunk?"

If you are considering whether to ask an open-ended "Why" question you should remind yourself that by doing so you will abdicate your control over the witness. This is something you should never do lightly. If you should ever decide to do so, you should make the decision only after calm and thorough deliberation. In Ex. 5–19 the cross-examiner asked why a witness despised his client for the very worst reason. The cross-examiner had lost control of himself to the point where he asked "Why?" out of exasperation and rage at the witness. To avoid losing control of the witness, it is elementary that you must avoid losing your own self-control.

THE "RULE" AGAINST ASKING QUESTIONS DURING CROSS-EXAMINATION TO WHICH YOU DO NOT KNOW THE ANSWER

In Exs. 5–3 and 5–5 through 5–22 the cross-examiners did not know what answer the witness would probably give to their questions. "Do not ask a cross-examination question without knowing the answer" is one of the Ten Commandments of Trial Advocacy laid down by Professor Irving Younger in his lectures throughout the country. Professor Paul Bergman refers to the Commandment as the familiar Golden Rule and recommends that in effect it be amended to read, "Do not ask a cross-examination question when you will not be able convincingly to refute an undesired answer."[2] Most writers on trial advocacy endorse the basic rule. The high stakes at risk in asking a question in violation of the rule are illustrated by the following two examples centering on courtroom clocks.

Example 5–23:

SEEING IS BELIEVING

Philip H. Corboy

Some time ago I was trying a railroad crossing case. The witness I was cross-examining was an elderly man who wore glasses that

continued

Example 5-23 (cont'd.)

looked like the bottoms of Coke bottles. I knew he could not possibly have seen in detail that which he claimed to have seen at 11:30 on a dark, dreary, misty, cloudy night. He not only described the number of box cars, but their various widths and heights. He could not have possibly seen what he said he saw.

Behind me in the courtroom I knew there was a clock that was 12 to 14 inches in diameter. It would be difficult for somebody on the witness stand without 20/20 vision to see the clock, let alone see the time. I nonchalantly, without looking, raised my right arm and pointed to the rear of the courtroom and said, "Mr. Witness, you have told us what you have seen in great detail; now will you be kind enough to tell me what time that clock behind me says." The man immediately answered, "The minute hand says 27 after 11 and the second hand says 33 after 11, so I make the time out to be 11:27:33." His answer was so accurate that the jury undoubtedly would believe the observations of the accident which he had testified to.

Example 5-24:

ONLY TIME WILL TELL

Patrick F. Kelly

I recall years ago as a young lawyer in a defense firm my cross-examination of the plaintiff in a personal injury trial. He was an elderly man who had crossed a darkened highway at the time my client's vehicle struck him. Our obvious defense was that the old gentleman just did not see what was there to be seen. The plaintiff's lawyer, wrapping up his direct examination, alluded to my suggestion of this defense. To the rear of the courtroom was an old clock, and the plaintiff's counsel asked the plaintiff if he could see alright, to which he said, "Yes, Sir," and, "You can see that clock?" to which he said, "Sure."

My intuition was that the plaintiff couldn't read the clock. So on cross I simply said, "What time is it?" The witness was unable to respond. His eyesight was so poor that he could not read the clock in the courtroom. The demonstration of his poor eyesight was a demonstration of the defense of contributory negligence.

In Exs. 5–23 and 5–24 Attorneys Corboy and Kelly took the identical gamble. Neither knew whether the witness' eyesight was good enough to read the clock in the courtroom and neither was in a position to refute an undesired answer which correctly read the clock. Mr. Corboy lost the gamble and may have lost the trial as a result. Mr. Kelly won the gamble and undoubtedly won the trial as a result.

Should You Gamble on Long Shot Questions to Which You Do Not Know the Probable Answer?

The fifty percent rate of success between Attorneys Corboy and Kelly in asking eyesight questions without knowing how the witnesses would probably answer and without being able to refute the undesired answer is unrealistically high. All the attorneys who asked this sort of question in Exs. 5–3 and 5–5 through 5–22 lost their gamble. The admonitions by writers and lecturers against asking such questions reflect their experience that gambling with such questions almost always fails. Does the low probability of success mean that you should literally adhere to the Golden Rule and never ask such questions? Professor Bergman says, and I agree, that you should ask such questions if the alternative is almost certain defeat.

In deciding whether you are in this predicament, you should keep in mind that a jury may not believe a witness even if cross-examination does not demonstrate that the witness is not credible or even if there is no cross-examination. Furthermore, you should weigh the probability of defeat without asking the question against the probability that the answer to the question itself will spell defeat. For example, questions asking why a witness seems hostile to the cross-examiner or his client, as in Exs. 5–19 to 5–22, have a very high probability of eliciting disastrous answers. If a client has a worthy basis to go to trial rather than concede or settle, and if you have prepared for trial thoroughly, you usually need not ask cross-examination questions whose answers are unpredictable and irrefutable. When both sides avoid such questions, the trial can be a rational means for determining the truth rather than a gambling device.

DO NOT "OPEN THE DOOR" TO PREJUDICIAL SUBJECTS WHICH OTHERWISE ARE INADMISSIBLE

Not only can you open disastrous floodgates by asking questions when you do not know what the likely answer will be, but also you can open disastrous floodgates by asking questions on a subject you know all about. Not infrequently you will know all too well some prejudicial fact that would dramatically reduce your client's chances for victory if the jury learned about it. Indeed, you often would advise your client not to go to trial if the fact were admissible. But when you are confident that the law of evidence renders the fact inadmissible, you may go to trial.

To prevent the jury from getting even an inkling of the prejudicial fact from which they might infer the worst, you should ask the judge in advance of trial by a motion in limine to rule that the fact is inadmissible and that your opposing lawyer should not refer to it within the hearing of the jury. It will often be the case that the judge will deny the motion in limine on the ground that, say, the relevancy cannot be determined until more is learned about the case from opening statements and the introduction of evidence. If your prospects for victory depend on exclusion of a prejudicial fact, you should make an alternative motion. This motion will request that the judge order your opposing lawyer (a) not to offer the prejudicial fact in evidence within the hearing of the jury in open court; but, (b) when he reaches the point in the trial when he wishes to put the fact in evidence, to request permission to approach the bench. At the bench a colloquy on its admissibility can take place without the jury hearing anything about it before objection can be made.

By these motions and other pretrial planning, you should do your best to assure that a prejudicial, inadmissible fact does not reach the jury. However, in the heat of battle be wary that your own cross-examination questions do not nullify your best-laid plans. If what you ask, or evidence you present, involves the inadmissible subject, you will have "opened the door" to the subject, i.e., made it admissible.

Example 5–25:

WHEN YOU HAVE CLOSED A DOOR, DON'T BE THE ONE WHO FORCES IT OPEN

F. Lee Bailey

During the Patty Hearst bank robbery trial, a substantial bombing was the work of the New World Liberation Front, a successor

continued

Example 5-25 (cont'd.)

revolutionary group to the Symbionese Liberation Army (which had originally kidnapped Miss Hearst). Its comunique demanded that Miss Hearst refrain from testifying, and that Randolph Hearst furnish $250,000.00 for the defense of William and Emily Harris. I attempted to bring this development out in the direct examination of Patricia, who took the stand in her own behalf, to buttress her claim that her fear of the Harrises had been and was at that time pervasive. My opponent succeeded in convincing the trial judge that such evidence was too remote from the bank robbery to be relevant.

During the cross-examination of Miss Hearst, attorney and defendant were at loggerheads. When the prosecutor pressed Miss Hearst stridently as to why she had assumed a revolutionary posture in the moments soon after her arrest, she explained that Emily Harris was close at hand and that she was forced to continue to play her assigned role for fear of retribution by Emily. In his attempt to debunk this unreal fear of Emily, the prosecutor said, essentially, "You don't mean to tell us that you still feared the Harrises?"

Miss Hearst looked at me. I rose and suggested that she should be allowed a full answer to that question. The prosecutor's First Assistant literally yanked his coattails, and exhorted him to withdraw the question. He moved to withdraw. The trial judge ruled that it was too late. Miss Hearst was then allowed to explain the fact of the bombing (of which the locked-up jury was ignorant), the threat to herself, and the demand upon her parents. It was a classic example of the maxim, "When you've closed a door, don't ever be the one that forces it open."

You May Need to Use Redirect to Introduce Previously Inadmissible Evidence to Which Your Opponent Has Opened the Door

Notice that the lawyer who benefited from the door-opening cross-examination question, Mr. Bailey, was so pleased by the question that he requested the judge to allow it to be answered before the prosecutor sought to withdraw it. By interrupting before Ms. Hearst answered, he may have tipped off the prosecutor's First Assistant that the inadmissible subject would be included in the answer. Nevertheless, the judge permitted Ms. Hearst to testify during cross-examination about her fear. However, if your opponent in cross-examination merely opens the door, but does not elicit the previously inadmissible evidence, you yourself must be alert to introduce the helpful fact in redirect. Consider the alertness of the lawyers who

received a windfall when cross-examiners opened the door in the next
three examples.

Example 5–26:

THE CROSS-EXAMINER OPENS THE DOOR
TO A LITANY OF GORY CHARGES
AGAINST THE DEFENDANTS

Jack I. Zalkind

In 1968 I prosecuted the case of *Commonwealth v. French*, 357
Mass. 356, 259 N.E.2d 195, which involved the infamous government informer, Joseph Barboza.

In planning my direct examination of Barboza, I realized that I
could not introduce any evidence pertaining to the reasons why
Barboza became an informer, since that would be irrelevant and
immaterial at this point of the trial. My opportunity, however,
presented itself when a defense attorney on cross-examination of
Barboza asked the following question:

"Isn't it true that the reason why you turned informer was
because you were promised leniency by the District Attorney?"
Barboza's answer was an emphatic "No."

I did not expect that he would be asked what his reasons were.
However, on redirect I asked the following series of questions and the
following answers were given.

"Mr. Barboza, on cross examination you were asked whether or
not an alleged promise by the District Attorney of leniency forced
you to become a Government witness, and your answer was that it
did not. Now I ask you on redirect examination, if a promise of
leniency was not your reason, what were your reasons for becoming
a government witness?"

Of course, there were many objections by defense counsel; but
the late Judge Forte ruled that, since the defense counsel elected to
open up this area, an explanation was required; and therefore, the
question could be answered. Barboza then went forward to answer
by saying:

"Number 1, I believe that the defendants were trying to kill me
and my wife and family. Number 2, I believe that the defendants were
responsible for the killing of two of my close friends. Number 3, I

continued

Example 5-26 (cont'd.)

believe that the defendants were responsible for stealing $70,000 from my friends who were trying to raise bail money for me. Number 4, I believe that they were responsible for blowing up my lawyer's car which caused him to lose his leg."

There were many other reasons brought forth by Barboza which were extremely harmful to all of the defendants and which certainly would not have come out if defense counsel had not opened up this area in cross-examination.

Example 5–27:

CROSS-EXAMINATION ABOUT DELAY IN FILING A CRIMINAL CHARGE OPENS THE DOOR TO DAMAGING INFORMATION

Chief Justice G. Joseph Tauro

One of the important rules of cross-examination is: don't open the door to damaging evidence which is inadmissible except if you interrogate on the subject.

A graphic violation of this rule occurred in my court room. The trial was for the crime of driving so as to endanger the lives and safety of the public. Juries are reluctant to convict on this charge unless serious injuries in fact result. Yet ordinarily evidence that such injuries *in fact* resulted is inadmissible, as distinguished from evidence that the driving was so dangerous that such injuries *might* result.

In the prosecutor's direct examination the investigating officer was not permitted to testify that as a result of the defendant's driving a passenger in another car was thrown onto the pavement and suffered serious, nearly fatal injuries. The investigating officer did testify that he had arrived within minutes at the scene of the accident. On cross-examination, defense counsel prodded the police officer with the fact that he had not charged the defendant with the offense at the scene, but instead had waited for two days before filing the charge. Defense counsel never asked the reason for the delay.

On redirect examination, I permitted the prosecutor to ask the officer why he had not preferred charges on the night of the incident.

continued

Example 5-27 (cont'd.)

I did so on the ground that defense counsel had opened the door to this area in his cross-examination.

The devastating answer was, "We expected to have a 'fatal' on our hands because of the serious injuries. That was the reason for the delay."

Jury verdict: Guilty

Example 5–28:

THE ADOLESCENT GIRL HAD HER REASONS

Judge Andrew R. Linscott

In a statutory rape case, the indictment mentioned many times over a six-month period when the defendant was accused of having had sexual intercourse with the victim, a girl of about 14 years of age.

The defendant's attorney cross-examined the victim at length on the issue of failure to make fresh complaint. It was obvious that the girl had many opportunities to tell her family and friends.

Consent was not an issue. There was obviously no force and no violence.

On redirect, the district attorney asked the following question, "Will you please tell us, if you can, why you never told anybody about sexual relations with the defendant?" The girl, who had been shy and withdrawn, now looked directly at the jury and said in a firm voice, "Because I liked what he was doing and I was afraid if I told anybody it would stop."

In statutory rape cases where force and violence are not in issue, and the only question is whether the events happened, the attorney in cross-examining the victim must consider carefully whether it would be worthwhile going into fresh complaint at all.

Here, after about 20 minutes spent on the subject on cross-examination, the answer given by the girl on redirect was devastating.

The cross-examiners in Exs. 5–26, 5–27, and 5–28 all opened doors to the definite detriments of their clients. They should have anticipated that the subjects of motivation to become an informer, delay in filing a charge, and failure to make fresh complaint would open the door to very prejudicial redirect testimony. The way to avoid the prejudicial redirect is to studiously avoid door opening cross-examination.

DO NOT CROSS-EXAMINE EXCESSIVELY ON A PERIPHERAL SUBJECT WHICH MAY CAUSE THE JURY TO ATTACH UNDUE IMPORTANCE TO THE SUBJECT

The cross-examiner who does not open the door to a decisive subject that sinks his ship may nevertheless torpedo his case by excessive cross-examination on a relatively peripheral subject. His exaggerated attention to this subject may well cause the jury to give it disproportionate importance.

Example 5–29:

PROTRACTED CROSS-EXAMINATION ON THE RECANTATION BY AN ELDERLY WITNESS—THE EFFECT ON OTHER ISSUES

Judge Albert J. Engel

In one of my first jury trials, I defended a trucking company against a suit by a guard at Continental Motors Corporation in Muskegon, Michigan. Continental produced war materials during the Korean War. Plaintiff while working for Continental walked onto the bed of a truck owned by my client, fell through a hole therein, and seriously fractured his leg. Although he was covered by Continental's workmen's compensation, he sued the trucking company on the theory that it had negligently provided a truck with a hole in the bed. Our defense was that the hole in the bed had been actually caused by Continental's improper use of unloading equipment, that the truck was under Continental's control, and that Continental had not released it for repairs. A critical issue in the case was whether my client had been denied permission to remove the truck to repair it, and this depended upon the testimony of the Continental Traffic

continued

Example 5-29 (cont'd.)

Manager, a man who at the time of the trial was in his 70s and in failing health.

Under Michigan law an employee is forbidden from suing for recovery from his employer over and above what he is paid by workmen's compensation, but is permitted to pursue an action against a third party for the same injuries if that party's negligence contributed to them.

In preparation for trial, our investigators had interrogated the traffic manager who confirmed the facts that he was aware of the hole in the bed of the truck and had told the owner of the trucking company that they could not remove the truck from Continental's operation that week due to the press of emergency work. At trial, however, when I asked the man concerning his conversation with the owner of the trucking company, he denied all knowledge of it. I was completely nonplussed. My efforts to refresh his memory were without avail and were met with the vociferous objection of opposing counsel. My law partner, who had been sitting in on the case with me, counseled that we should excuse him for the time being, put on another witness and simply survive until the noon recess.

At noon the traffic manager came to me and asked me if I was upset with him. My answer was that I was. He asked why. I told him that he had either lied to me during the investigation of the case or he had lied to me during the trial. "Why?" he asked. I told him it was because he had testified that he had not had any conversation with my client or known of the condition of the truck before the accident. He then replied, "But of course I knew. What did I say?" I then repeated what he had testified. "But that's not true," he said. "That's what you told the jury," I replied. It was quite apparent that the old gentleman was addled and that he had become so flustered in the course of his examination that he had completely misunderstood what he was being asked.

When he asked me what he could do about it, I recalled that some collateral research I had recently done had revealed to me that under Michigan law a witness who discovers he has testified untruthfully at trial has an independent right to clarify his testimony and to rehabilitate himself, quite independently of the rights of the party who called him. I told him this, and accordingly on his own the witness went to the trial judge who called a conference in chambers. Over strong objection, the judge ruled that the witness could be recalled and could make such recantation as he wished. Accordingly,

continued

Example 5-29 (cont'd.)

he was recalled. It was at this point that opposing counsel's tactical error appeared.

Rather than simply accepting the recantation before the jury and perhaps even suggesting that that recollection was as infirm as the first, opposing counsel flew into a rage and berated the poor old gentlemen until all at once the entire trial seemed to be focused on whether the witness was telling the truth or was lying. Actually there were many, many other perilous issues in the trial, but all were subsumed in the one question: was the recantation honest? It seemed apparent to me, as it must have to the jury, that the witness was not coached. He recited what he had done during the noon hour. He recited going to the judge. He apologized profusely to the jury. He testified what the true state of the facts was, and the severe cross-examination he underwent only increased the jury's sympathy for him and his credibility.

Had opposing counsel simply accepted the recantation gracefully and not himself made so pointed an issue of the witness' credibility, he probably could have survived the setback and gone on to a favorable jury verdict, in my judgment. Instead the jury was out only about fifteen minutes before returning a verdict for the defendant.

The cross-examiner's ill-advised choice to focus on but one of many perilous issues, namely, the credibility of Continental's elderly traffic manager, undoubtedly signalled to the jury that the verdict should depend just on that one issue.

DO NOT APPEAR TO ABUSE THE WITNESS LEST THE JURORS SYMPATHIZE WITH THE WITNESS

As noted on page 131, the jurors may not be objective judges of cross-examination, for cross-examination pits a witness who is a lay person like themselves against a professional, the trial lawyer. Jurors are quick to empathize and sympathize with lay witnesses who are as unaccustomed to being in court as they are. In Ex. 5–29 a severe cross-examination berated an elderly witness. In Judge Engle's judgment the result was that the witness' credibility increased and the jurors sympathized with him.

How far cross-examination can go before engendering sympathy for the witness depends on many circumstances, particularly the nature of the witness. At one extreme on the spectrum are the very young or very old witnesses. At the other extreme are very assertive or belligerent witnesses and trial lawyers who are witnesses. (The aphorism that lawyers make bad witnesses may spring from the fact that jurors have as little reason to identify with the lawyer-witness as with the lawyer-cross-examiner.) Take a witness who is a bereaved child as an example.

Example 5–30:

UNWISE CROSS-EXAMINATION OF A
BEREAVED SON ABOUT A MOST
SYMPATHETIC SCENE

Edward Bennett Williams

I once tried a case involving a man who had been killed by a street car in Washington. There was some suggestion that he might have been drinking before he was hit, but there was no proof of this. He did have a tendency to drink too much but there was no evidence that he had had a drink when he was hit by the street car.

I put the man's son on the stand. Although he had not witnessed the accident, he had come upon the scene shortly thereafter, and he testified.

When the defense lawyer took him over on cross-examination, he said to him, "You went out in the street, didn't you? Your father was lying there, wasn't he?"

The boy answered, "Yes."

The lawyer said, "You went out and leaned over him, didn't you?"

"Yes." ...

The lawyer said, "You were sniffing for alcohol, weren't you? Looking for a bottle, weren't you?"

"No, sir."

"Weren't you bending over looking in his pockets, trying to get a bottle out of his pocket?"

"No, sir."

"Did you smell alcohol on him?"

---

continued

Example 5-30 (cont'd.)

"No, sir."

"Well, witnesses have testified that you leaned over him, lying there in the road. *Why* did you lean over him."

The boy said, "Because he was my father and he was dying, and I leaned over and kissed him."

That jury—well, that jury was ready to come out of the box to grab that lawyer. They wanted to get him and flog him.

There was no recovery from that. There could be no recovery.[3]

A similar lesson can be learned from the cross-examination of a young teenager who had recently been blinded. The subject of the cross-examination, which is another circumstance along with the nature of the witness which determines at what point the jury will sympathize with a witness, is what the teenager saw.

Example 5–31:

THE LAST VISION OF A BLIND BOY

Frederick W. Allen

The plaintiff's intestate and another young boy were engaged in watching a college student firing a small caliber rifle at a box located in an abandoned quarry where construction materials were stored. Unfortunately, the box contained dynamite which exploded, fatally injuring our client and blinding his companion. Suit was instituted against the various contractors involved with the project upon which the dynamite was being used.

One of the issues in the case was whether there was any warning on the box to indicate that dynamite was stored therein or that the contents were dangerous.

At the trial for the wrongful death of our client, the blind boy was called as a witness and testified that the box had no warning of any kind. He was in his early teens and was assisted to the witness stand by his mother and his newly acquired seeing-eye dog. He was an extremely bright, intelligent young man and was an excellent witness. He testified that the box bore no warning. It was obvious that cross-examination could only reinforce the story that the boy

continued

Example 5-31 (cont'd.)

> told. Most of the attorneys for the defendants realized this and quickly and quietly waived their cross. One of the finer trial attorneys in this jurisdiction, probably convinced by his client that there was such a sign and believing that the boy would confirm this if given the opportunity, very gingerly made an attempt to develop this.
>
> He questioned the boy very quietly on a few unimportant matters and finally asked the following:
>
> "Isn't it possible, _____, that there was a sign on that box, and that you just don't recall seeing it?"
>
> Without a pause, the boy quietly answered: "Mr. _____, that is the last thing that I ever saw and I know there was no sign on that box."
>
> A recess had to be declared as most of the jurors were openly sobbing. The case was settled during the recess. Perhaps the question had to be asked, but the result was so catastrophic that one wonders.

The jury in this example sympathized with the lad's blindness, which was evident the moment he entered the courtroom with his seeing-eye dog. The cross-examiners could not prevent the jury from learning of the witness' affliction. They could only try to prevent the jury from focusing solely on his blindness. All but one of them did so by waiving cross-examination. The one who tried to interrogate gingerly, however, caused the jury to focus very intensely on the tragic consequences of the explosion.

In another case the witness' affliction was not evident when she took the witness stand. But the cross-examiner erred in dramatizing it by using an extrinsic document during his cross-examination of her.

Example 5–32:

A CROSS-EXAMINER FAILS TO FORESEE THAT A LETTER, WHICH SUPERFICIALLY IMPEACHES A WITNESS, WILL EVOKE JURY SYMPATHY FOR THE WITNESS

An anonymous judge

I have been asked to recall an instance of a tactical error by an attorney in the trial of a case before me. What comes to mind is an example of what may be called overkill.

continued

Example 5-32 (cont'd.)

I think back to a case that was being tried to a jury some years ago. As I recall the incident, it involved a charge of armed robbery of a supermarket and went something like this:

The brother of the defendant had previously been convicted and at the time of my trial had been incarcerated. The defendant on trial before me was accused of having driven a red automobile to an area near the supermarket, and to have been acting as a look-out and also as a possible get-away driver. A well-known defense attorney subjected each witness to intensive and prolonged cross-examination. Woe betide any unwary witness who had put thoughts or remembrances on paper. The attorney would almost invariably use the papers as prior inconsistent statements to deflate the effectiveness of such witness' testimony.

It so happened that the government called as a witness the divorced wife of the incarcerated brother. At the time of the alleged offense her marriage had been intact and she had two minor daughters.

Under questioning by the Assistant District Attorney the brother's divorced wife identified an automobile rental contract for a red car bearing a designated registration number. She testified that she was now appearing at the trial under subpoena and stated that she had in fact gone to the automobile rental agency on the significant weekend and had hired the red car for a period of several days. She testified that she had done this as a result of conversation with her then husband and with his younger brother, the defendant now on trial. She said she had resisted the request that she obtain an automobile for the use of the defendant but that her husband struck her and insisted that she get the car for his younger brother. Thereupon she did so.

The aforesaid defense attorney took her on cross-examination toward the end of an afternoon and subjected her to questioning as to her bias against the defendant. She testified that since the time of the alleged robbery her marriage had been dissolved in divorce courts.

In the cross-examination she readily admitted that her feelings toward the defendant were not friendly and that she blamed him for his influence over her former husband. However, she did maintain that her testimony about the auto rental contract was the truth.

At the end of the afternoon, the defense counsel requested the court to tell the female witness to return the next morning as he hoped to have some letters of the witness about which he wanted to question her.

continued

Example 5-32 (cont'd.)

> The next day the defense counsel produced a two or three-page letter which the witness identified as one of her own letters written to her former husband while he was incarcerated. The defense attorney then said to her, "Madam, I ask you to read this letter to the jury." She turned to me and said, somewhat tearfully, "Judge, do I have to do this?" The lawyer appeared confident of the effect of this upon the jury. However, surprisingly, and before I could answer her question, she quickly composed herself, straightened her shoulders and said, "I want to read it."
>
> She then proceeded in a steady voice to read the letter to a jury which became increasingly involved in what the letter contained. In effect she had written to the husband that she missed him deeply and that their two daughters missed having him at home. She described in detail her efforts to support the girls and their activities in school and outside school, emphasizing again that she didn't entirely know what to do without him and that life without him was difficult and a burden. After a page or two of this type of material she then wrote that she felt that his brother, the defendant, had not been a good influence on his life and that she had feelings against the brother with regard to what had happened to the husband and to their life together.
>
> The relevant parts of the letter did no more than restate what the witness had readily admitted on the previous day. But the confident reading of the whole letter evoked sympathy rather than disbelief of the witness on the part of the jury. I sensed that the tactics of the defense attorney in attempting overkill in impeaching the credibility of the government's witness had misfired, and that in fact the letter which the witness read had struck a human chord in the experience or interest of the jurors which could hardly adversely affect their opinion of the witness.
>
> It's something to consider before you give an adverse witness an opportunity he or she may unexpectedly welcome.

Cross-Examining a Woman

Until the second half of the twentieth century, trial lawyers pretty universally felt that a male cross-examiner had to cross-examine a woman witness rather gingerly. That is, they felt that jurors would consider women witnesses to be abused by a cross-examiner's questions which, if put to a man, would not seem abusive.

Example 5–33:

JURY SYMPATHY FOR AN UNEDUCATED FEMALE

Paul T. Smith

As a young lawyer, I recall a time when I was associate counsel with one of the outstanding practitioners on the criminal side of the court. The defendant in this particular case was charged with the rape of an elderly lady who had obviously spent considerable time in the District Attorney's office in preparation for her testimony. During the course of his cross-examination, the outstanding counsel for the defendant led the witness up to the point where the criminal act was to have taken place. He asked the witness, "Then what did the defendant do?" The witness answered, "He then 'coursed' me."

Defense counsel, in what turned out to be devastating to the defendant, pursued this and asked, "What do you mean 'coursed' you?" The victim looked around with a pious expression on her face seeking help and the Judge ordered her to answer. She responded, saying: "He," and then used the past tense of a four-letter Anglo-Saxon word. The reaction of the jury was apparent. Here was this uneducated lady who had made every effort to express herself in a fashion which would not be offensive to the jury and was making every effort to use what she thought would be refined language, being pursued by a cross-examiner to a point where she had no choice but to respond in language which so graphically described the defendant's act as to generate sympathy from the jury. The outstanding defense counsel told me afterward that it was one of the major mistakes he had made in his career.

If the witness had been a man, this cross-examination probably would not have produced jury sympathy for the witness.

Effect of an Educated Witness on Jury Sympathy

There probably would have been little jury sympathy too if the witness had been an educated person, for education is another circumstance affecting at what point the jury will sympathize with a witness. A jury may think it fair game for you to go after a highly educated "professional" expert witness tooth and nail; after all, his contribution to the trial depends on his expert knowledge, and he purports to know more about a relevant subject than you since your education and experience are not on the relevant subject.

The usual David and Goliath roles of witness and lawyer during cross-examination are reversed for expert witnesses, and may be equalized if not reversed for other highly educated witnesses. The usual David and Goliath roles, however, fit the uneducated witness and his cross-examiner; the requirements for admission to the Bar mean that all lawyers are giants in education compared to uneducated witnesses. In such trial matchups, most jurors like everyone else will be rather quick to find the giant guilty of bullying.

Be Familiar with the Attitudes and Values of the Jurors

In describing some of the circumstances affecting how far you can go in cross-examination before you generate juror sympathy for the witness, I have mentioned that trial lawyers have considered juries to be far more protective of female witnesses than males. In some places today, or before very many tomorrows, that may no longer be true. What has or may bring about the change is the feminist revolution of the second half of the twentieth century. You cannot rely on the assumption that yesterday's circumstances will continue to cut the same way today and tomorrow. You must constantly reassess the values and morals of the people who live in the district from which the jury for your trial will be selected. You must be a master student of human nature and the civilization in which the jurors live. If you are, you will have a pretty reliable sense of where the jury will draw the line between proper and abusive cross-examination. If you do not live where the jurors do, you should associate yourself with local counsel who can advise you on what jurors will probably find offensive.

The power of juror sympathy for an abused witness to govern the verdict should not be underestimated.

Example 5–34:

MISPLACED SYMPATHY

An anonymous trial lawyer

I was representing an impoverished family against a railroad. Of course, under these circumstances you would assume that the

continued

Example 5-34 (cont'd.)

> sympathies of the jury would be with the family. It was the wrongful death of their mother. However, the way both the judge and I tried the case resulted in the jury having sympathy for the railroad instead of having sympathy for my client. The engineer was caught in so many lies and so many attempts to justify what he did that the jury thought that the engineer was being abused. There were just too many nails in the coffin. The jury began to feel badly for the engineer, and equated this sympathy for the engineer with the railroad.

The cross-examiner thought that jury prejudice against the large corporate railroad, and sympathy for the plaintiff family, would outweigh jury sympathy for the engineer, a witness who seemed to the jury to have been abused. The cross-examiner was mistaken. He thought the jurors would accept his telling, hard-hitting cross-examination in light of the nature of the parties, a poor family against a railroad. He underestimated the effect on jurors of seeing a fellow human being, a lay person like themselves, being destroyed on cross-examination right in front of them.

DO NOT QUESTION SO HOSTILELY OR EXTENSIVELY THAT YOU STIMULATE THE WITNESS TO BECOME A BETTER ADVOCATE FOR THE OTHER SIDE

Jury sympathy is not the only disadvantage of abusive cross-examination. Another disadvantage is that the witness may become a more articulate or persuasive advocate for the other side.

Example 5–35:

AN UNCOOPERATIVE WITNESS TURNS AROUND

Judge Marie M. Lambert

In thinking back over my many years of trial experience, the case that stands out in my mind as to when a person should not have cross-examined is a case in which a defendant cross-examined one of my doctors. In that case the plaintiff had sustained a rather severe

continued

Example 5-35 (cont'd.)

head injury necessitating the placing of a steel plate in his head. The doctor who was testifying on my behalf was the hospital doctor who was not inclined to be cooperative or helpful and whose attitude was that it was a waste of his time to come in to testify as to injuries and damages in a negligence case.

I had put the doctor on the stand and asked him a few questions; he had a very perfunctory explanation of the injury; and he had warned me that if I went further with him it would not help my case because his attitude would be to minimize the injury. After asking a few questions and asking him to describe the operation and the after effects, I sat down. The attorney for the defendant proceeded to attack the doctor as follows:

"Doctor, are you familiar with an electroencephalogram?" The doctor stated, "Yes."

"And Doctor, did you do an electroencephalogram on this man?" The doctor answered in the negative.

"Doctor, are you familiar with a pneumoencephalogram?" Answer, "Yes."

"Did you do a pneumoencephalogram on this man?" The answer was, "No."

"And doctor, are you familiar with a brain scan?" The answer was, "Yes."

"Did you do a brain scan on this man?" And the doctor answered, "No."

"And doctor, do you mean to say that you did none of the neurological tests?" And the doctor's answer was:

"Young man, there was no need to do the neurological tests. When this man was brought into the operating room, his brain was hanging outside his skull. I could visually see the damage to his brain. I took the brain and physically put it back into the skull and I thereafter scooped out portions of the brain with a scoop that resembles an ice-cream scoop and sutured up the skull and inserted the plate. There was no need for any of this testing because huge portions of the brain had been destroyed and the man was to all intents and purposes a vegetable from a mental point of view."

An unduly extensive or challenging cross-examination of the opposing party can tranform him from a harmless to an effective witness.

Example 5–36:

DO NOT PUT BLOOD BACK INTO THE VEINS OF A DYING ADVERSE PARTY

C. R. Beirne

In this case I was representing the plaintiff who was the only available witness to testify to an accident. When the case came to our office the man was in the hospital and dying. We immediately filed suit and took his deposition at the hospital. My direct examination was fruitless—the man was unable to make any coherent statement about the occurrence. My adversary took care of the matter by a challenging cross-examination. As the dying man was being cross-examined, I could almost see him coming to life as the adrenaline started to flow when he realized he was being challenged by an adversary. He narrated the necessary facts to get the case to a jury and it was ultimately settled.

An expert witness is especially likely to become a zealous partisan if the cross-examiner attacks his qualifications.

Example 5–37:

AN EXPERT'S DISPASSIONATE MANNER IS TRANSFORMED WHEN HIS QUALIFICATIONS ARE ATTACKED

Judge Norris L. O'Neill

In a recent negligence case which I tried with a jury, the plaintiff's orthopedic doctor testified in a very matter of fact, unexceptional, and rather dispassionate manner in regard to certain soft tissue injuries to plaintiff's back incurred in an accident. The doctor was a renowned orthopedic expert. The demand before trial was $7500.

On cross-examination the defendant's counsel asked the doctor the following: "Isn't it true that you are not a real expert in problems of the back, like a chiropractor?"

continued

Example 5-37 (cont'd.)

> This so enraged the doctor that he became a true partisan for the plaintiff. He was no longer the detached observer but an active participant and he proceeded to greatly enlarge his prior meager testimony.
>
> The jury verdict was $25,000.

Attacking an expert's qualifications may do more than stimulate him to become more partisan. It also may result in the expert disclosing additional credentials which make it more likely that the jury will embrace his opinions.

Example 5–38:

THE EXPERT DID NOT ATTEND MEDICAL SCHOOL BUT TEACHES AT ONE NOW

Julius B. Levine

Dr. Leonard M. Paul, a vocational psychologist who holds a Doctorate, related to me a cross-examiantion which focused in part on his qualifications. The lawyer initially addressed him as Mr. Paul. After being reminded several times that the expert witness was a "Dr.," the lawyer asked, "But you are not a medical doctor, are you?" Dr. Paul replied that while he is only a small town psychologist, he does have staff privileges at one of the Philadelphia teaching hospitals. The lawyer proceeded to dig himself in still deeper by asking, "But you did not go to medical school, did you?" Dr. Paul's answer, "No, but I teach at one now."

DO NOT UNDERESTIMATE THE CAPABILITY OF THE WITNESS

In planning and executing cross-examination, the capability of the witness should not be underestimated. The second of the trial errors in Chief Justice Tauro's Foreword was his decision to cross-examine a medical malpractice plaintiff. He based the decision, at least in part, on his client's advice that the plaintiff was simple minded. Her answer to his question turned out to be brilliant—it supplied for the jury the "expert testimony" that the defendant had committed malpractice which her case had lacked.

Even if you are not advised that the witness is dull-witted, you might incorrectly lower your guard in questioning a witness whose occupation is not very cerebral, as in the following two examples.

Example 5–39:

PROFESSIONAL HIERARCHIES

Judge Fred M. Winner

I presided over a case in which Roxanne Reynolds said that her civil rights were violated by a Denver Police Department order which said that convicted prostitutes had to report every so often to the city hospital for a venereal disease examination. Roxanne demurely testified on direct examination that she was a prostitute who had been wronged by that order. On cross-examination the first question was, "So you're just a common whore?" and she responded, "No, I am not." Next question: "I thought that's what you testified to on direct." Answer, "No, I said I was a prostitute." The next question (which shouldn't have been asked) was, "What's the difference?" with the reply, "It's the difference between a lawyer and a shyster." It took a while to restore order in the courtroom.

Example 5–40:

A DUAL CAREER WITNESS

Earle C. Cooley

An important issue in a case I once defended was what caused a pipe to explode when an acetylene torch was being used to cut it. The police photographer slipped in during direct testimony that the pipe was loaded with a white powder that he said was ammonium nitrate. The judge would not strike his testimony. On cross-examination, my voice dripping with venom, I asked the cop when he had received his degree in chemistry. You can imagine my humiliation when I learned that he held both a Bachelor's and a

continued

Example 5-40 (cont'd.)

Master's degree in chemistry from Northeastern University. He who goes for the jugular on the basis of an obvious assumption learns to tiptoe around such assumptions in the future.

If Mr. Cooley had not assumed that the photographer was not also a chemist, he would not have asked him whether he had a chemistry degree. In that event Mr. Cooley would have been able to argue to the jury that they should not find that ammonium nitrate was in the pipe since the photographer had not been shown to have the qualifications or capability to identify the substance.

Error in appraising a witness' capability sometimes manifests itself when the cross-examiner attempts to be humorous, as in the next two examples.

Example 5–41:

THE OPPOSING PLAINTIFF GETS THE LAST LAUGH

Judge Samuel Adams

The defendant corporation, whom I represented, was a manufacturer of pin setting machines used in bowling alleys. Incidental to the purchase of a bowling alley by the plaintiff, the defendant had agreed for a stated consideration to "rehabilitate" some pin setting machines.

The plaintiff brought a breach of contract action against the defendant in which he alleged in substance that the defendant had failed to fully rehabilitate the machines by the agreed upon date on which the bowling alley reopened; that for some three months after the reopening the machines worked sporadically and as a result the plaintiff lost considerable business. Among the charges made against the machines were that they returned customers' bowling balls chipped or gouged, that they swept away "deadwood" and sometimes standing pins just before a customer was about to bowl for a spare, and that the machines often did not reset the appropriate number of pins. All of these failures by the machines had according to the plaintiff considerably irritated his customers.

continued

Example 5-41 (cont'd.)

> Included in the business loss damage claim was lost revenue from vending machines. In reviewing the sales of the miscellaneous items available from these machines, I asked the plaintiff this question:
>
> Q: "I note that the sales of aspirin went down too, so the customers could not have been too badly irritated?"
>
> A: "Things had become so bad that the customers started bringing their own aspirin."
>
> While humor can sometimes help your case or at least enhance your image as an attorney in the eyes of the jury, there is probably nothing more helpful to the other side's case than when your attempt at humor is topped by the opposition.

Example 5–42:

> ### THE EXPERT'S HUMOR TOPS THE CROSS-EXAMINER'S RIDICULE
>
> **James Krueger**
>
> The personal injury plaintiff had seen, in addition to her orthopedist, a chiropractor. Defense counsel thought that he would score a great deal of points in demolishing the chiropractor by advising the jury of the basic concept of chiropractic which, in the old school, was thought to believe that all human ills result from skeletal malalignment.
>
> In pursuing this line of inquiry, defense counsel asked the chiropractor whether, if one fell out of a tree and landed so as to injure oneself and be left with a skeletal malalignment, one could contract tuberculosis as a result? The chiropractor stopped, thought a little bit, and agreed that such was true—if the person falling had fallen upon another person who already had tuberculosis.

DO NOT WORD QUESTIONS AMBIGUOUSLY

Although you work with words and with meanings of questions more than most witnesses do, be careful not to underestimate the capability of a witness to misinterpret a question.

Example 5–43:

THE DOUBLE MEANING OF "HANDICAP" IN GOLF AND IN COURT

B. B. Markham

I was employed to defend a pathologist who had diagnosed cancer of the penis in a 52-year-old man. The general practitioner had discovered the lesion on circumcision and he biopsied the lesion and the end result was a diagnosis of cancer. The general practitioner recommended a urologist who amputated the penis. Thereafter, through a comedy of errors, the surgeon informed the patient that he was happy to tell him that he did not have cancer. This resulted in a lawsuit. Some other doctors were also defendants. We had a very elderly jury selected on the theory that the old men would say what was the difference if the plaintiff had lost his penis and the old ladies would conclude that they all ought to be cut off.

In any event, when I cross-examined the plaintiff, it occurred to me that most of these elderly people would recognize when a person was referred to as "an old sport." Consequently, I started cross-examining the plaintiff on his activities as an athlete, discovered that he had played football, was a baseball player in a semiprofessional league, and the cross-examination was going along very well. This was all going to lead to the conclusion wherein I would refer to him as "quite an old sport." However, I made the classic mistake of asking one too many questions. I inquired as to whether or not the plaintiff played golf, to which he answered, "Yes"; then I asked him what his handicap was, and he gave me a puzzled look and replied his handicap was, "He had to take his trousers down to go to the bathroom."

Example 5–44:

AN INNOCUOUS, AMBIGUOUS QUESTION CAN BE DEVASTATING

Judge Alfonso J. Zirpoli

Counsel was cross-examining the police officer who had arrested the defendant while he was driving away from a service station

continued

Example 5-44 (cont'd.)

> after an alleged theft of tires. He began his examination as follows:
>
> Q: When and where did you first see the defendant?
>
> A: About two years ago at midnight I apprehended him as he was coming out of the back door of a Safeway supermarket carrying a case of whiskey.

Steps to Minimize Ambiguous Questions Which May Result in Injurious Answers

Examples 5–43 and 5–44 illustrate that communication between the cross-examiner and the witness may be very fragile and subject to misunderstanding, real or contrived. To minimize injurious answers resulting from misunderstandings, you should do several things.

a. If the witness will not answer less favorably if he knows in advance what the questions will be, you should interview him before he testifies. In the interview you should preview for him the questions you plan to ask to elicit each segment of his information. Doing so should prevent neutral witnesses or witnesses favorably disposed toward your side from giving a harmful answer to a misunderstood question. But the pretestimony interview will not prevent such an answer by a witness who is unfavorably disposed toward your side. A witness of this stripe will be overjoyed to be asked an ambiguous question which he can answer injuriously to your side.

b. Another step to avoid an answer purportedly arising from a misinterpreted ambiguous question is for you to review the questions you are planning to ask witnesses with your client. If in Ex. 5–44, for example, the lawyer had said to his client that he was planning to ask the arresting police officer when and where he had first seen him, the client undoubtedly would have advised him to reframe or drop the question so that the officer would not be invited to testify to arresting him two years earlier for another theft. This client could help on this question, but obviously clients cannot be sufficiently kowledgeable and sufficiently skilled semanticists to steer counsel away from all ambiguous questions.

c. Neither consulting the witness nor consulting the client can be relied upon to prevent all ambiguous questions. In addition you must address the problem head-on—you must use as much care as possible to phrase your questions so that they are not ambiguous in the context of the trial. Instead of asking the plaintiff "what his handicap was," the plaintiff should have been asked "whether his golfing ability has been rated" and, if so, "what rating he has been given." Similarly, instead of asking the aresting police officer, "When and where did you first see the defendant?", he should have been asked, "On the day of the alleged theft of tires, when and where did you first see the defendant?" You must continually work hard to phrase precise questions. It is imperative to minimize the possibility of real or contrived misunderstanding, for a misunderstood question can be as devastating as a wrongly conceived one.

CROSS-EXAMINATION MAY BE USED OFFENSIVELY, ALTHOUGH IT IS USUALLY MORE RISKY THAN DIRECT EXAMINATION OF A WITNESS WHOM YOU HAVE SELECTED AND PREPARED

Typically the major purpose of cross-examination is to minimize the effect of direct testimony by discrediting its content or by impeaching the credibility of the witness. That is, the major purpose is to defend against the direct testimony. Hitherto we have been dealing with defensive cross-examination.

However, there may be room for offensive cross-examination. The purpose of offensive cross-examination is to establish the claim or crime, when the plaintiff or prosecutor is cross-examining, or to establish a defense when the defendant is cross-examining. In some jurisdictions, the law does not allow offensive cross-examination on all subjects which would be permitted on direct examination; these jurisdictions limit the scope of cross-examination to subjects mentioned in the witness' direct examination except if the court in its discretion permits otherwise. An example is Federal Rule of Evidence 611(b). In other jurisdictions, however, the scope of cross-examination is not limited. Even in jurisdictions with limited scope of cross-examination, there may be offensive cross-examination on subjects partly mentioned in direct examination.

Assuming that the law allows offensive cross-examination, it is by no means always advisable that you always engage in it. If the witness to be cross-examined is the only person who can testify to an indispensable element of your claim, prosecution, or defense, he must be examined. Often there is a choice between cross-examining the witness on the element or recalling him later for direct examination on the element. Cross-examination has the considerable advantage over direct that leading questions may be used if the witness is unfavorably disposed toward you.

But if another reliable witness is available to give the same testimony, should you offensively cross-examine a witness who is neutral or unfavorably disposed toward your client? Consider the following example.

Example 5–45:

ASKING TOO MUCH OF AN ADVERSE WITNESS

Chief Justice Walter H. McLaughlin, Sr.

In the days when leaving the scene of an accident after causing personal injury, without disclosing your identity, was a mandatory jail sentence, I was defending a driver for that offense. The facts very simply were that while he was driving an automobile, and probably slightly intoxicated, he sideswiped a boy about 11 or 12 years old riding a bicycle who was a baseball player on the Cambridge Red Sox. There was no doubt that he had hit the bicycle. There was no doubt that the boy had been injured. The driver kept on going.

The only defense to a situation like that was to establish that he had no knowledge that he had caused an accident. I proceeded to cross-examine the injured boy vigorously in that area and in approximately the following format:

Q: This was a cold day, wasn't it, sonny?

A: Yes it was.

Q: It was a very cold day, wasn't it?

A: Well it was cold but not that cold.

Q: Well, the driver had the window of his car closed didn't he? (Meaning and intending to establish that he didn't hear the contact with the bicycle because the window was closed.)

A: No, his window was open.

Q: Well on a cold day you don't drive an automobile with the window open, do you?

A: He did.

Q: Well weren't you distracted from noticing the window when the car hit your bicycle?

A: No. I noticed it and it was open.

continued

Example 5-45 (cont'd.)

> Q: Are you willing to positively say the window in his car was open?
>
> A: Yes, because when he hit me, I hollered at him and he stuck his head out the window and said, "Go on home you little son of a B or I will kick you in the ass."
>
> I thereupon proceeded to negotiate myself a plea.
>
> I knew at the time and still believe that children that age instinctively tell the truth. I also knew that a witness that age had to be handled very, very gingerly. I thought I had done so, but I asked too many questions. It would have been better to have left that area unexplored with the victim and in direct examination of my defendant put in that his window was closed and he didn't hear any crash.

Note that Chief Justice McLaughlin's cross-examination made commendable use of leading questions; he exploited the advantage of using cross-examination rather than direct examination. Nevertheless, he concluded that it would have been wiser to have had his own client testify on direct that he had not known that his car had collided with the bicycle than to have tried to make the same point during cross-examination of a witness who was unfavorably disposed to his client. There is a substantial risk of injurious answers to offensive cross-examination even from a neutral witness except if he has been thoroughly interviewed on the subject before testifying, just as should be done in preparation for direct examination.

Chief Justice McLaughlin also candidly confessed that he had asked too many questions. After receiving the unfavorable answer that the car window was open, he should have stopped since he then was in the position of a typical defensive cross-examiner who has received an injurious answer. His next two questions made cogent points he could have argued in summation to persuade the jury that the boy was mistaken, and the defendant was correct, about the window. He should have saved the points for summation. By putting them as questions to the boy, he may well have lost them as convincing summation points, since the boy's denials sapped their strength. The Chief Justice's last question was far less leading than the rest, and presented the boy an opportunity to say why he was positive that the window had been open. He did so with such telling corroboration that the Chief Justice had to scramble for a plea bargain.

All trial lawyers will undoubtedly agree that the Chief Justice did ask too many questions. You might, however, disagree with the Chief Justice's belief that 11- or 12-year-old children instinctively tell the truth—on the witness stand at any rate. You may feel that some children testify other than to the truth because an adult, usually a parent, has promised them a reward or threatened them with a punishment. Finally, all trial lawyers also will agree with the Chief Justice that an 11- or 12-year-old witness has to be cross-examined very, very gingerly. Earlier in this chapter on page 178, Ex. 5–30, it was pointed out that a very young witness receives the sympathy of jurors earlier than witnesses with almost any other characteristics. Jurors, like most people, are very protective of the very young. He who does not cross-examine a child gently runs a high risk of an unfavorable verdict.

SUMMARY

Cross-examination is the epitome of the adversary system. It typically pits you against a witness selected by your opponent to do maximum harm to your client. In this most confrontational of trial settings the results of the contest between you and the witness will tend to be relatively magnified by the jury. The same gain scored by you, or loss inflicted by the witness, during direct or redirect examination will probably grip the jury's attention and memory far less. It is remarkable if during cross-examination a witness selected by one side winds up helping the opposing side. Even if this does not materialize, it is exciting to watch the witness fend off the opposing side's assaults during cross-examination.

Your affirmative goals during cross-examination may be offensive or defensive. To use cross-examination offensively is to try to elicit from the witness testimony on a subject not covered during direct which helps your side. The probability of success in this effort generally is low since usually you have not prepared the witness, who is unfavorably inclined toward your side. You will not find yourself pursuing this goal very frequently. You will be better advised to present your offense through the direct examination of witnesses you have selected and prepared. The defensive use of cross-examination is the pervasive one. The defensive goal is to minimize the injury that the direct examination has inflicted to your side by discrediting the testimony or the witness or both.

In addition to these two affirmative goals, this chapter has underscored a negative goal: to avoid the pitfalls of cross-examination. Ill-advised or ill-executed cross-examination can wreak havoc in many ways such as the following:

a. It can provide the adrenalin to convert an indifferent witness on direct examination into a zealous, earnest partisan for your opponent during cross, especially if you attack the witness' expertise.

b. Excessive cross-examination on a peripheral subject can cause the jury to attach undue significance to that subject at the expense of more central subjects which are more promising for you.

c. Free wheeling cross-examination can open the door to otherwise inadmissible evidence which is prejudicial to you.

The foolproof route to avoid these pitfalls and others similar to them is to waive cross-examination altogether. This route should be followed when the direct testimony has not harmed you. This route should also be followed when the harm from the direct is outweighed by the likelihood that the testimony on cross-examination will hurt you even more, whether owing to a pitfall or to your opponent's decision to save his witness' most telling testimony for cross. The latter consideration in Ex. 5–4 led Mr. O'Brian to waive cross-examination and thus silence the big guns of the star witness against him, Wendell Wilkie, who was the Republican Presidential candidate in 1940.

When the direct examination has injured you and your cross-examination, rather than deepen the injury, is likely to minimize it, you should cross-examine. However, you should cross-examine in a manner which recognizes that the witness is usually as ominous as a loyal operative for your adversary. Given the opportunity, he will hurt you. You must take every precaution to deny him that opportunity and keep him under your control.

The following are time tested means to control the witness:

a. Ask him only leading questions.

b. Do not ask the antithesis of leading questions, open-ended questions, of which the most disastrous are questions asking "why" or for an explanation. Be particularly careful not to ask the witness to explain his hostility to you or your client.

c. Formulate your questions so that the only responsive answer is "yes" or "no."

d. If the witness embarks on an unresponsive, long answer, interrupt and cut him off. If you do not do so, you are endangering your case or defense just as much as if you asked a "why" question.

e. Do not ask the witness in effect to repeat his direct testimony or, heaven forbid, to enlarge upon it.

f. An effective device for preventing the witness from harming you during a cross-examination which you have begun is to stop—either do not cross-examine any more or do not interrogate any further on the topic at hand. If the witness has given you an answer that hurts on the topic, don't ask any more on that topic. Do not let the witness dig your grave deeper. On the other hand, if favorable testimony on a topic has been given, stop questioning further about the topic. If you continue to question about the topic, you may ask a one-question-too-many which enables the witness to disavow or neutralize the helpful testimony he or she had given you.

Moreover, by failing to stop and by asking the one-question-too-many, you extricate the opposing counsel from the redirect examiner's dilemma. That dilemma is whether to be silent in redirect about the cross-examination testimony favorable to the other side with the consequence that it stands uncontradicted or whether to interrogate about it in redirect with the possible consequence that the witness will reaffirm and expand it rather than disavow it. If the opposing counsel does not elicit a disavowal on redirect and if you have stopped short of a one-question-too-many during cross, then the favorable testimony is intact for you to argue in your closing argument. It is often the cross-examiner's impatience to drive the effect of the favorable testimony home to the jury immediately by asking more questions during cross which impels asking the one-question-too-many. Summation, not cross-examination, is the proper place to argue the meaning of the testimony.

For cross-examination to succeed in its mission to minimize the injury inflicted by the direct, it is not necessary (as well as usually impossible) to discredit every injurious subject of the direct. If you discredit one of the subjects or even a part of one, or if you impeach the witness' credibility, you often would do well to stop at that point. Then you will have avoided all possible pitfalls and yet frequently be in a position to argue in summation that since some of the witness' testimony was discredited, none of it is reliable.

When you use appropriate cross-examination questions, the

witness says very little except "yes" or "no." Hence, during cross-examination, unlike during direct, you are the center of the jury's attention. Under the influence of the mass media the jury may look forward to your exhibiting a measure of adversariness. However, you must restrain yourself from attacking the witness abrasively. Witnesses' capabilities should not be underestimated. If you question them with a fire breathing tone and a hostile demeanor, they may well exercise augmented vigilance in adhering to their direct testimony which has hurt you. To avoid thus making your task more difficult, and possibly to lead witnesses to let their guard down, your cross-examination style often should not be adversarial but sincere, fair, collaborative, or even friendly.

By the same token, if the jury feel that you are abusing a witness, they will be quick to extend sympathy to the witness and a backlash against you. How far you can go with a witness before the jury will perceive you to be bullying depends on the nature of the witness. At one end of the spectrum are young children who must be cross-examined very gingerly. At the other end of the spectrum are highly educated, professional expert witnesses for whom a no-holds-barred cross-examination is fitting.

This chapter tries to help you to become a better cross-examiner by drawing lessons from errors committed by first-rate lawyers. Hence it is heavy on the pitfalls which lurk in cross-examination and light on the benefits cross-examination can yield. Be sure not to lose sight of those benefits—impeaching the credibility of the witness and discrediting his testimony. They are usually worth pursuing. Some witnesses can be successfully impeached during cross-examination, provided you have the basis to do so before you begin your cross. Likewise, some direct testimony successfully can be shown during cross to have been incomplete, misleading, or even occasionally false, provided you have the basis to do so before you begin your cross. But you must be discerning about your basis to impeach or discredit. What seems like a clue to successful cross-examination may turn out to be a devastating trap, as in Exs. 5–6, 5–7, and 5–8.

REFERENCE NOTES

1. See, e.g., "The Jury Will Disregard...," News, 73 American Bar Association Journal 34 (November 1, 1987); W. Thompson, G. Fong, and D. Rosenhan, "Inadmissible Evidence and Juror Verdicts," 40 Journal of Personality and Social Psychology 453, 460, 461 (1981); V. Hans and A. Doob,

"Section 12 of the Canada Evidence Act and the Deliberations of Simulated Juries," 18 Criminal Law Quarterly 235, 251, 252 (1976); R. Keeton, *Trial Tactics and Methods*, 2d ed., Boston; Little Brown and Company, 1973, pp. 167–168; cf. T. Morse, Jr., K. Lanzer, and K. Mc Hugh, "A Snapshot of a Jury," 21 Boston Bar Journal, pp. 5, 7, 12 (September 1977).

2. Paul Bergman, *Trial Advocacy In a Nutshell*, St. Paul, MN: West Publishing Co., 1979, pp. 183–186.

3. Albert Love and James Saxon Childers, Eds., *Listen to Leaders in Law*, pp. 122–123 © copyright 1963 by Holt, Rinehart and Winston.

WINNING CLOSING ARGUMENT

THE CULMINATION OF YOUR TRIAL WORK: ARGUE AND TIE TOGETHER THE EVIDENCE

Closing argument or summation should be the culmination of your planning for the trial. As soon as you take on a new case you should open a file entitled Argument. You should write a memo to this file on why a jury would want to find for your side. You should place additional points for argument in the file, and modify them, as you find further facts and applicable law from the initial investigation stage through actual testimony at trial. The closing argument is your opportunity to use the arguments you have developed over months or years to tell the jury what you have proved or what your opponent has failed to prove that entitles you to a verdict. You can summarize and emphasize the obvious points in your favor which the evidence has shown.

Beyond the obvious points, you can tie together exhibits and direct and cross-examination which the jury may have received from numerous witnesses, testifying weeks apart from each other. By drawing inferences from evidence or by reorganizing or marshalling evidence which did not appear to be connected when separately introduced, you can show that a point on the merits has been established or that the credibility of a witness has been impeached, which some of the jurors may never realize without your help.

Show the Significance of Your Cross-Examination in Which You Did Not Ask One-Question-Too-Many

You also can clarify for the jury the significance of answers to an individual direct or cross-examination question or a discrete series of questions whose significance some jurors will not have recognized unless you explain it. To avoid asking the fatal one-question-too-many, you should stop your questioning short of fully showing the point you are driving at. Your closing argument, however, is the place where you will fully explain your point. Examples 5–8 through 5–18 in Chap. 5 illustrate where points for argument were lost by one-question-too-many. The points attempted to be made by the backfiring questions should have been made in argument instead.

FOUR VARIABLES TO ADAPT TO IN PLANNING AND MAKING SPEECHES

When you make your points in argument, you should recognize that you are making a speech to persuade the jury to reach a verdict in favor of your client. A great deal has been written about how to make this forensic kind of speech, starting with classical rhetoricians such as Isocrates, Aristotle, Cicero, and Quintilian. Modern rhetoricians would advise the trial lawyer in planning and executing his summation to keep in mind the four variables of every speech situation, namely, the speaker, the occasion, the audience, and the speech. The effectiveness of your summation is diminished if you do not adapt to each of these variables.

Variable one: the speaker The speaker obviously is not a variable to the lawyer himself. But the speaker is a variable in the sense of the jury's expectation of what the lawyer will be like when the summation is delivered. If a jury in the south expects that a lawyer may drop to his knees when beseeching for a favorable verdict, he will not hurt his case in doing so. But if a northern jury does not expect such a physical display, the lawyer who does so risks alienating the jurors.

Variable two: the occasion The occasion as a variable is usually out of the control of the lawyer. The law defines the scope and purpose of closing argument, which the judge usually conveys to the jury. If you exceed the scope of argument, you do so at your peril. For example, if you refer to facts which were not admitted in evidence, your opponent will successfully object or the judge on his or her own initiative may admonish you. When either happens, the jury will trust you less and the interruption may prevent your overall speech from being as unified and smooth as it might have been.

Variable three: the audience The third variable, the audience, is the jury and judge. Chapter 1 on Jury Selection Techniques and the part of Chap. 5—The Keys To Successful Cross-Examination—on appearing to abuse the witness point out that you should be ever mindful of the composition of the jury and the characteristics of the jurors and present your case accordingly. You could best adapt your closing argument to the jury if you knew their throughts and reactions as you were speaking. Since this is impossible, you should do the next best thing, namely, watch the jury's body language as they react to your summation and adapt your argument accordingly.

Example 6–1:

WATCH THE JURY'S REACTION TO YOUR ARGUMENT

Judge Shirley Hufstedler, formerly U.S. Secretary of Education

This incident occurred during the trial of a wrongful death action by the parents of a four-year-old child. The parents had just purchased a metal-skinned vacation trailer. During the construction of the trailer a nail had been driven through a piece of electrical wiring and into the metal skin. The child was electrocuted when he touched the skin of the trailer. The little boy was a beautiful child, and the loss of the boy was a terrible tragedy in the life of the parents.

The jury were an unusually thoughtful and intelligent group. The plaintiffs' lawyer decided to ring the cash register by tugging the jury's heart strings. He very emotionally read Eugene Field's sentimental poem, "Little Boy Blue." He was so enraptured by his reading of the poem that he did not see the jury's faces harden. Nor did he realize that he had insulted them. Only the strength of the liability case saved that lawyer's day. The jury returned a verdict in the plaintiff's favor in spite of the lawyer. In my view if the liability question had been at all shaky, the plaintiffs would not have received a dime.

The lawyer in Ex. 6–1 should not have allowed himself to be so caught up in reading the poem that he forgot to keep his eye on his audience. He mistakenly let the poem consume all of his attention rather than paying attention to the effect it was having on the jury. There was nothing wrong with the lawyer's advance plan to use the sentimental poem in his argument. Many juries probably would be stimulated to award a larger amount of unliquidated damages after hearing the poetic expression of the value of a boy.

However, what is true of many juries or audiences may not be true of the actual audience a lawyer faces. Judge Hufstedler had concluded that this particular jury was unusually throughtful and intelligent. If the lawyer had reached the same conclusion before making his argument, he should have been flexible and discarded his plan to read the poem lest he insult the jury's intelligence. Even if he had not foreseen their reaction to the poem, as he was reading it he should have noticed their facial expressions, as the judge did, and flexibly but gracefully found it unnecessary to read the rest. In sum, he should have adapted his summation to the third variable in every speech situation, the audience.

In another trial the lawyer's summation was not at all out of step with the jury. Yet he still had difficulty with his audience.

Example 6–2:

THE JUDGE MAY COOL YOUR ZEALOUS ARGUMENT

Judge John J. McNaught

In Middlesex County I tried an accident case in which my client suffered a permanent and painful injury to one of his lower extremities. Totally immersed in the drama, I argued to the jury that in assessing damages they should keep in mind that this man, for the remainder of his lifetime, would suffer pain with every single step that he took, and the judge interrupted and said: "Every *other* step." That took the starch out of the remainder of that argument.

The audience addressed in summation and opening statement in a jury trial is not the jury alone but the judge *and* jury. If you overlook the judge as a member of the audience, you may indeed find the starch taken out of your argument. Jurors view the judge as the impartial umpire between zealous advocates. They may well view his ruling on a part of an argument as bespeaking his evaluation of the whole argument or the trustworthiness of the lawyer making it. Such a view by the jury of an unfavorable judicial remark or ruling in the course of a summation is a good reason for you to be ever aware of the judge in your audience. You should do your utmost to avoid a negative expression about you by the judge in the presence of the jury.

The judge as part of your audience may cause your closing argument to have an even more direct effect on the outcome of a case. In Judge Hufstedler's Ex. 6–1, an emotional appeal in a summation for the plaintiffs came close to leading the jury to return their verdict against the plaintiffs. The emotion turned the jurors off. In the following example, another emotional appeal in a summation for the plaintiff resulted in the judge not permitting the jury to return a verdict for the plaintiff. The judge felt that the emotion turned the jurors on excessively.

Example 6–3:

AN ARGUMENT WHICH PUTS TEARS IN JURORS' EYES LEADS TO A SAD RESULT FOR THE CLIENT

Michael A. Musmanno

I was representing a twenty-two-year-old girl who had been hurled through the windshield of the automobile in which she was riding when it was hit by a truck traveling on the wrong side of the road. Prior to the accident, Mary Walker had been a vision of superlative beauty, now she was tragically disfigured....

The following was part of my summation: "Members of the jury, Mary Walker comes into court for justice. One year ago on April 15 she could not appear in public without becoming the cynosure of every eye. Her loveliness was so extraordinary that it attracted like a shaft of gold from the sky breaking through a dark and foggy day. Now she cannot appear in public without attracting the attention which no one desires.

"Prior to this horrible accident Mary Walker was a ravishingly beautiful girl. She evoked throughts of Venus, Mona Lisa, Helen of Troy, and all that entrancing parade of beauty gracefully treading the

continued

Example 6-3 (cont'd.)

flower-strewn path of history's charming womanhood. Here is her picture" (proffering photograph) "taken a month before the accident. Breath-taking isn't it? Look upon those features fit for a Greek goddess, perceive the coral lips, the capturing smile, the perfect blending of harmonious lines. Even this untouched photograph tells of the roses and cream in her complexion, of the glorious health in her sparkling eye, of the wondrous luster of her hair. You heard witness after witness describe with a sigh the gorgeous beauty of this once happy girl.

"Beauty. Ah, beauty, the dream of every girl, the yearning of every maiden, the longing and aspiration of every lass as she appears on the stage of life.

"This girl had beauty, but now it has disappeared behind the curtain of the past. Never to have been beautiful is not so piercing a tragedy as to have possessed this most priceless gift of the gods and then lose it. That merciless gasoline truck cut beauty out of the face of Mary Walker as the vandals once ripped Mona Lisa from her frame and left an empty quadrangle of wood.

"This is an age of beauty. On comeliness of form and harmony of feature are today conferred rewards never even imagined in the past. With motion picture directors, stage producers, and commercial artists constantly seeking girls of facial splendor, blemishless skin, and perfect teeth, every pretty girl has become a potential financial treasure. We do not know whether Mary Walker aspired to the stage or screen, but we do know that with her sheer enchantment of grace she possessed the potentialities of riches founded on sheer pulchritude.

"But the bloom and radiance which were hers have been scraped away by the broken glass cruelly dashed into her face by that monster truck. She is no longer beautiful. That rosebud mouth of hers is deformed, the coral lips are jagged, her smile turns into an unwanted leer. That matchless skin with its rose-petal texture has been roughened with merciless scars. Her dainty chin, which she had so joyously tossed in girlish abandon, is branded. As long as she lives, Mary Walker will bear these ugly slashes which disqualify her at once in the ever-present contest for faultless beauty. Miss Walker can and will be referred to as 'the girl with the scarred face.'"

I stopped speaking. My heart-stricken client had broken into unrestrained sobbing which mounted to frenzy. Even against what the candid mirror told her, she still hoped she might once again be
continued

Example 6-3 (cont'd.)

beautiful. "Perhaps it was unkind of me to say what I have said," I went on after a pause, "but my expression was the creation of pity. Many will voice it out of malice." There was never any doubt about the liability of the truck owner. The only question the jury had to decide was the amount of the verdict they should award the plaintiff....

Never did I plead with more feeling and fervor for a sister human being. "Members of the jury, Mary Walker is a young girl with her whole life ahead of her. She was struck down by a merciless fate traveling in a truck on the wrong side of the highway.... My friends, render such a verdict that when you yourselves stand before the Great White Throne on Judgment Day you will be satisfied with the justice you rendered unto this little girl with her poor scarred face and her pain-racked form."

When I ended my speech, a dead silence, interrupted only intermittently by the stifled sobs of Mary Walker, had settled on the courtroom. Two or three of the women jurors were dabbing at their eyes with handkerchiefs as they looked on the hapless little girl who had come into their lives. Would they ever be able to forget that pathetic countenance? What could they do for her? Although they could never restore to Mary the bloom of beauty which was once hers, they could plant a lilac bush or two in the bleak garden which had at one time been a riot of roses and dreams.

But suddenly another truck rumbled into the picture—and it seemed to be traveling on the wrong side of the road too. My opponent, the attorney for the truck company, rose and addressed Judge Moore on the bench: "May it please the court, I ask for a mistrial on the ground that Mr. Musmanno has inflamed the jury. In the present state of their excitement to which his speech has brought them, they will be incapable of rendering a verdict which will be just to both sides."

"Your Honor," I replied, "Mr. Pierce's motion is absurd. I have said nothing which is not supported by the evidence. Your Honor has the right in his charge to make any reference to my speech which he deems necessary. I see no reason why, after a week in court, Mary Walker should again be required to undergo the ordeal of another trial, which in itself will leave another scar on her sensibilities and on her soul."

But Judge Moore heeded not my protest or the beseeching eyes of my client. As the jury gasped in astonishment, the black-robed

continued

Example 6-3 (cont'd.)

> arbiter of justice declared: "The motion of Attorney Pierce is granted,
> and I declare a mistrial...."
>
> Miss Walker simply could not come into court again. The torture
> of another trial, listening to the doctors say she would never again be
> beautiful, and feeling the world sink beneath her feet at pronounce-
> ment of the word "ugly" went beyond what she could endure. She
> preferred anything but another trial. Thus we were compelled to
> accept from the truck company a settlement which was not even a
> beauty patch on the face of loveliness....[1]

Variable four: the speech The fourth and final variable in all speech
situations is the speech itself. The speech made as a closing argument,
like all speeches, must be prepared and delivered on two levels. One is
the content—what you say. The other is the style—how you say it.
Rhetoricians universally agree that the content should contain an
introduction, a body, and a conclusion. Just what should make up
each of these parts of the summation depends on the particular trial.
You must adapt to the case at hand. No two trials are identical, even if
they are both trials on possession of cocaine charges, or even if one is
a retrial of the other. The witnesses never testify identically, by word
or by demeanor. The lawyers never phrase their questions identically.
Whoever tries to argue this month's trial with last month's summation will be as stale and unpersuasive as yesterday's coffee and toast.

Nevertheless, there are components of the introduction, body,
and conclusion which effective trial lawyers often use after carefully
considering whether they are appropriate for the particular trial.
What follows is a list of some of these components. This list is
suggestive, not exhaustive.

THE INTRODUCTION

The introduction most frequently begins with counsel, on behalf of
his client, thanking the jury for their attention and patience during
the trial. Opening on a light note allows the audience to miss a few
words as they adjust to the speaker's voice with no harm to the client.
If in a particular trial you have objected noticeably more than your
opponent, you are well advised to add that you trust that the jury will
not hold against your client the instances when you may have taxed
their patience to make an objection. You should explain that one of
your duties as one of the trial lawyers was to invoke the law of

evidence in response to evidence offered by your opponent, and that objections are the legal mechanism for doing so. (You also should have requested an instruction to the same effect by the judge to the jury.)

Set the Mood for Your Argument

A final component of your introduction should be a statement that puts the jury in a favorable mood for the balance of your argument. What is favorable turns on what kind of case is being tried and which side you represent. For example, if the testimony ended with laughter by the jury, plaintiff's counsel in a wrongful death action should try early in his summation to lead the jury into a serious mood. Seriousness promises to result in greater damages than levity. A way to induce seriousness is to exalt the role of the jury, e.g., to point out that they are sitting in judgment because King John of England was compelled to grant the right to trial by jury in the Magna Carta in 1215 at Runnymede. Another method to induce seriousness is to inform the jurors that the Constitution, not a repealable act of the Legislature or the Congress, but the Constitution itself, makes ordinary local citizens as jurors, not career officials, the final judges of the facts in dispute between the parties.

In a criminal case counsel for the defendant will want the jury continually and ultimately to evaluate whether the government's evidence measures up to the standard of proof beyond a reasonable doubt. Hence counsel's introduction will usually stress that, as the judge will instruct the jury, the burden of proof is on the government and the quantity is the heavy one of beyond a reasonable doubt. Conversely, the prosecutor, who argues first and anticipates that the defense counsel will stress the government's burden of proof, may decide that the introduction ought to steal the opponent's thunder by conceding he or she has the burden of proof and confidently stating that the jury will find that the government's evidence exceeds the standard of proof beyond a reasonable doubt.

THE BODY OF THE SUMMATION

Use the Judge's Charge on the Law to Organize the Body of Your Argument

The body of your closing argument typically should match the evidence with the law in a way that convinces the jury that your side should win. Two organizational techniques should help the jury reach this conclusion. One is to use the judge's charge on the law as the framework for the summation. The charge is frequently given after the summations. But when you sum up, you usually will have a pretty firm idea of what the charge will be, since in most trials there is no dispute on what the governing law is. Also, rules of court generally require the judge to announce to counsel his or her rulings on their requests for instructions before summations commence.

Use of the charge as the framework of the body of the summation can be illustrated for recurring kinds of civil and criminal cases. In a civil case the judge will charge that the jury must decide whether plaintiff proved, first, liability, e.g., that the defendant was negligent and its negligence was the proximate cause of plaintiff's injuries, and, second, damages. The corresponding summations would argue that the evidence proved, or did not prove, negligence, proximate cause, and damages. In a criminal case the judge typically will instruct the jury that they must decide whether the government proved beyond a reasonable doubt, first, that the defendant committed the act charged and, second, that at the same time the defendant had the requisite state of mind. The corresponding summations would argue that the evidence proved beyond a reasonable doubt, or failed to prove beyond a reasonable doubt, that the defendant committed the act at a time when he or she had the requisite state of mind.

The advantages of using the charge as the organizing framework of the summation are two-fold. One is that if you organize your argument around the very same questions the judge presents to the jury, then the jury will more readily think of your answers when answering those questions. The other advantage is that you may gain credibility with the jury by appearing to be on the same wave length or "side" as the judge. By the jury hearing the defense lawyer say that negligence is defined as failing to behave as a reasonably prudent person would behave under the same circumstances and then hearing the judge charge them that negligence is defined as failing to behave as a reasonably prudent person would behave under the same circumstances, the jury may tend to equate the defense summation with the judge's instructions.

The Persuasiveness of Arguing as the Judge Will Instruct

If you succeed in being equated to the judge by the jury, it is highly likely that you will win a favorable verdict, because most juries place great confidence in what the judge says and desire to return the verdict they think the judge favors. They look at him as a good, impartial, knowledgeable person who is vastly more experienced in judging cases than they are. For this reason a jury would be a very receptive audience indeed if the judge were trying to persuade them as a lawyer does in summation. To the extent the jury looks at you in summation as on the same wave length or "side" as the judge, you also will be very persuasive. The jury will look at you too as a good, knowledgeable person. The rhetorician Quintilian taught that the perfect orator is one perceived by his audience as a "good" and "able" person. If in your summation you track the judge's instructions, usually you will be perceived as a good, able person. Juries like other audiences are persuaded by just this kind of speaker.

The organization of the summation is not the only opportunity to gain credibility by draping oneself in the robes of the judge. For example, since the judge will charge the jury that they must decide the case solely on the evidence they receive and the law he gives them, your summation should ask the jury to limit the bases of their decision in exactly this way. And if you learn that the judge's charge invariably uses a particular analogy, say, the analogy of scales of justice to explain the burden of proof, you should use the same analogy in your summation. In the usual case the more you sound like the judge, the better your chance to win.

Marshal the Evidence as an Organizational Technique

A second important organizational technique for the body of the summation is to marshal the evidence. Neophyte trial lawyers frequently review the evidence witness by witness and exhibit by exhibit in the order in which they were introduced. When a witness or exhibit in a negligence case has provided information on negligence, proximate cause, and damages, they dutifully recite the input on each of the three issues before going on to the next witness or exhibit. This approach requires the jurors to hold three groups of information in suspension in their minds as the closing argument proceeds to cover what may be very numerous exhibits and witnesses, and it requires the jurors continually to assign each point the lawyer discusses to the correct group. It requires a memory and mental dexterity beyond the capacity of many jurors. Their incapacity to follow the lawyer will prevent him from making the points he is driving at.

If you marshal the evidence instead, you should find that the jurors see your point. You marshal the evidence by dealing with each issue, e.g., negligence, separately and by reviewing the evidence from witnesses and exhibits bearing on that single issue before proceeding to another issue. In reviewing the evidence even on a single issue you should not mechanically recount the contribution of each witness or exhibit in the order in which they were introduced, but you should refer to them in the order which enables you to weave the tapestry you want the jury to see.

Recurring Elements in Effective Summations

The body of a closing argument may marshal the evidence and be organized around the judge's charge on the law. But it must do much more to be effective. It must make convincing arguments about the evidence. What they will be will turn on the particular facts of each case. However, a number of elements in convincing arguments recur very often.

Appeal to common sense and common knowledge For example, if your client has been indicted as the kingpin of an enormous racketeering enterprise and you have proven that he regularly worked 50 hours a week as a clerk in a busy department store, you should ask the jury to use their common sense in deciding whether he had the time to conduct the multitude of nefarious acts charged.

Argue inferences You should argue that the jurors should draw inference Z, of which there is no eyewitness testimony, from circumstantial evidence X and Y, of which there is eyewitness testimony. Many uninitiated jurors believe that eyewitness evidence alone must support a verdict. If you can win only if the jury draws inferences, then you must stress that it is a misconception to believe that eyewitness evidence is required. Examples of inferences that are close to home, such as concluding that it is raining from seeing windshield wipers operating on cars, can go a long way toward dispelling the misconception.

Use analogies In arguing damages for loss of a leading model's arm, there are many ways to suggest the jury translate the injury into an amount of money damages. An example of an effective analogy would be to suggest that the jury consider the money value it would place on loss of a leg of a race horse like Native Dancer or Secretariat or on destruction of one of the arms in the painting of Mona Lisa, and to remind the jury that our civilization values a human being such as the plaintiff over a race horse or a painting.

Attack or support the credibility of witnesses It is a rare verdict indeed which does not depend on the credibility of witnesses. Hence another element you usually should argue in your summation is that the crucial witnesses in your favor are credible and that those opposed to you lack credibility, i.e., you will compare the credibilities of the witnesses when the comparison helps your side. Even if the verdict will turn on a single witness, that witness' credibility alone usually should be addressed in the summations. In arguing credibility, four factors may be discussed with regard to virtually all witnesses.

1. How well or poorly did the witness perceive what he or she testified about?

2. How well or poorly did the witness remember what he or she perceived?

3. How correctly did the witness communicate from the witness stand what he or she remembered?

4. Did the witness' demeanor before the jury bespeak veracity?

Science has not provided principles for linking demeanor with veracity; therefore, the law does not exclude arguments based on any aspect of the demeanor of the witness. To make a telling argument on this score, you must draw the jury's attention to a characteristic of the witness, e.g., rubbing his or her hands while testifying, see *Quercia v. United States*, 289 U.S. 466, 468 (1933), or courageously acknowledging unpleasant facts as in Ex. 5–32, which you hope will strike a responsive chord with the jury. In such an argument you are making a judgment about human nature. You are saying, for example, that people who rub their hands while talking are lying. You must be cautious in formulating such arguments, for if the jury disagrees with the putative law of human nature underlying the argument, they may lose respect for you and, therefore, the rest of your argument. (If you make this argument, you should also be careful not to rub your own hands while addressing the jury!)

In respect to some witnesses, additional factors may affect their credibilities, and you should argue them. The additional factors are the bases for impeaching and rehabilitating witnesses defined by the law of evidence, such as prior convictions, prior inconsistent or consistent statements, and financial or penal bias. It usually does little good to labor to get evidence of this character admitted in evidence without arguing in summation how it discredits or accredits the witness.

Minimize the Effect of Weaknesses in Your Case or Defense

Invariably some of the information which reaches the jury hurts your client's case. You may wish that it would simply vanish, but it will not. You must do your best in closing argument to minimize its effect. The harmful information may be irrelevant to the issues for decision and yet may be capable of dominating the jury's decision. For example, assume that when defendant's car ran into plaintiff's and caused plaintiff serious injuries, the passenger in plaintiff's car was someone else's wife. Plaintiff's summation should try to counter this embarrassing fact by reminding the jury that they have taken a solemn oath to decide the case solely by applying the law to the relevant facts, and that therefore it is their duty to give no weight whatsoever to the irrelevant fact of the identity of plaintiff's passenger. (It would also help if plaintiff's wife sits loyally, if not lovingly, by his side throughout the trial.)

Other harmful information may be all too relevant. Your summation should address these weaknesses when you can minimize them. If, for example, the government's chief witness has a long criminal record and has committed the same crime for which defendant is being prosecuted but is testifying under a grant of immunity, defense counsel will score heavy blows against the witness' credibility. Counsel will charge that the witness not only is generally unreliable in light of his or her criminal record but also has fabricated the story implicating defendant in exchange for immunity from prosecution and punishment. To save his or her own neck, the witness lied, will be the thrust of the defense position. The prosecutor's closing argument should concede that the witness is not the ideal witness and should say candidly that the government would have preferred that the witness had been a winner of the Nobel Peace Prize rather than an admitted law-breaker. But the prosecutor should add that the government has to take its witnesses where it finds them and that witnesses to crimes committed in hell cannot be expected to be angels. The prosecutor can also try to rehabilitate the witness' credibility by explaining that the immunity does not cover perjury on the witness stand and that the fear of a perjury indictment should have deterred the witness from lying.

What should your summation say about the weaknesses which cannot be minimized? Your choice is to ignore them or to concede them. If opposing counsel did not argue these points, it is probably wise not to mention them, since the jury may overlook them if not reminded of them in closing arguments. Of course the order of argument may be such that you must predict in advance rather than waiting to see whether opposing counsel will argue these points.

If opposing counsel may turn out to argue the points, it is much better for you to concede the points before your opponent excoriates you with them. For example, if your opening statement had asserted that plaintiff had sustained injuries to his teeth, jaw, and knee, but the expert evidence was that plaintiff's sole injuries were to his jaw and knee, your silence during summation about plaintiff's teeth would enable defendant in his subsequent summation to argue as follows: the plaintiff's summation tried to convince you that he has dreadful injuries to his jaw and knee; but did you notice that his summation said nothing about his teeth and yet his opening state-ment listed injuries to his teeth right along with his jaw and knee; he didn't say anything in his summation to support his claim about his teeth because there was no evidence of any injury to his teeth; thus that claim in his opening was misleading; therefore, you have the right to ask yourself whether he is misleading you about his jaw and knee too.

As plaintiff's lawyer you can steal the thunder from this argu-ment if in your summation you frankly concede that it turned out that, when the doctors testified, they attributed all of the injury to the jaw rather than the teeth; and you therefore are withdrawing any claim for injury to teeth. In addition, by conceding what you cannot overcome, you appear like Quintilian's "good" person, if not the most "able" person. To maximize the benefit from a concession, you should make it early in your closing argument. Otherwise some jurors may close their minds to earlier points you are making because they do not trust you on account of the point you are prepared to concede.

Ordinarily your summation will both emphasize the evidence and inferences that indicate you should win and minimize those pointing in the other direction. There may be room for reasonable lawyers to disagree on exactly which of multiple arguments you should make. However, there is no disagreement that you should not make a summation which puts all your eggs in one basket when you are not bereft of additional arguments.

Example 6–4:

OVERDRAMATIZING ONE ARGUMENT MAY OBSCURE OTHERS

George Williams and Bernard G. Segal

The incident occurred during the trial of a personal injury action by the patron of a beauty parlor against the proprietor of the shop. The plaintiff, a woman in her early thirties, claimed to have sustained permanent loss of her hair as the result of the application of a hair straightening preparation in the defendant's shop. The defense was that the preparation was a reputable product generally used in beauty shops for hair straightening purposes and that the defendant had meticulously followed the manufacturer's instructions in applying the product to the plaintiff's scalp and that in any event the plaintiff might have exaggerated the extent of the unfortunate consequences which she claimed to have flowed from the treatment.

In the course of his closing argument to the jury, defense counsel referred to the fact that the plaintiff had sat throughout the entire trial with her head wrapped in a bandanna. Counsel raised the question whether plaintiff's hair loss was really permanent and suggested that since the trial was taking place several years after the application of the product perhaps the plaintiff had not exhibited her scalp to the jury because her real condition was inconsistent with her claim.

In his rebuttal argument, counsel for the plaintiff informed the jury that his client had kept her head covered throughout the trial because her condition so mortified her that she was unable to bring herself to exhibit her scalp to the jury. Counsel then said that since his client's integrity had been directly challenged, he hoped that she would not object to what he was about to do; whereupon, with a flourish, counsel removed the bandanna from plaintiff's head. To the great embarrassment of defense counsel, plaintiff was as bald as a billiard ball.

It was so dramatic and decisive for plaintiff's counsel to have bared his client's head during his rebuttal argument that the jury may have focused solely on this defense and overlooked the other two defenses. The jury was probably exceptionally moved to see the plaintiff's loss because it was revealed for only a brief period before they began deliberations. Experienced personal injury lawyers agree that their clients' impairments make the maximum impact on the jury when exhibited for but a brief period. If a parapalegic, say, is present throughout a nine day trial, wheels himself in and out of the courtroom up to eight times a day, and talks animatedly with his counsel, the jury's horror at his disability may well abate. The jury in this example had no time to become blasé at the baldness. Selection of the argument that plaintiff may have kept her head covered because the hair she had lost had grown back may have caused the jury to attach undue importance to that issue, as had the cross-examination on whether the elderly Traffic Manager had lied in his recantation in Ex. 5–29.

Stay Away from Risky Arguments That Enable Your Opponent to Destroy Your Case in Rebuttal

The decision to argue that the plaintiff may not have been bald is reminiscent of another, more common error of cross-examination. The argument was not a typical summation point, because it implicitly challenged plaintiff to display her head to the jury rather than commenting about evidence which had previously been presented to the jury. In the latter sort of argument there is no risk about what the evidence will turn out to be. But the argument in Ex. 6–4 was very risky, since apparently defense counsel had not learned before trial by informal or formal discovery what her head would look like, just as the cross-examiners in Exs. 5–3 and 5–5 through 5–24 did not know how the witness would answer. Moreover, the lawyer making the argument totally abdicated control over the outcome of his challenge inasmuch as he had no ability to refute the display of a bald head. He did not even have the ability cross-examiners sometimes have to refute an undesired answer by further cross-examination or by calling additional witnesses.

The poor judgment of making the perilous argument in Ex. 6–4 is evident too from the fact that the jury had seen the plaintiff sit throughout the entire trial with her head wrapped in a bandanna. There was a very good chance that without defense counsel mentioning this fact the jury would have inferred on its own that she did not let them see her head because she had something to hide, which was that her hair had returned. The best argument can be the one left unsaid. If a juror thinks of it on his or her own, pride of authorship may well cause this juror to advocate it to the other jurors with greater zeal and tenacity than if a lawyer had presented it.

Order of Multiple Arguments

Usually you should plan to make multiple arguments, some accentuating the positive about your case, others minimizing the negative. In what order should you make your multiple points, and should you present the positive first or the negative first? There are no clear-cut answers to these questions, although rhetoricians and trial lawyers have struggled with them since ancient times. Enlightening relevant materials are collected by G. Bellow and B. Moulton.[2] The disagreement on the order of presenting points of the same kind most often centers on whether to present them in order of strongest to weakest or weakest to strongest. The former order relies on the psychological principle of primacy, i.e., the jury will be most influenced by what it hears first; the latter order relies on the psychological principle of recency, i.e., the jury will be most influenced by what it hears last. The adherents of both orders probably would agree that the points in the middle will have the least impact by virtue of their position. If you are not confident that either primacy or recency will be most effective, you can try to capitalize on both by placing strong arguments at the beginning and at the end.

Do Not Ignore Your Opponent's Arguments

Cicero and many modern lawyers feel that positive points should be made before negative points. They say that the order of the arguments should suggest confidence and not seem defensive. But there are reasons to think it is better to refute your opponent's case before reviewing your own. While listening to arguments, audiences may think of opposing points. If the opposing points have been refuted, this tendency will not get in the way of accepting the argument. Furthermore, if you have refuted the other side, you will have shown that you do not have blinders on but have recognized that there are two sides to the case. Your attention to the points in favor of the other side may demonstrate that you are realistic and fair-minded. If the jury perceives you in this way, they should accept your positive arguments far more readily than if they view you as a hired gun blindly espousing only your side.

The Cronology of Summations

The selection among arguments should take into account a final factor, the chronology of summations by opposing counsel. Typically the lawyer for the party with the burden of proof has the right to argue first. Then the opposing lawyer presents his summation in which he may both advance the arguments he selects and rebut the arguments just made by his opponent. Lastly the lawyer who argued first may give a rebuttal that in some states is to be limited to answering his opponent's summation.

The depth of the wound defense counsel inflicted upon himself in Ex. 6–4 was partly caused by the chronology of summations. He made his argument that the bandanna covering plaintiff's head may have been hiding her regrown hair following her argument in chief, but before her rebuttal argument. In her rebuttal her counsel removed the bandanna with a flourish to reveal that she was as bald as a billiard ball. Thereafter, under the summation chronology which is used in that jurisdiction and which prevails generally, defense counsel had no opportunity to concede that he had no defense that the hair had regrown but to remind the jury that he should win nevertheless because of his other defenses, namely, that it was not negligent for his client to have used the hair straightening preparation and that his client had not applied it negligently to the plaintiff's hair. The summation chronology meant that the jury's last impression was that defendant had been completely wrong and plaintiff had been completely honest about her hair loss. This made it very easy for the jury to forget the negligence issues in the trial. It would not have been easy for them to have done so if the summation chronology had been reversed, i.e., if defense counsel had argued first and last, and so had had an opportunity to revive his negligence defenses after the display of plaintiff's bald head.

Counsel for both sides appeared to try to gain advantages from the conventional summation chronology in the following example.

Example 6–5:

STRATEGY, COUNTER-STRATEGY, VERDICT

Judge Anthony Grillo

The plaintiff's case involved a personal injury claim. The medical testimony was fragile. The claim for destruction of earning

continued

Example 6-5 (cont'd.)

capacity was also questionable. (The plaintiff operated a small restaurant.) Nevertheless, the medical evidence and the evidence with relation to lost wages were sufficient to make out a prima facie case and precluded a directed verdict for the defendant. At the conclusion of the trial, the attorney for the plaintiff did what is often done. He gave a succinct argument to the jury as to his client's claim and, of course, referred to the evidence supporting the plaintiff's contentions. This was done apparently in order to save his forceful argument until after the defendant's attorney made his argument. (In this jurisdiction the plaintiff argues first, the defendant gives his argument, and the plaintiff has a last "shot" to rebut the defendant's position.) This leaves the jury going into the jury room with the plaintiff's attorney's argument ringing in their ears, so to speak.

The court asked the defense counsel to proceed at the conclusion of the plaintiff's argument, and defense counsel stated: "The defendant waives argument."

I assume that this tactic was employed by defense counsel in an attempt to say silently to the jury: "This case has absolutely no merit, and I will not dignify the plaintiff's argument by any further comment." Then again, since the plaintiff's attorney had made a fairly brief summation in his first argument, the defense attorney's tactics made it impossible for the plaintiff's attorney to make his best arguments in rebuttal because there was nothing to rebut, the defendant's attorney having waived argument. I assume that the defense counsel felt the case was so thin that, combined with the short argument of the plaintiff's attorney, the verdict would be for the defendant.

However, the jury returned a substantial verdict (about $70,000 as I recall) for the plaintiff. One can only guess as to whether the jury took the view that the defendant could not in good conscience contest the claim of the plaintiff and thus suggested to the attorney that he make no final argument. That is to say, the jury might have felt that the opposition to the plaintiff's claim was disingenuous. Who knows? I think that defense counsel lost sight of the pragmatic factor that would tend to elicit sympathy involved in this matter. Plaintiff testified that the only way he could keep his restaurant in business was by having his wife and his son leave their home to run the restaurant when he was incapacitated. While I appreciate that we charge the jury that sympathy should not enter the picture, sympathy does sometimes play a part in verdicts. Defense counsel would have made a home run if his theory proved correct, but unfortunately it boomeranged.

Judge Grillo seems to feel that the defense counsel might well have won the verdict if he had not waived argument, despite the jury's likely sympathy for the plight of the plaintiff and his family. The judge offers no explicit reason for this view. However, the judge's implicit reasoning is that in argument defense counsel could have impressed upon the jury its duty under its solemn oath to give absolutely no weight whatsoever to sympathy for the plaintiff. It is true that the judge's charge instructs the jury to the same effect, but with juries as with children, sometimes two exhortations go further than one.

Closing Argument Should Rarely Be Waived

Defense counsel's loss of the verdict may be explained by jury sympathy for the plaintiff and his family or by jury interpretation of waiver of summation as a concession of the validity of the plaintiff's case. While either explanation may be correct, a third might explain the verdict as well. It is that waiver of summation surrenders the advantages of making a summation which are sketched at the outset of this chapter. Defense counsel forwent his only opportunity to tell the jury why he should win the case. If he had argued, he could have stressed the paintiff's burden to prove both his personal injuries by medical evidence and destruction of his earning capacity, and he could have emphasized that the evidence failed to do so. The jury verdict may have been in the plaintiff's favor because the jury may have failed to notice, or may have forgotten, these potentially lethal weaknesses in the plaintiff's case. Although defense counsel's decision to waive argument did control plaintiff's summation by denying him a rebuttal, it also surrendered defense counsel's opportunity to try to "control" the jury by making them aware of, or refreshing their recollection of, the shortcomings of the plaintiff's case.

Comparison with Waiver of Cross-Examination

The waiver of argument in Ex. 6–5 shares two characteristics with the waiver of cross-examination in Example 5–4. In Example 5–4 John Lord O'Brian had concluded that Wendell Wilkie's direct testimony had omitted his main points, and that Mr. Wilkie planned to work them into his answers during cross-examination. Mr. O'Brian denied him the chance to make those points by deciding not to cross-examine him. Likewise, defense counsel in Ex. 6–5 apparently concluded that plaintiff's counsel had saved his best and most forceful points for his rebuttal, and denied him the chance to make them by deciding against giving a summation. In addition, waiver at both stages may lead the jury to infer that the party cannot dispute the direct testimony or the opposing summation. Here, however, the comparison between waiving cross-examination and waiving summation ends.

What the jury hears you say in your summation should always help your client because you totally control it. There is no witness to upset the applecart by giving an unexpected answer during summation. To waive summation is to waive what should be a blessing to your case. Cross-examination, on the other hand, may turn out to be a mixed blessing at best. Chapter 5 illustrates the host of deadly pitfalls which lurk in cross-examination. Most of the pitfalls arise from failing to keep the witness under control. Despite the cross-examiner's most heroic efforts, there is always the danger that the witness will slip in an answer that will be more deleterious than all of the witness' direct testimony. The only foolproof way to keep the witness under control is not to cross-examine at all. The absence of an uncontrollable force like a witness during summation renders waiver of summation far less likely to be wise than waiver of cross-examination.

The opportunity in summation for you to pull everything together for the jury, to show them why they should find for your client, is an opportunity you should have been preparing for since the client first walked into your office. You should rarely, if ever, waive it.

Objections to Closing Argument

Does this mean that a defense counsel who does not waive summation is defenseless against a lawyer like plaintiff's in Ex. 6–5, who apparently plans to make the bulk of his argument in rebuttal, which can be extremely persuasive since it reaches the jury last and is free from response? Not necessarily. Defense counsel could give his summation. Then in a state limiting rebuttal to replying to defendant's arguments, defense counsel could object any time plaintiff's rebuttal exceeded this limitation. Favorable rulings will go far to prevent plaintiff's counsel from firing his big guns during rebuttal, and this will have been achieved without paying the extreme price of waiving summation. However, the fact that the jury will probably hear some improper rebuttal before an objection cuts it off means that the objection alternative will not entirely silence the big guns, as does waiver of summation.

The use of the objection alternative may require paying another price. An objection to a summation is an interruption of a speech which may interrupt the speaker's train of thought. Juries like audiences in general tend to consider interrupting the speaker to be discourteous. In the context of closing arguments where both sides have equal time in which to make their speeches, an objection may look like unsportsmanlike conduct. Therefore, the objection to improper rebuttal is likely to carry the price of some diminution in jury respect for defense counsel. But a favorable ruling by the judge will minimize this price. Conversely, an unfavorable ruling may increase the price, for the jury may read the judge's overruling of the objection as signifying his agreement with them that it was improper for defense counsel to have interrupted his opponent's speech. Since in states limiting rebuttal the line between improper and proper rebuttal is not always clear, use of the objection alternative to Ex. 6–5 is not without danger.

Objections During Closing Arguments Should Be Sparingly Made

Like objections which interrupt your opponent's opening statement, objections which interrupt summations should be sparingly made. In general they should not be made unless they will be held to have been waived if made later or unless the damage will be incurable later and you are confident that the judge will sustain the objection. Whenever the benefit from objecting can be substantially achieved by deferring the objection until opposing counsel has completed his speech, that course should be followed. That course, which circumvents the discourtesy of interrupting a speech, supposedly would have been to no avail for defense counsel in Ex. 6–5. If he had waited until the end of a rebuttal in which plaintiff's counsel had not limited himself to answering defense counsel, and if defense counsel had then successfully objected that plaintiff's own big guns were improper rebuttal, the jury would have been unable to expunge from their minds plaintiff's improper rebuttal arguments, despite an instruction from the judge to do so.

An example of an erroneous point in a summation, to which objection should be deferred until the end of the speech, is when plaintiff argues that in awarding damages for personal injuries the jury should take into account the taxes plaintiff will have to pay on the damages. If a successful objection is made immediately after this point, the jury has nevertheless heard it and may not expunge it from their minds. Furthermore, the interruption not only makes defense counsel look unsportsmanlike, but it also may cause the jury to think that the taxability of damages is a far larger element in the case from the viewpoint of the defendant, who is hoping to win on liability, than is the fact. If the objection is not made until plaintiff has finished his speech, and then the judge instructs the jury to disregard the argument about taxability, defendant's objective of correcting his opponent's misstatement of law will have been attained with less dramatization of the tax element and without interrupting plaintiff's speech.

THE CONCLUSION

Tell the Jury the Exact Verdict You Desire

Thus far we have discussed the introduction and body of a summation. Like any speech it will be incomplete unless it has a conclusion. Your conclusion at a minimum should tell the jury the verdict you are asking for your client. It does little good if your closing argument has convinced the jury to find for your client but has not informed the jury how to do so. As part of learning how the judge will charge the jury you should learn what the verdict form(s) will be before arguing. Then during argument you should expressly recite to the jury the recipe for returning a verdict for your client. When a general verdict form is used, your recital will be as simple as that the foreperson should sign the verdict form for defendant. When a special verdict form or general verdict form accompanied by interrogatories is used, your recital should go through each and every question and say how it should be answered. It may seem tedious, but all the pretrial and trial effort is for nought if the jury intends one verdict but inadvertently answers questions bringing about the opposite.

Occasionally the law in its wondrous mystery requires the jury to return verdicts which do not on their face seem just. When you are seeking such a verdict, it may not be enough for you to give the jury the mechanical recipe for it. You must do more to persuade the jury that the verdict will work out to be just. Take the instance in which a plaintiff seeks damages against two defendants who are jointly and severally liable, and assume that the governing law permits him to collect his damages wholly from either defendant or in part from one and the balance from the other, but does not permit him to collect from both more than his total damages. The corresponding verdict is required to be against each defendant in the amount of the total damages, which undoubtedly seems unjust to a jury. If you are requesting such a verdict, you should graphically illustrate that your client will not be able to collect more than the total damages by showing the jury two Execution forms. You should explain that if the jury returns the verdicts you are requesting, the clerk will issue an Execution, which is the legal means to enforce verdicts, against each defendant, and that if your client collects the full amount of the verdict from one defendant, he will be under a legal duty to nullify the Execution against the other defendant, which you can symbolize by literally tearing up one of the Executions in front of the jury.

Warn the Jury If You Will Not Have an Opportunity to Refute Your Opponent and Remind Them of Their Promises When Selected

When your opponent has the last word, the conclusion of your summation is the place to bring to the jury's attention that your opponent will have an opportunity to speak after you and that you will have no opportunity to respond. You may wish to invite the jurors to respond in your place by thinking of what the evidence in fact shows about the subjects opposing counsel may choose to argue. Another helpful element in the conclusion is to remind the jurors of the undertakings they made during their voir dire examination. Even if there had been only minimal voir dire, the jurors would have promised that they would decide the case impartially. If there had been more extensive voir dire, the jurors can be reminded of their more specific promises which will help obtain a favorable verdict, such as not to hold a party's race against him.

Ask the Jury to Find for You, and in
Accordance with the Judge's Charge

The closing words of effective summations usually express confidence that the jury will return a verdict for the side arguing. You may declare that such a verdict is the only just or fair one. Furthermore, if you feel that the jury is typical in that they respect the judge and will endeavor to follow her instructions, you might ask the jury to decide the case solely on the evidence presented to them and in accordance with the law the judge gives them, which of course is exactly what the judge will charge. You could add that if the jury does so, the verdict will be for your client.

DELIVERY

So much for what is to be said in a closing argument. There remains the question of how it is to be said. A cardinal rule for everything you do in trying a case is that you must be yourself.

Example 6–6:

BE YOURSELF

Leon Jaworski

For several years I had an able assistant to accompany me to the courtroom. In most of the cases I was then trying, he did both fact investigation and law research for me. He was of great assistance in the many cases we tried together.

After a period of time, I thought it unfair to let him play "second fiddle" and therefore I selected another assistant and let him have a docket of his own. It was not long before I noticed that he was not as effective in the courtroom as a man of his ability and experience should have been. The mistake he made was in trying to emulate me in the cases he had watched me try.

A trial lawyer must not forsake what is natural for him to do in favor of copying someone else's methods and techniques in court. I have never seen such an adoption work effectively. The trial lawyer should use his own talents and such techniques as are natural to him. This is the lesson this able young man learned and is a lesson every young trial lawyer should remember.

Deliver Your Summation As Conversation Writ Large

Mr. Jaworski's sage advice surely applies to the summation. If you try to speak like someone else with whom you do not share major qualities of character and personality, you will be perceived by the jury as insincere. That perception will doom your summation to failure. On the other hand, you may deliver your closing argument according to your own style and yet speak differently than in an informal conversation. It is natural to speak differently in a formal courtroom to a jury of strangers about a verdict that will affect your client's life, liberty, or property than when making small talk with a friend. Your goal is to develop a good rapport with the jury as in conversation, but it has to be conversation writ large. The different setting means that your summation will be more formal, more earnest, and perhaps more passionate at points, your voice will be louder, and your gestures will be larger.

In planning your summation, how long should you plan to speak and where should you plan to stand? Consider Ex. 6–7.

Example 6–7:

DO NOT STAND SO AS TO INVADE THE JURY'S SENSE OF PRIVATE SPACE OR SPEAK TOO LONG

Mayo A. Darling

I was trying a motor vehicle case in which the respective cars were going in opposite directions. The street had a painted center line. The plaintiff, a passenger in the adverse vehicle, was thrown out of the car and sustained a fractured pelvis. There was no quarrel about her injuries; the real question for the jury was, "Who was on the right side of the center line at the time of the collision?"

My argument to the jury was very short. I told them that I did not question the nature or extent of this young lady's unfortunate injuries, and that if they decided that the defendant was on the wrong side of the road they should return a verdict for her. If instead, however, they decided that the defendant was on his own side of the road, they should return a verdict for him...and I sat down.

My opponent argued, believe it or not, for almost one and a half hours! He was the type who leaned over the rail about midway, so

continued

Example 6-7 (cont'd.)

> that he was almost in contact with the two middle jurors. I could see various of them looking up at the clock from time to time, clearly indicating that they were fed up with what he had to say.
>
> Prior to argument I thought the evidence was just about even—if not 50–50 perhaps the plaintiff's case was a little stronger. But the jury was out less than a half-hour, and came in for the defendant.
>
> I have always believed that my opponent simply talked himself out of a verdict.

Plaintiff's counsel might well have won the verdict if the judge had not left him free to argue for an hour and a half. Unable to punish lawyers directly, the jury may take out its displeasure with a lawyer on his client. Rules of court frequently set time limits, subject to modification by the judge. Judges often impose time limits in the absence of a rule of court. Example 6–7 illustrates that judges may do lawyers backhanded favors when refusing to enlarge the customary time limit. After all, except when a speech is entertaining, audiences universally prefer a short speech over a long one. The ideal length of any speech is easy to state but not so easy to put into practice. The ideal is that the speech be long enough to cover the subject but not so long that the audience loses interest.

How Close to Stand to the Jury

Plaintiff's counsel in Ex. 6–7 committed a second error in delivering his closing argument. "He...leaned over the [jury] rail...so that he was almost in contact with the two middle jurors." He undoubtedly invaded their sense of private space. They probably were offended. They may well have even used body language like crossing their arms and legs to tell him so, but he apparently did not read it. You should never stand so close to jurors as to make them uncomfortable. If the judge directs or permits you to hand a juror an exhibit, you should back away immediately afterwards. During summation you should be close enough to the jurors for all of them to see and hear you easily. At this distance you probably will not invade any juror's sense of private space, although if you sense that you may be doing so you should move still farther back and speak correspondingly louder.

Changing Your Position; Eye Contact

Do not stand in the same place throughout your closing argument. It is too boring for the jury. Movement contributes variety, and variety holds the attention of the listener. Leaving an outline on a podium or counsel table gives you a reason to move back there from time to time. And it is far preferable to use an outline than to forget a significant point. However, you should not try to argue by reading from a script. The lack of eye contact will be soporific to the jury, and they cannot be convinced while they are asleep.

Jurors do not often speak out when lawyers irritate them in delivering their summations, whether it be by reading a script or invading a juror's space. The silence of jurors notwithstanding, they are distracted by improper delivery and find themselves thinking of the distraction rather than the content. A rare instance in which a juror did speak out stands as a reminder of the need to avoid distracting delivery.

Example 6–8:

THE JURY ARE DISTRACTED BY INAPPROPRIATE DELIVERY

Judge Homer Thornberry

I remember, during an argument before a jury, that defense counsel became very loud to the extent that a juror sitting in the front row exclaimed, "Don't talk so loud. You are hurting my ears." The poor lawyer never recovered. He stammered, apologizing a great deal, and then just sat down. I do not recall the outcome of the case, but I am sure the lawyer did not help his client's cause.

This example does not reveal to whom defense counsel was shouting. If it was directed at the juror, it may well have seemed louder than it was because it appeared to be accusatory of the juror. If it is consistent with your personal style to shout and pound the table, jurors will tend to react far better if it is directed to your opponent rather than to the jury. Shouting and pounding is most appropriate when you are flaying opposing counsel for, say, having misstated what the evidence was, or berating the opposing party for giving misleading testimony. Such an emotional delivery will convey the most conviction when you gradually build up to a peak as you detail your opponent's wrongdoings. Beginning a summation at a very high emotional level simply does not ring true.

However fine-tuned the emotional level, however eloquent the overall delivery of the summation, the way in which it is spoken cannot be expected to carry the day in the face of far superior content. If through thorough preparation you can demonstrate that the content of your opponent's eloquent summation was inaccurate, the verdict will go to accuracy over eloquence, to substance over form.

Example 6–9:

SUPERIOR SUBSTANCE PREVAILS OVER ELOQUENT DELIVERY

Judge Roszel C. Thomsen

In an important criminal trial, an experienced attorney made a long and eloquent closing argument for the principal defendant to the jury, in which the lawyer purported to summarize the testimony of the witnesses with respect to the controlling facts of the case. The consensus of the audience was that he had won an acquittal for all the defendants.

The U.S. Attorney was to make his closing argument the following morning. Overnight the U.S. Attorney and most of his staff worked until 3 A.M. checking the facts as stated by the lawyer against the transcript of the testimony of the several witnesses.

In the morning the U.S. Attorney made a short closing argument. Almost all of his argument was devoted to reading passages from the closing argument of the defendant's attorney and passages from the transcript of the testimony of the several witnesses, pointing out the contradictions.

The jury found all the defendants guilty.

SUMMARY

Closing argument is the culmination of your efforts. Throughout your work on a case you should be planning what you will tell the jury to persuade them to return their verdict in your favor. Since argument is prohibited in your opening statement, your closing argument is your first opportunity to look the jury in the eye and tell them what you have proved or your opponent has failed to prove which entitles you to win. It is also your last chance to persuade them to find for you. In your summation you should not only sound your principal themes but also tie together testimony and exhibits which were introduced in evidence at unconnected points. Similarly, you should fully explain the significance of answers by witnesses which you left as they stood without hazarding a fatal one-question-too many.

Unlike direct and cross-examinations, during closing argument you are totally in control. Possibilities of surprising answers to questions and of witnesses who arrive too late for a meaningful interview before testifying are behind you. If you have prepared thoughtfully for your summation over the months or years that you have been working on the case, and if during the trial you have modified that preparation to reflect unanticipated twists and turns in the evidence, then your summation will be the capstone of your trial presentation. Your exclusive control over it and its importance mean that you should rarely, if ever, waive it.

You are on center stage making a forensic speech when you argue. Hence you are well advised to keep in mind the four variables of every speech, namely, the occasion, the audience, the speaker, and the speech. A fifth variable of a closing argument is the chronology of speaking between you and your opponent(s) and the availability of a rebuttal. In regard to the audience as a variable, Exs. 6–1, 6–2, and 6–3 illustrate both that you must adapt to the composition of your particular jury in deciding whether an emotional appeal will be effective and that even in a jury trial the judge is an integral member of the audience whom you overlook at your peril.

Your closing arguments, like all good speeches, need an introduction, a body, and a conclusion. What they should be depends on the case at hand. Often the introduction will thank the jury for their attention, ask that objections not be held against the client, and try to create a favorable mood by exalting the role of the jury.

The body of the closing argument is where you demonstrate that the credible evidence and the applicable law stated or to be stated in the judge's charge require a verdict for your side. Your discussion of the evidence should not only emphasize the evidence in your favor and place it in its most favorable light but also minimize the effect of the evidence which militates against you or even concede a minor issue which is not decisive. If you do the latter, the jury should conclude that you are not an overzealous advocate who is of no help to them. Instead, they should regard you as an able and fair-minded professional who has considered both sides of the case and in whom they can have confidence.

You should endeavor to organize your discussion of the evidence on the framework of the judge's charge. The more the jury get the impression that the judge and you are in accord, the better for your client. Your organization of the evidence should marshal it issue by issue. Thus your summation can bring order to the relative chaos of evidence which is necessarily presented witness by witness rather than issue by issue. Your discussion of the evidence need not be confined to the literal contents of the testimony and the exhibits. In arguing the significance and reliability of the evidence you may appeal to the jury to use their common sense, to draw sound inferences, and to judge the credibilities of the witnesses. You often will find it helpful also to argue by analogy. An objection to a closing argument which interrupts the speech should be sparingly made lest the jury condemn you as unsportsmanlike.

The conclusion to the closing argument should inform the jury of the precise verdict you are asking them for and express confidence that they will find for your client. If the verdict does not on its face seem just, such as that against multiple defendants who are jointly and severally liable, explain that the law limits the use of verdicts so that no injustice is done. In some instances you will be well-advised in your conclusion to remind the jurors of the promises they made during their voir dire examinations and to forewarn them that you will have no opportunity to refute your opponent's subsequent argument or rebuttal.

As you talk with the jury, watch their reaction to what you are saying. It will very rarely happen, as it did in Ex. 6–8, that jurors will speak out during your closing argument. But their body language may provide a signal that you have struck a responsive chord or that you had better cut short a particular line of argument. By the same token the jury will be watching you. Your delivery of your closing argument, however eloquent or silver-tongued, cannot be expected to compensate for deficient evidence, thought, or organization. However, as the jury watches you they can be distracted from paying attention to your thoughts by awkward or inappropriate delivery. Usually your delivery will be satisfactory when you are yourself, although you must be conscious that you are engaged in conversation writ large.

REFERENCE NOTES

1. Michael A. Musmanno, *Verdict!*, pp. 219—222. Copyright © 1958 by Michael A. Musmanno. Reprinted by permission of Doubleday Publishing, a division of Bantam, Doubleday, Dell Publishing Group, Inc.

2. G. Bellow and B. Moulton, *The Lawyering Process,* Mineola, NY: The Foundation Press, Inc., 1978, pp. 908—910.

CHAPTER SEVEN

TRIAL STRATEGY: MISCONCEPTIONS AND MISEXECUTIONS

Chapter 3 makes plain that meticulous and patient preparation for trial is necessary to maximize your chance to win. However, the most thorough preparation may be to no avail because of poor strategic planning or execution before trial or at trial. For example, it is not always advisable in framing pleadings to assert all available claims or defenses. Even though you may have evidence to support a claim or defense, you should consider whether the subject you could add to a case would hurt your client's more promising claims or defenses. If you conclude that the value of a claim or defense is outweighed by its adverse impact on other more important matters between the parties, then do not assert it.

Example 7–1:

THINK CAREFULLY BEFORE PUTTING YOUR DEFENDANT'S REPUTATION ON THE LINE IN A COUNTERCLAIM FOR LIBEL

Louis Nizer

I have in mind as a tactical error counterclaims by defendants in libel suits. Ordinarily, a defendant's reputation is irrelevant. It is the plaintiff's reputation for which damages are sought. However, if the

continued

Example 7-1 (cont'd.)

defendant counterclaims for libel, he thereby puts his own reputation on the line since his entitlement to damages depends on how good his reputation is.

An illustration of the error is the *Quentin Reynolds v. Westbrook Pegler* case in which I represented Reynolds. Pegler counterclaimed against Reynolds for libel. Pegler asserted that Reynolds' review of a book "said in effect that Pegler was morally guilty of the homicide of Hayward Broun."

At the trial in my opening statement I turned the jury's attention to Pegler himself. I knew how effective Reynolds would be, and what an extraordinary series of witnesses was ready to testify on his behalf. But I wanted the jury to know that it was Pegler we were waiting for, and I wanted Pegler to know it, too.

So, after explaining Pegler's counterclaim against Reynolds, I said: "Now we are very glad in a way, ladies and gentlemen—it is a curious thing to say, but we are very glad that we have a counterclaim in this action, because Mr. Pegler thereby puts his reputation and character on the line. He says that his reputation and character have been injured, and when the time comes we are going to examine Mr. Pegler's reputation and character, and what he does and what he writes, and what he stands for from the beginning of his life to now. We don't mind putting Mr. Reynolds under a microscope. We are going to do it—anything at all that they wish to ask him. But we are going to take the same privilege and put Mr. Pegler under a microscope in this court and find out what his reputation and character are. I invite you, ladies and gentlemen, I entreat you, to wait for the time when Mr. Pegler takes the stand and watch him carefully. Listen to every word carefully."

As I turned from the jury for a moment, I caught a glimpse of Pegler. His eye was twitching. After the intervening testimony Pegler finally was turned over to me for cross-examination. Since Pegler had made the mistake of filing a counterclaim for libel against Reynolds, it became relevant—which otherwise it would not have been—to ask what was Pegler's reputation which he said was injured?

We had researched Pegler's life and activities. I had read thousands of his columns and indexed them. I had read everything I could find which had been written about him. Since he accused Reynolds of being a slacker and a coward, it was quite proper to look at Pegler's own war record. This is what cross-examination of him revealed:

continued

Example 7-1 (cont'd.)

> Q: At one time in your life you were also a war correspondent, were you not?
>
> A: Yes.
>
> Q: That was during World War I?
>
> A: Yes.
>
> Q: And you were at that time how old, sir?
>
> A: I think twenty-three.
>
> Q: And unmarried?
>
> A: Unmarried.
>
> Q: And healthy?
>
> A: Yes.
>
> Q: ...When you became a war correspondent, did you first try to enlist as a soldier in the Army?
>
> A: No.
>
> Q: ...Or any other military branch of service?
>
> A: No.

Pegler's gift for insult and offensiveness got him into trouble as a war correspondent and his accreditation was canceled.

We skirmished over changes in his testimony and he shouted: "Your Honor, may I be protected from this harassment? Could he stand down there?"

COURT: There has been no harassment.

I returned to the main line of cross-examination. After he was discharged as a war correspondent, what did he do?

> Q: Well, during that period that you were in London without accreditation as a war correspondent, and without enlisting, did you consider...that you were a coward?
>
> A: No.

Knowing that great infantry battles were impending:

> Q: Did you try to enlist in the Marines?
>
> A: No, sir.
>
> Q: In aviation?
>
> A: No, sir.

continued

Example 7-1 (cont'd.)

> Q: In the infantry?
>
> A: No, sir.
>
> Q: The only attempt you made to enlist was in the Navy; is that right?
>
> A: That is right.

Although six feet tall and in perfect health, he obtained a clerical job. He was stationed in an office building.

> Q: You never had a gun?
>
> A: No, sir.
>
> Q: When you got the assignment to render clerical service at a hotel office building in Liverpool for the United States Navy, did you protest to anyone?
>
> A: Of course not.
>
> Q: Did you request to be assigned to any fighting ship?
>
> A: No.
>
> Q: To any fighting service, either in the Navy or in the Army?
>
> A: No.
>
> Q: So that it is fair to say, Mr. Pegler, that your war record consisted of being a war correspondent in civilian capacity between 1917 and 1918 when the United States was at war, and at which time you did not enlist, and thereafter when you enlisted, your war service consisted of being a clerk in a hotel building in Liverpool for the United States Navy?
>
> A: That is right.

At this moment the only comment permissible was a meaningful pause. It was not until the testimony was completed and I was permitted to sum up to the jury that I could contrast the forty-year-old Reynolds' participation in the mutilating struggles of the Second World War with the twenty-three-year-old Pegler's service at a Naval typewriter in the First World War. Yet it was Pegler who set himself up as a standard-bearer of patriotism and reviled Reynolds for dodging duty and danger.

I probed into other inconsistencies of Pegler.

> A: ...I don't say Reynolds was not loyal and patriotic. I say he is a big dope. He doesn't know the difference.

continued

Example 7-1 (cont'd.)

> Q: Now isn't it a fact, Mr. Pegler, that you have joined...organizations which you later felt were Communistic?
>
> A: No—oh, the Newspaper Guild, yes.
>
> Q: Well, isn't there another one [Friends of Democracy] that you found is subversive?
>
> A: No, just rotten.
>
> Q: ...And how long had you been listed as a member on the letterhead before you discovered you were a dope?
>
> A: I didn't say I discovered I was a dope and I never was.
>
> Q: Did you consider...that your name on the letterhead committed you morally and politically to that organization?
>
> A: No.
>
> I read to him his answer in his deposition before trial in which he said, "A. I joined it, I gave...authority to use my name on a letterhead...which I consider to have committed me morally and politically to their organization."
>
> Q: Did you make me that answer?
>
> A: Yes. I am mistaken now in my present answer.
>
> I quoted some of his prior answers on the Newspaper Guild and elicited the confession:
>
> A: I was mistaken under oath...
>
> And as for being "taken in" by "questionable" organizations, I asked him:
>
> Q: That can happen to any man, can't it?
>
> A: I don't know. Maybe some of them would be smarter than I was.
>
> Q: In any event, your name on the letterhead meant to you that you were being represented as one of the sponsors and supporters of this organization.
>
> A: ...I am afraid that could have been so.
>
> Why had he waited three years before retiring from a "Communistic organization" he had been roped into? When he couldn't find the explanation, I supplied it from a column he had written: "I know
>
> *continued*

Example 7-1 (cont'd.)

who the Communists are, and I waited for a long time before I became convinced that they were actually enemies of the freedoms which are inherent in Americanism."

Of course, he was more embarrassed by his excuse for waiting than by his original error in joining.[1]

Weigh the Consequences of Joining a Defendant or Filing a Counterclaim Even If It Is a Compulsory One

Mr. Nizer so devastatingly exploited Mr. Pegler's strategic error in asserting a counterclaim which put his own reputation at issue that Mr. Pegler's prospects for successfully defending against Mr. Reynolds' suit must have become very dim indeed. Mr. Pegler's lawyer may have decided to make the counterclaim because it was a compulsory one under the applicable procedural law. However, the fact that a counterclaim is compulsory does not require that you make it. You may elect not to make it, which constitutes a waiver of your client's claim. To protect yourself you should obtain your client's assent to this waiver in writing, for it means that his claim is barred from being asserted in any subsequent legal action. That waiver may be far better for your client than the consequences of filing the claim as a counterclaim, like those sustained by Mr. Pegler.

Unlike compulsory counterclaims, the law does not generally require closely related claims against different defendants to be joined in the same lawsuit, on pain of waiver. Joinder of claims and defendants is permissive rather than compulsory. You may decide to join your client's claims against several defendants to avoid the duplication of expense and delay entailed by separate suits. But before you do so you should ask yourself whether countervailing undesirable consequences may flow from the joinder. Consider the next Example drawn from the entertainment world.

Example 7–2:

THE BEATLES AS LITIGANTS MAY BE JUST ANOTHER VERSION OF THE SUE ME, SUE YOU BLUES; BUT SUE THEIR LAWYER PERSONALLY AND YOU SEE SPEEDY ACTION

Albert S. Pergam

Abkco Industries, Inc. had a management contract with three of the Beatles and the Beatles' group of companies including Apple Corps Limited in the late 1960s and early 1970s. The Beatles and their companies had a falling out with Abkco and sued Abkco in England on the ground inter alia that they had been induced to enter the management contract by misrepresentations. The firm of solicitors representing the Beatles was Frere Cholmeley; its senior partner on the case was Michael Boreham.

Eight days after the Beatles sued in England, Abkco retaliated by suing the Beatles in New York for past and future commissions and for compensation in quantum meruit. We represented in New York John Lennon, George Harrison and Richard Starkey of the Beatles. We on the Beatles' side thought that the English forum would be more hospitable to them. Abkco thought its chances were better in New York. Thus a race was on to determine in which forum the case would go to trial first.

For the first year or so it was a close race. But in December 1974 Abkco ill-advisedly joined a new defendant whom it alleged was personally liable as a co-conspirator for $20 million, claiming he wrongly induced his clients to breach their contract with Abkco. The new defendant was the Beatles' solicitor, Michael Boreham. This threat to Mr. Boreham, his reputation and pocketbook, stirred our English legal team much more effectively than had our efforts to implement our strategy and move the English case forward. Mr. Boreham's litigating partners had a real incentive to push our barristers. We won the race.

Since Abkco's claims against the Beatles appear to have been much more important to it than its claim against Mr. Boreham, it should not have sued Mr. Boreham until the race between the English and New York forum had been decided. Suing the Beatles' solicitor may have been unwise strategy for another reason, too. The Beatles' side of the litigation may have interpreted the suit against one of their lawyers as a signal that Abkco had evaluated its prospects in the case as very poor. This could have hardened the Beatles' position in any settlement negotiations.

The basis for this interpretation is a generalization about litigation strategy which has been colorfully expressed as follows: when liability is in your favor, hammer away at liability; when damages are in your favor, hammer away at damages; and when neither are in your favor, hammer away at the opposing counsel. Striking the opposing counsel, however, can be counterproductive, as it was in Ex. 7–2.

A Double Edged Sword—Protect a Winning Verdict Against Reversible Error in the Record

A strategic lesson conveyed by the performance of Mr. George V. Higgins, the prosecutor in Ex. 5–8 in Chap. 5, is what he refers to as "avoid[ing] the possibility of tainting my case with reversible error." For this reason he decided not to show his witness mug shots to determine whether she could identify a defendant who had been indicted for bank robbery. Mr. Higgins explains in Ex. 5–8 that at that time the state of the law on photographic show-ups was such that, if her testimony had identified the defendant on the basis of the mug shots, a conviction might well have been reversed. Mr. Higgins' decision was eminently sound. *When the admission of evidence or an instruction to the jury by the judge at trial may turn out to be a reversible error on appeal, do not offer the evidence or request the instruction if the remaining evidence or instructions give you a good chance to win the verdict at trial.*

When you have persuasive evidence which is of borderline admissibility, it is a great temptation to use it even though the appellate court may rule it inadmissible. You may feel proud that you have detected in other jurisdictions, in the lower appellate courts of your own jurisdiction, or in academic writings some movement toward creating favorable new law or favorably modifying previously settled law. Then it is a great temptation to request that the judge instruct the jury to apply the new law. These temptations must be resisted if you can win without risking that the appellate court will disagree with the trial judge. A victorious verdict at trial proves to be a pyrrhic victory on appeal when, in the view of the appellate court, the verdict was based on erroneously admitted evidence or erroneous instructions.

Salvage a Losing Verdict Through Reversible Error in the Record—the Other Edge of the Sword

Using questionable law or questionably admissible evidence at trial is a double edged sword. To be sure, it can transform a winning verdict into a reversal on appeal. But it also can transform a losing verdict into a reversal on appeal. This may come about if you offer evidence of questionable admissibility or request an instruction of questionable law, the trial judge excludes the evidence or refuses to give the instruction, and you lose the verdict. You can win a new trial on appeal if you can convince the appellate court that the trial judge's ruling on the evidence or requested instruction was reversible error. If you do so, you are taking advantage of "error in the record" of the trial, which you have made possible by the offer of evidence or requested instruction. For the purpose of getting a second shot if you lose the verdict, you should be vigilant to find opportunities in the course of a trial to "put error in the record." The advantage of "error in the record" of course does not accrue to trial lawyers who have no right to appeal. Criminal prosecutors are a prime example, for generally they cannot appeal a not guilty verdict.

The double edges of the reversible error sword mean that you frequently will be in a dilemma. If you have evidence of borderline admissibility or law of borderline acceptance, you must judge whether to offer it by balancing the following choices: if you offer it, your victorious verdict may be reversed on appeal; but if you withhold it, your appeal of a losing verdict may fail owing to the absence of the evidence or instruction ruling as the reversible error. From time to time, you may find yourself fortunate enough to be walking a tightrope between the double edges of the reversible error sword. This may happen if you offer the evidence or request the instruction but the trial judge refuses to give the instruction or rules the evidence inadmissible. In this happy scenario, you have not risked reversible error and yet may have "put error in the record." Trial lawyers usually would opt for this scenario. However, except in the very rare case in which you can predict in advance that the trial judge will rule against you, this option is not available when the lawyer must judge whether to offer the evidence or request the instruction. At that point you must offer the evidence or law and risk reversal of victory or withhold them and forego rulings which might reverse defeat. In making this judgment you must weigh your chances of victory without the evidence or law against your chances of defeat at trial and reversal on appeal without adverse rulings by the trial judge on the evidence or law.

The judgment is easy if you see a slim chance to win at trial without the evidence or law. You must use it. You also must make a strong effort to persuade the trial judge to admit the evidence or give the instruction. You do not serve your client well if after a half-hearted effort the trial judge rules against using the evidence or law, your client loses the verdict, and the appellate court reverses the verdict and orders another trial because of the trial judge's erroneous ruling. At the new trial the evidence or law will be used. But your client is only in the same position he would have been in if you had made a better effort in the first trial with the result that the trial judge had then ruled in favor of using the evidence or law. The client in a larger sense is in a worse position owing to the expense and delay of the appeal. The judgment also is easy if you foresee a slim chance of defeat at trial without the law or evidence. Then there is no reason to risk reversible error by using questionable law or evidence of questionable admissibility.

But in most trials when you must judge whether to use borderline law or evidence, neither defeat nor victory is extremely probable. When you make this difficult judgment, you should not be criticized if on hindsight your judgment turns out to be wrong. You should only be criticized if, when you made your judgment, you did not appreciate that either decision was risky, i.e., that you were subject to a double edged sword.

You can walk the tightrope between the double edges of the reversible error sword, escape any pretrial error in strategic planning of the claims and parties, thoroughly prepare for trial, and yet find all your exemplary efforts frustrated because you commit an isolated strategic mistake in the course of the trial itself.

Example 7–3:

DO NOT SACRIFICE AN OVERARCHING
STRATEGIC GOAL FOR A LESSER ONE

Jared M. Billings

The subject of this tactical error deals with the use of an impeachment witness during the liability portion of our trial. Having

continued

Example 7-3 (cont'd.)

deposed the defendant driver in this intersectional collision case, we knew that the defendant driver would testify to facts A, B, C, and D at the time of the trial. Following the deposition of the defendant, and before the trial, we discovered the identity of a liability witness who would serve to impeach very convincingly the testimony of the defendant driver.

This impeachment witness was very believable, and it was our strong belief that his testimony would convince the jury that the defendant driver was not telling the truth in regards to a few crucial facts. It was further our hope that by calling this person as an impeachment witness, the dramatic effect of doing so would utterly destroy the defendant's testimony and his case. Because he was an impeachment witness, under our rules, we did not have to list him as a witness on our pretrial list of witnesses. Our strategy was based on the assumption that the defense attorney would call the defendant driver as a witness during the defendant's case.

Unfortunately for our plan to impeach the defendant so dramatically and convincingly, the defense attorney did not call the defendant driver as a witness. Accordingly, we were not allowed to call our witness as an impeachment witness, as there was no testimony during the defendant's case to impeach. Also, the trial court would not allow us to reopen our case to call this witness as one of our own additional witnesses.

Since we had called the defendant briefly as a witness during our own case, the defense attorney had the opportunity at that time to examine his defendant during our case, and then decided not to recall the defendant. Upon reflection, it probably would have been better for us not to have called the defendant as our own witness; in this event the defense attorney would have called the defendant during his case, which would have allowed us to impeach this witness by the dramatic means I described earlier.

Keep Your Strategic Priorities Straight

When Mr. Billings concludes that upon reflection it would have been better not to have called the defendant as their own witness, he is saying that they misweighed two of the goals they were pursuing. On was to use the defendant "briefly as a witness during our own case." The other was to have the defense attorney call the defendant as a witness so that the impeachment witness could be called in rebuttal. They sacrificed their more important strategic goal to obtain a lesser goal. Your eye must always, even in the heat of battle, be on the overarching objective.

Calling an Adverse Party as Your Witness—It May Help, but the Party Can Be Well Prepared for It and the Party's Lawyer Should Adapt Flexibly

Mr. Billings' move in calling the opposing party as a witness in his case in chief had been rarely done under the classical common law of evidence. Under that legal regime calling the other party was fraught with danger, since you could not impeach your own witness or put leading questions to him and you were deemed to vouch for the credibility of each witness you called. Today, however, most jurisdictions have abolished these rules of evidence in respect to the opposing party. An example of the abolition of these rules is Federal Rule of Evidence 611(c) which provides that if you call an adverse party as a witness, you may interrogate him by leading questions. See Federal Rule of Evidence 607.

Although Mr. Billings' decision to call the opposing party as his witness turned out to be counterproductive for him, some lawyers exercise the right as a stratagem to foil their opponent. Their purpose usually is different from Mr. Billings', since he called the defendant but briefly, presumably to supply a single or very limited number of facts. They call the adverse party and typically elicit his whole story—the heart of what he would have testified to on direct examination by his own lawyer.

They do this for several reasons. They may want the adverse party to commit himself before their client does. They may feel that the adverse party will make a far worse impression on the jury answering their leading, cross-examination questions than his own lawyer's carefully rehearsed direct examination. They may also call the adverse party on the expectation that they will throw off the opposing lawyer's plans for presenting testimony on various subjects in the most persuasive order and way. They surely are correct that after they have elicited an adverse party's entire knowledge on a subject, his own lawyer will probably decide not to bore the jury, or risk a successful objection on the ground of repetition, by presenting his testimony on the subject again by his direct examination.

I once witnessed the demoralization of the opposition when I called the adverse party as a witness. I called him "accidentally" when he unexpectedly turned out to be the only available witness who could supply some facts my plaintiff needed to be sure to survive a motion for a directed verdict. I cannot take credit for having planned the successful use of this strategem. It turned out that the facts I elicited from the defendant were central to the "script" he and his inexperienced trial lawyer had planned for his direct examination. When subsequent to my cross-examination they attempted to present their planned testimony with omissions for the parts covered by my examination, it was painfully plain that their confidence had been badly undermined.

You must be prepared for what happened to this defendant's counsel. Your opponent may call your client as his or her witness, too. You must forewarn the client not to be surprised if called as a witness by the other side. You should remind your client that everything you have mentioned in preparation for cross-examination in general, such as those things discussed in Chap. 3 on page 76, applies to this kind of cross-examination as well.

Moreover, you must know the case well enough to adapt your subsequent direct examination of your client to the fact that your client will have already given part of his testimony. By no means should you be tongue-tied to a script. An outline is what should be on the paper before you, and one which can be readily modified by, for example, checking off and deleting the points testified to in your opponent's case in chief. To be an effective trial lawyer, you must be flexible. To be sure, you must be well-prepared. However, trials are not plays performed by actors with memorized lines. They are living processes in which adaptation, and informed spontaneity, often are decisive.

In Mr. Billings' Ex. 7–3, the defense attorney adapted to the fact that Mr. Billings' side had called the defendant by eliciting all the testimony he desired from the defendant through examining him immediately after Mr. Billings' examination of him. The defense counsel flexibly shifted the order of his witnesses by presenting his client's testimony during the plaintiff's case in chief rather than the defense case in chief, once Mr. Billings had given him the option to elect between these two places. My commentary immediately after Ex. 7–3 took the position that the reason Mr. Billings' side failed to execute their planned coup by calling an impeachment witness in rebuttal was that they sacrificed their more important strategic goal to obtain a lesser goal.

The Risks in Resting Your Fate on Predictions of the Strategic Moves by Opposing Counsel

Their failure to execute the planned coup in rebuttal may not entirely be attributable to misweighing their two goals. They also may have miscalculated the reaction of the defense attorney to their decision to call the defendant in plaintiffs' case in chief. They may have thought that even though the defense attorney would have the right to examine his client following their brief examination, he would choose not to do so but to adhere to his plan to call his client as part of the subsequent defense case in chief. The defense counsel's reaction frustrated their strategy which had been planned carefully before trial.

Chief Justice Tauro related in the Foreword a similar mistake he remembers observing when he was a law student. Attorney Tom Kelly was sure that his opponent would object to his question to a witness, "Mary, do you know of any woman in this county who drinks more than you?" When the opposing lawyer failed to object, the witness' response refuted Mr. Kelly's suggestion that she was the county drunk, while at the same time reflecting adversely on Mr. Kelly's wife and so perhaps leading the jury to lose a degree of confidence in Mr. Kelly. It is risky business to rest your fate on a prediction of what your opponent will elect to do. It did not pay off for Tom Kelly or in Ex. 7–3. Nor did it pay off in Ex. 5–4. However, it did succeed in Ex. 4–4.

Unfortunately, there is no guarantee of the success of your carefully planned strategy even when its execution rests only on yourself.

Example 7–4:

REMEMBER TO CARRY OUT YOUR HIGH-PRIORITY PLAN

Julius B. Levine

I represented the plaintiff in his claim for personal injuries and property damage arising out of a motor vehicle collision. Part of my client's injuries reflected an unusual coincidence rather akin to the classical egg shell skull case: he was a 21-year-old musician who played the French horn in a military marching band; and two of his

continued

Example 7-4 (cont'd.)

injuries were to a knee and his lip and mouth. He believed that these injuries had dashed his realistic ambition before the collision to rise to the very highest rank among musicians. In his view they put in doubt his ability to perform well enough even to make a living.

I asked musical experts who had been familiar with my client's level of performance before the collision to compare his ability to perform after his lip and mouth injuries. They agreed with his pessimistic assessment. On the other hand, the physicians and surgeon who had attended his other injuries in the hospital immediately following the collision had paid no attention to his lip and mouth except to note that they had been cut but not seriously enough to require stitches. Hence the defendant's counsel insisted that the lip and mouth injury was of no consequence—physically or monetarily. He could count on the attending doctors to testify that this injury was insignificant.

After a rather difficult search I located a neuropathologist who was an accomplished amateur musician on the baritone horn, a similar instrument to the French horn. He examined my client's lip and mouth and listened to him play the French horn. He agreed that my client did not seem able to play now at a very high level, and certainly not at a level which would have merited the musical awards he had received before the collision. Furthermore, the neuropathologist was able to explain why small, otherwise insignificant cuts to the client's mouth and lip would disable him permanently from excellence on the French horn. The small cuts left small scars, which were permanent; they in turn prevented the client from forming the embouchure—the shaping of the lips and mouth to produce music on a wind instrument—necessary for high-quality performance.

Thus I faced the challenge to prove a very significant injury about which opposing doctors were very skeptical. The same was true about the injury to my client's knee which had slammed into the dashboard during the collision. Right after the collision the only visible damage to the knee was a one-inch superficial cut. Not until about ten days later did it bother the plaintiff. It was about a month before he was hospitalized for the knee. This delay contributed to the view of the defendant's doctors that the collision did not give rise to his knee problem. Another contributor was the fact that plaintiff had sustained trauma to the knee approximately ten years earlier.

Still another damage challenge was my client's claim of aggravation of an old injury to his other knee. After he had been unable to

continued

Example 7-4 (cont'd.)

use the first knee for about a year and a half following the collision, an old injury to his other knee had flared up. His orthopedic surgeon attributed it to the increased burden it had been bearing since the first knee had been out of commission. The opposing doctors figuratively arched their eyebrows very high in skepticism about this claim.

The day before trial had been scheduled to begin one of those uncontrollable developments in litigation occurred: I telephoned the office of one of my key medical experts, an orthopedic surgeon who had evaluated the plaintiff's injured knees, to remind him that he would be testifying in a few days. A few weeks earlier when I had received notice of the trial date he and I had conferred to prepare his testimony. He then confirmed his availability for the trial date and the following few days, although he added that three weeks later he would be attending a conference in Brazil. This time when his secretary answered I said that I did not have to speak to the doctor personally but merely needed her to remind him that I would need him in court in two or three days. To my astonishment she replied that he was in Brazil at a conference and would not return for a week.

On the basis of the sudden, unanticipated unavailability of an indispensable witness, I moved immediately for a week's continuance of the trial. The defendant's counsel opposed the motion on the ground that the schedules for weeks ahead of his numerous expert and lay witnesses as well as his own schedule had been set on the premise of this trial date. The judge ruled that, inasmuch as my newly unavailable witness would testify only on damages, the trial would be bifurcated: the liability issue alone would be tried without a continuance; and if plaintiff prevailed on liability, damages would be tried on a date after the doctor's return from Brazil.

The trial began. At the end of a three-day, hard fought liability trial the jury returned a verdict finding the defendant 100 percent at fault. We went on to the damages trial. Neither side objected to the date set by the court. Our orthopedic surgeon had returned from Brazil and testified along with approximately five other medical expert witnesses.

It was a sharply contested, five-day trial. All of the challenging damages claims which I outlined above were fully fought—first-class musical ability permanently destroyed; delayed permanent damage to a knee which prevents a member of a marching band from marching; and triggering off permanent impairment of the other knee

continued

Example 7-4 (cont'd.)

which had been previously injured. I prepared as well as I could for the damages trial in the conventional way. But I also adopted an unconventional strategy in one respect.

My client's car was injured in the collision, as well as his body. The potential maximum recovery for his car, about $900, paled in significance compared to his personal injuries. Ordinarily I would have proved the car damage by a discovery request for admission or a request at a pretrial conference for a stipulation from the defendant that the difference in the car's fair market value before and after the collision was $900. But in this case I studiously avoided inducing the defendant to remove the car damage as a contested issue. In fortunate furtherance of my strategy, his lawyer did not volunteer to do so, even though he had not prepared any evidence on the car damage. I had done so and called an expert on car values. He duly testified that the car's fair market value had dropped by $900.

By this unconventional strategy I was in a position to make the following argument to the jury: "The defendant questions just about all of our claims of damages. For example, he contends that small cuts in the mouth and on the lip can't convert a star musician into a 'has been.' He says that slamming a knee into a dashboard when there's no trouble with the knee until 10 days later cannot be the cause of terrible knee impairment; there must have been some intervening cause, he says, and so forth. But, ladies and gentlemen of the jury, ask yourselves: has defendant produced reliable evidence to dispute our proof of these very serious injuries? Or is he just stubbornly opposing them to avoid paying?

"An affirmative answer to this last question is evident from one of our damage claims which the defendant has not devoted time in his summation to. That is our claim for $900 damages to my client's car. You will remember that one of our witnesses was an expert in car values. To recover this $900 of damages from defendant, we brought an expert to court to testify that the collision damaged plaintiff's car in the amount of $900; and I have asked you to include this $900 in your verdict. Even though defendant has not, and cannot, claim that the collision did not cause the car damage, he still required us to prove it. Even though he has no quibbling, hair-splitting basis on which to say that it was too small a dent, or that the damage was noticed too long after the collision, he has not conceded that the earlier jury verdict of his 100 percent liability means that a verdict of at least $900 must be returned against him now. And since he resists

continued

Example 7-4 (cont'd.)

paying even the undisputed car damage, doesn't the conclusion become compelling that he doesn't have well grounded, good faith bases to oppose the rest of plaintiff's damages either; but he does so simply because he stubbornly does not want to pay what he's liable for?"

Maybe an argument along these lines would not have been terribly persuasive to the jury. At any rate by careful planning and by going to the trouble of using an expert in car values I was in a position to make the argument in my rebuttal at the damages trial. But my mistake was that I did not make it. During the summation by opposing counsel I decided to give a high priority to answering a number of his points. Upon finishing my discussion of his points I planned to make the above car damage argument. Before I finished, however, the judge interrupted to inform me that my time was up and I had to sit down.

The verdict on damages was for less than we had hoped for.

In this example I should have paid better attention to the time remaining as I gave my closing argument. Even though my rebuttal of the points made by opposing counsel may have deserved a high priority, I should have been sure to have saved time for the rather brief argument that I had planned to make for months—and that I had decided deserved a high priority under far calmer and cooler conditions in my office than those of the clamor and heat at trial. To be sure, we must adapt to what happens at trial and cannot be hidebound to our pretrial preparations. On the other hand, when nothing happens at trial to discredit our pretrial preparations, as was true in my case, we must remember to carry them out at trial. That is not a difficult lesson to understand.

Your Desire for a Bifurcated Trial May Well Turn on Which Side You Represent

The implications of the order for a bifurcated trial, which was made in my case, are not so easy to understand. From the standpoint of judicial administration this ruling was a veritable Judgment of Solomon. It assured the plaintiff the benefit of the doctor's damages testimony, while assuring no disruption of the schedules of defendant's witnesses and counsel if defendant won on liability and only minor possible disruptions if defendant lost on liability.

From my standpoint the bifurcation ruling was a mixed blessing at best. I would not lose the testimony of a key damages expert. But the liability issue in my case was a close one. Plaintiff contended that the collision resulted from defendant's vehicle being partly on the wrong side of the road. Defendant contended that plaintiff's excessive speed caused the collision. Comparative negligence was the applicable law: this particular statute provided that if plaintiff was 50 percent or more at fault, defendant was not liable.

The statistics indicate that plaintiffs win a significantly smaller percentage of personal injury - negligence trials when liability is tried alone than when liability and damages are tried together. Commentators explain these statistics by the hypotheses that in a unitary trial (a) the jury may compromise in a weak plaintiff's liability case by returning a verdict finding defendant liable but awarding less than full damages or (b) the jury may decide liability out of sympathy to plaintiff after learning about his or her damages.

Bifurcation thus translated for me into a diminution in the odds for victory. It also meant that the jury was unlikely to give short shrift to defenses against our damages as a result of devoting more attention during a unitary trial to evidence about liability. Despite my misgivings, the liability verdict was 100 percent in our favor. Still, the subsequent disappointing damage award meant that the overall result in this case did not depart from the conventional wisdom that defendants are likely to win bifurcated personal injury-negligence cases.

SUMMARY

Strategic choices inevitably must be made as you conduct litigation. Before you file an action against multiple potential defendants, you should think through thoroughly the consequences of joining them in a single action or suing them separately at the same time or at different times. As Ex. 7–2 illustrates, joining a less important defendant may render it much harder to win against more important defendants.

Similarly, if you represent a defendant, before you file your answer you should not only consider whether your client has a compulsory counterclaim but also anticipate the consequences of filing the particular counterclaim in the overall action. In Ex. 7–1 the counterclaim for defamation put the defendant's reputation on the line. Since his reputation was questionable, he would have been better served if the counterclaim had not been filed. If it was a compulsory counterclaim, one result of not filing it would have been that he would have been barred from suing on it in the future. But another result would have been that his chances to win the pending lawsuit against him would have been markedly better.

In trials in which you may put forward evidence of questionable admissibility or a questionable requested instruction of law, your objective should be, on the one hand, to avoid reversal on appeal of a verdict in your favor. On the other hand, your objective also should be to have "error in the record" which you can use on appeal should you lose the verdict. When these objectives conflict, you must make a difficult judgment, which, however enlightened, may not extricate you from the double-edged sword without damage.

Strategic considerations often enter into your decision on which witnesses to call and whether to present them in your case in chief or in rebuttal. As you make your plans about witnesses, you should bear in mind that your opponent may call the same people you plan to call, including your client, before you get to them. You should prepare your witnesses for this possibility, and you yourself must be ready to examine them after your opponent in a fashion that renders the effect of their total testimony as favorable to your side as possible.

In Ex. 7–3, plaintiff's counsel planned to call a key witness in rebuttal in order to maximize his effect in impeaching the defendant. That strategy was based on the assumption that the defendant's lawyer would use the defendant as a witness in his case in chief. When the defendant's lawyer did not do so, the plaintiff was prohibited from calling his key witness at all. By basing his strategy on his prediction of what the opposing counsel would do, plaintiff's counsel wound up worse off than if he had had no strategy to maximize the impact of the witness but had simply called him in his case in chief. Other instances in other chapters also underscore the riskiness of basing strategy on a prediction of what opposing counsel will do.

In Ex. 7–3, the defendant's counsel did not behave as predicted because the plaintiff's counsel called the defendant as a witness in the plaintiff's case in chief. Although by doing so the plaintiff's counsel realized a strategic objective, it was less valuable than the strategic objective which was thereby lost. Plaintiff's counsel had failed to act in accordance with the priorities of his objectives. I made the same mistake in Ex. 7–4 when I allocated scarce time in summation to some rebuttal points at the expense of a much better point I had planned to argue since early in the preparation of the case. Example 7–4 also demonstrates that the best laid plans made during the preparation stage come to naught if you do not carry them out.

You must get your strategic priorities straight and not neglect them. For instance, if your side of a case is less likely to prevail in a bifurcated trial than in a unitary trial, it behooves you to do all you can to be sure that all of your necessary damages witnesses are available—in person or by deposition—when the unitary trial is scheduled to begin. Otherwise, your motion for a continuance may yield you but a pyrrhic victory: an order for a bifurcated trial.

It is well to use sound strategy to enhance your case or defense. But you must be vigilant against falling into a pitfall as you conceive and execute your strategy.

REFERENCE NOTE

1. L. Nizer, *My Life in Court*, pp. 24, 42, 43, 109, 110, 111, 113, and 114 © copyright 1961 by Louis Nizer.

INDEX

Bias:
  of judge, 1, 2
  of jury 1, 2, 9-11, 13-14, 15, 18, 19
  of witness, 48-49, 63-66, 161
Bifurcated trial, 250-55, 257
Burden of proof, 33-34, 38-39, 42, 45, 80-81, 112, 130, 157, 211, 213, 221

Closing argument, 21, 124, 125
  chronology, 221-22, 233
  compared with cross-examination, 224
  content, 124-25, 134, 154, 159, 160, 161-62, 190, 196, 203-4, 210-17, 219, 221, 226-28, 233-34, 253-54
  delivery, 228-32, 234
  judge reaction, 206-7, 209-10, 233
  jury reaction, 205-6, 219-20, 223, 225, 231
  organization, 210, 211-14, 220, 226, 233-34
  purpose, 203-4, 211, 216, 217, 223, 233-34
  scope, 204-10, 223, 225
  style, 205, 211
  waiver, 222-224
Competence of counsel, 45
Counterclaim, 237-42, 255-56
Credibility:
  of counsel 25, 26-27, 28, 34-35, 42
  of defendant, 103-4, 247
  of witness, 26, 34, 47-48, 59, 63-68, 83, 84, 102, 125, 128, 130, 133, 142-43, 162, 177, 181, 216-16, 246-48
Cross-examination:
  of celebrity, 134-35
  of client, 60-62
  content, 124-25, 126, 130-31, 134, 169, 177, 204, 249
  control of witness, 131-34, 142-43, 166-67, 198-99
  pitfalls, 136-39, 141-94, 198, 224
  purpose, 123, 125, 128, 133, 134, 194, 197
  related to closing argument or redirect-examination, 125, 154-56, 160, 204

scope, 194
style, 123-24, 139, 177, 182-83,
    185, 196-97
waiver, 132-33, 134-36, 180, 198,
    224
witness preparation, ii, 62-63,
    66, 75-76, 82-83

Demonstrations, 78-79, 94-95,
    101-3, 114-15, 127-29, 130
Depositions, 56, 120, 143, 150,
    165, 187, 241, 247
Direct examination, 114, 118, 130,
    233
content, 137-38, 194-95, 196,
    197, 248
organization, 114
Directed verdict, 25, 37
Discovery (see also deposition),
    38, 62, 66, 111, 113-14, 120,
    150, 177, 219
Federal Rule of Civil Procedure
    (FRCP)
    FRCP 30, 113
    FRCP 32, 150
    FRCP 34, 113
    FRCP 36, 114
    FRCE 45(d)(1), 113

Equal protection clause, 2, 18-19
Error in the record, 245-46
Ethics, viii, 4, 45
Evidence:
damaging, 27-28, 42, 108-13,
    130-31, 147, 149, 170-75,
    238-42
documentary, 85, 88-90, 91-94,
    108-9, 110-11, 119, 120,
    180-82
examining, 108-113, 120
exhibits, 21, 25-26, 31, 73-74,
    133

inadmissible, 40-41, 43, 103-7,
    109, 170, 171-72, 173-74,
    244-46, 256
law of, viii-ix, 93, 134, 170, 172,
    194, 210-11, 246, 248
Federal Rule of Evidence (FRE)
    FRE 607, 248
    FRE 611(c), 248
    FRE 612, 93
    FRE 801(d)(1)(A), 59
preparation, 36, 45-47, 56-59,
    60-61, 62-63, 66, 85-93, 94,
    107-9, 111, 113, 120
presentation, 21, 42, 109-10, 111,
    112, 114, 119, 120, 127-28,
    130-31, 203, 213
proof of elements, 34, 37,
    46-47, 55, 94, 194
testimonial, 21, 34-35, 100, 114,
    119, 125
Expert witnesses, 55, 76-83,
    92-93, 114-15, 148, 155-56,
    157-58, 159, 183-84, 187-88,
    200, 250-54

Interview (see witness, interview)
Investigation, 60-62, 68-69,
    83-85, 86-89, 90, 92-94

Judge:
bias, 1, 2
comments of, 24-25, 162-63,
    206
conduct of voir dire, 5
discretion, 5, 12, 17, 41, 100,
    209-210, 230
selection of, 1, 2
Jury:
attention, 22, 25, 29, 124-25,
    130, 131, 157, 197, 200,
    229-30, 231
challenges:
    for cause, 2, 3, 4, 5, 18

effect on jury, 2, 12, 18
equal protection clause, 2, 18-19
peremptory, 2, 3, 6, 8, 9-12, 18
composition, 2, 3-4, 5, 18
  minority view, 3, 11, 18
  majority view, 3-4, 18
inferences by, 38, 98-99, 100, 106, 107, 119, 219, 221-22
instructions, 40, 98-100, 119, 142, 211, 212, 213, 226, 244-46, 256
investigation of:
  informal, 4, 10, 14, 18
  social science, 4, 14, 18
misconduct, 8-9, 19-20, 116-18
perception of counsel, 2, 5, 7, 12, 14-15, 16, 18, 34, 35, 39, 42-43, 107, 124, 125, 130-31, 135, 140-41, 175-79, 184, 205-6, 212-13, 220, 225, 229-30, 234
perception of witnesses, 48, 49-51, 53, 55, 59, 80-83, 94, 128, 132, 135, 177-80, 180-85, 197, 200
values, 4, 6-7

Legal taboos, 71-73, 103-104

Motions:
  for continuance, 252, 257
  for directed verdict, 25, 37, 222, 249
  in limine, 40-41, 43, 107, 170
  for mistrial, 19, 57-58, 103-5, 117, 209-10
  for new trial, 8, 19-20
  to strike, 40, 41, 43, 58, 105, 142, 160, 164, 189
  to withdraw question, 171

Objections:
  dangers, 39-41, 105-9, 119, 142, 210-11, 225
  to closing argument, 204-205, 225-26
  grounds for, 40-41, 103-4, 105, 107, 126-27, 129, 141, 142, 146, 161, 172, 248
  to jury challenge, 5
  to opening statement, 39-41, 225
  timing, 39-41, 142, 225-26
  waiver, ii, 104-5, 141-42
Opening statement:
  argument, 21, 37, 41-42, 233
  contents, 21-23, 25-29, 33, 37, 217
  evidence, 21-22, 29, 37, 38, 217
  inadmissible evidence, 40
  objections, 39-41, 42-43, 225
  organization, 21-22, 25, 30-32
  primacy, 22-23
  timing, 23, 32-35, 36-39, 42
  tone, 23, 29-30
  waiver, 23-24, 36-37, 39, 42

Peremptory challenges:
  factors, 4, 6-8, 9-14, 18-19
  limitations, 2, 18-19
  use of, 2, 3, 4, 5, 6, 7, 8, 9-15, 18-19
Perjury, 59, 216-17
Pleadings, 237
Prediction of opponent's strategy, ii, 105-107, 134, 221-22, 246-47, 250
Primacy, 5, 17-18, 22-23, 25, 220
Privilege against self-incrimination, 35, 99

Questions:
  ambiguous, 191-94

dangerous, 126-28, 132-33, 134,
    136, 137-44, 145-47, 148-54,
    156-77, 184-91
hypothetical, iv, 77-78
leading, 7, 51, 52, 120, 131-32,
    142, 196, 198, 248
from learned treatises, iv
open-ended, 7, 18, 51, 52, 114,
    120, 141, 156-67, 196, 198
repeated, 114-18, 120, 126-27

Rebuttal, 219, 221-23, 224-25,
    233, 247-48, 250, 254, 256
Recess, v, 61, 101, 102, 103, 119
Recency, 220
Recross-examination, 146, 147
Redirect-examination, 128-31,
    140, 151, 154-56, 171-72,
    174, 199
Reversible error, 45, 145, 244-46

Settlement, v, 56, 59, 78, 91, 94,
    115, 119, 128, 131, 144, 151,
    180, 187, 210, 244
Subpoena:
    documents, 110-11
    rationale for using, 47-48
    witnesses, 36, 46-48, 68, 148,
        181
Summation (see closing
    argument)

Venire, 2, 5, 17, 18
Verdict, 3, 18, 27
View, 83-85
Voir dire of jury panel, 3, 4-9,
    14-20, 227
    argument, 17
    by counsel, 4-7, 14-15, 18

false answers, 8-9, 16, 19-20
by judge, 5, 18
oath, 4, 8
persuasion, 5, 16-18, 20
questions, 4-5, 6-7, 18-19

Witness:
    admonition by judge, 142-43
    adverse, 89, 143-44, 180-82,
        195-96, 248-49
    control of, 131-34, 142-43,
        166-67, 198-99, 224
    credibility, 8, 26, 47-48, 59, 63,
        68, 72, 83, 84, 125, 128,
        130, 133, 142-43, 162, 177,
        181, 188, 215, 246-48
    criminal conviction, 63, 65-66,
        162
    cumulative, 81-83, 94
    dressing appropriately, 53
    evaluating, 48-51, 55-56, 94,
        145
    hostile, 67-70, 195-96, 248-49
    impeachment (see Witness,
        Credibility), 48, 59, 63-66,
        125, 137-40, 155, 158, 161,
        162, 167-68, 180-82
    instruction or orientation, 51,
        53, 62, 63, 70-76, 77-78, 94,
        102-4, 120, 193, 249
    interview, 36, 49, 51-53, 54-55,
        57-70, 72-73, 94, 132, 193
    memory, 26, 37, 42, 54, 57-59,
        93-94, 176
    preparation, 26, 36, 45-47,
        49-51, 53, 54-55, 56, 61-63,
        70-78, 81-83, 86-88, 94-95,
        102-4, 197
    rehabilitation, 154-56, 176-77,
        215-16
    subpoena of, 36, 46-48, 148, 181
    unnecessary, 55, 69, 94, 97-88,
        100, 119
    written statement, 36, 57-60,
        94